WRITE AHEAD

Skills for Academic Success

2

Linda Robinson Fellag

Community College of Philadelphia
Philadelphia, Pennsylvania

Longman

Write Ahead 2: Skills for Academic Success

Pearson Education, 10 Bank Street, White Plains, NY 10606

Senior acquisitions editor: Laura Le Dréan
Development editor: Paula Van Ells
Vice president, director of design and production: Rhea Banker
Executive managing editor: Linda Moser
Production editor: Lynn Contrucci
Production coordinator: Melissa Leyva
Director of manufacturing: Patrice Fraccio
Senior manufacturing buyer: Dave Dickey
Photo research: Dana Klinek
Cover design: Ann France
Cover image: Jude Maceren/Stock Illustration Source, Inc.
Text design: Ann France
Text composition: Carlisle Communications, Ltd.
Text font: 11/13 Palatino
Text credits: See page x.
Photo credits: See page x.

LONGMAN ON THE WEB

Longman.com offers online resources for
teachers and students. Access our Companion
Websites, our online catalog, and our local
offices around the world.

Visit us at longman.com.

ISBN 0-13-027258-2

Printed in the United States of America
2 3 4 5 6 7 8 9 10—VHG—08 07 06 05 04

CONTENTS

SCOPE AND SEQUENCE

WRITING ASSIGNMENT	WRITING PROCESS FOCUS	GRAMMAR AND MECHANICS
How to be academically successful	Freewriting Overview of the writing process	Commas Capitalization
Making important choices	Brainstorming and listing	Simple present tense Present progressive Spelling vowel sounds
Components of culture	Brainstorming Parts of an essay: thesis statement, body paragraph, conclusion Graphic organizers	Sentence combining: compound and complex sentences
How birth order and gender affect personality and relationships	Introduction paragraph Thesis statement	Subject-verb agreement Gerunds Infinitives
Advantages and disadvantages of a technological device	Outlining Summarizing	Using present and past tense verbs together Articles and noun phrases
Problem-solution essay relating to natural resources	Cluster maps	Present perfect tense Comma splices
Steps necessary to perform a skill	Audience and purpose	Modals Commands Pronoun consistency
Changes in a place, object, or way of life	Venn diagrams Comparison/contrast essays	Comparatives of equality and inequality Transitions
Summary and response to a reading about security in public places	Summarizing Concept maps Paraphrasing	Reported speech Passive and active sentences

Introduction

Write Ahead is a comprehensive writing and language study series especially designed for immigrant learners of English, as well as learners who have had little formal instruction in English. The series prepares students to write fluently and accurately in academic English at these levels:

- *Write Ahead 1*   High beginning to low intermediate
- *Write Ahead 2*   Intermediate

Target Users

A growing segment of the ESL student population in the United States acquires English by immersion "on the streets." Naturally, their language learning needs differ markedly from traditional international ESL students. They lack "formal, metalinguistically oriented instruction" and use non-standard English dialects, as does the subgroup of U.S. high school graduates that has been labeled "generation 1.5 learners" (Harklau et al.). Indeed, these students of community colleges, universities, or high schools have startling gaps in their formal knowledge of English. Many are "ear" learners who have acquired the language informally. Their oral and aural abilities far exceed their reading and writing levels, and often their formal knowledge of the language is uneven or non-existent (Byrd and Reid). Furthermore, many have little experience with extensive writing in English (Harklau et al.). The components of *Write Ahead* were thoughtfully developed to utilize the language learning strategies and meet the pedagogical needs of such students.

Unit and Chapter Components

Chapter Goals. A list of chapter goals encourages teachers and students to preview the writing topics and language points covered in the chapter. Learning objectives are appropriate for busy immigrant English learners who need to see value and purpose in their educational tasks. At the end of each chapter, students reflect on the goals they are achieving and get extra help with goals they need more work on.

Approaching the Topic. Illustrations and questions encourage students to think about the reading theme and writing topic.

Reading for Writing. Each theme-based chapter opens with two readings, followed by a writing assignment and language activities. The readings model the writing assignment and provide ideas, vocabulary, grammer structures, and organizational features which students may apply to their writing. The articles and essays were carefully selected for high interest and relevance to students' lives.

Language for Writing. After reading, students study and practice vocabulary and lexicogrammar that they can use in the next writing assignment. Such activities include using a dictionary, finding synonyms and antonyms, studying word endings, and writing sentences. In *Write Ahead 2*, learners also study academic words from the chapter readings in order to prepare themselves for academic reading. Corpus research has found that generic academic vocabulary items appear across disciplines (Coxhead).

Writing Assignment. Each chapter contains a main writing assignment. Students read the assignment and then engage in a series of writing process activities that include

- Getting ideas by brainstorming, clustering, listing, and freewriting
- Organizing ideas into a paragraph with a topic sentence; writing different kinds of essays (expository, cause/effect, process, problem-solution, and comparison/contrast); using different types of support; writing an effective conclusion; and other elements
- Revising for content and development (independently and with peers)
- Editing to improve language (using an Editing Checklist)

The emphasis on the writing-process approach teaches students to revise and edit their writing, which they may be reluctant and ill equipped to do (Harklau et al.).

Editing. In the Editing section, students study and practice grammar and mechanics that will help them edit. Features of grammatical and mechanical topics include

- Grammatical presentations that provide special attention to errors made by students with non-standard dialects of English, such as the overuse of the *be* auxiliary or missing *-s* or *-ed* verb endings
- Mechanical topics that are problematic for "ear" learners, such as sentence end punctuation and spelling similar words
- Grammatical and mechanical presentations that are made accessible to learners with limited formal education by using as few metalinguistic terms as possible
- Overall practice with grammatical and mechanical structures that are appropriate for the intermediate ESL curriculum, as well as practice with beginning-level structures that learners may not have acquired earlier
- Grammatical topics related to the writing assignment, such as using present and past tense verbs together in describing important decisions and comparative forms in writing about changes in a subject from past to present

Journal Writing. Students build fluency by writing journal entries on topics related to the chapter theme, often in response to reading.

On Your Own. Each chapter includes More Writing Practice topics to facilitate extra writing practice on topics related to the chapter theme.

Other Components

Writing Evaluation Sheets. One-page scoring sheets for grading paragraphs and essays evaluate writing features that are presented in each chapter. Students can use the evaluation sheets to quickly check aspects of their writing before handing it in, and teachers can use the 100-point scoring systems to evaluate content, organization, vocabulary, grammar, mechanics, and format of student writing.

Do It Yourself. This section in the back of the book gives students extra practice in grammar and mechanics. The DIY is linked to the language structures presented in each chapter. If a student needs more work, he or she can turn to the DIY for a short presentation and extra exercises. The DIY also contains a Handwriting Guide. An answer key to the DIY exercises facilitates independent study.

Special Features of *Write Ahead*

In summary, *Write Ahead* meets the needs of immigrant English learners through these important features:

- Chapter themes and writing topics relate to adult immigrants' lives.
- Readings and example paragraphs and essays provide clear models and springboards for writing.
- Vocabulary activities build language for writing.
- Academic word study prepares students for academic work ahead.
- Students engage in the writing process, including revising and editing.
- Language presentations are written with little formal grammar terminology.
- Essential and troublesome grammar points are presented and practiced to fill in immigrant student's learning gaps.
- Special attention is given to mechanics since immigrant ESL students often have little experience writing or reading formal English.
- Writing Evaluation Sheets provide a quick check for students and teachers.
- The Do It Yourself section with answer key provides students with self-study language activities. The DIY also contains a Handwriting Guide.

Acknowledgments

I would like to express my gratitude to Laura Le Dréan, senior acquisitions editor of Pearson Education, for her support of the *Write Ahead* series. My sincere thanks also go to development editor Paula Van Ells, production editor Lynn Contrucci, and the rest of the Pearson Education team for their professionalism and careful attention to this text.

I also appreciate the suggestions made by the following reviewers:

Marsha Abramovich, Tidewater Community College, Virginia Beach, VA

Paula Baird, Tunxis Community College, Farmington, CT

Nanette Dougherty, The Jackson Heights School, Jackson Heights, NY

Kay Ferrell, Santa Ana College, Santa Ana, CA

Aileen Gum, City College, San Diego, CA

Mary Hill, North Shore Community College, Danvers, MA

Kelly Kennedy-Isern, Miami-Dade Community College, North Campus, Miami, FL

Debra McPherson, Cypress College, Cypress, CA

Cristi Mitchell, Miami-Dade Community College, Kendall Campus, Miami, FL

Michael Ringler, Hialeah-Miami Lakes Senior High School, Hialeah, FL

Paula Sanchez, Miami-Dade Community College, Kendall Campus, Miami, FL

Christine Tierney, Houston Community College, Houston, TX

As ever, I offer thanks to my family for their encouragement, and to my students at the Community College of Philadelphia, for the inspiration and motivation to develop materials to facilitate their academic success.

Linda Robinson Fellag

REFERENCES AND CREDITS

References

Biber, Douglas, et al. (eds.) (1999). *Longman Grammar of Spoken and Written English.* Essex, England: Pearson Education Limited.

Byrd, Patricia, and Joy Reid (1998). *Grammar in the Composition Classroom.* Boston: Heinle and Heinle.

Coxhead, Averil (1998). *An academic word list.* English Language Institute Occasional Publication No. 18. Wellington, NZ: School of Linguistics and Applied Language Studies, Victoria University of Wellington.

Web Vocabulary Profiler: http://www.er.uqam.ca/nobel/r21270/textools/web_vp.html

Harklau, Linda, Kay M. Losey, and Meryl Siegal (eds.) (1999). *Generation 1.5 Meets College Composition: Issues in the Teaching of Writing to U.S.-Educated Learners of ESL.* Mahwah, NJ: Lawrence Erlbaum Associates.

Nation, Paul (2000). *Learning Vocabulary in Another Language.* Cambridge, UK: Cambridge University Press.

Schmitt, Norbert (2000). *Vocabulary in Language Teaching.* Cambridge, UK: Cambridge University Press.

Schmitt, Norbert, and Michael McCarthy (eds.) (1997). *Vocabulary: Description, Acquisition, and Pedagogy.* Cambridge, UK: Cambridge University Press.

Text Credits

Photo Credits

Academic Success

- Write a topic sentence with a controlling idea.
- Organize a paragraph with major points.
- Start an academic word list.
- Recognize and write complete sentences.
- Mark sentence boundaries correctly.

Approaching the Topic

Academic success does not come easily. It requires motivation, commitment, and responsibility. In Chapter 1 of *Write Ahead 2*, you will learn strategies that you can apply to your own academic success.

1. Discuss these questions with your classmates.
   - A *goal* is "something that you hope to achieve in the future." What are your long-term academic goals? What are your academic goals this semester?
   - A *priority* is "the thing that you think is most important and that needs attention before anything else." What are your biggest educational priorities this year?

2. Study the meanings of these words:

- *Motivation:* eagerness and willingness to do something

  *Some students are smart, but they lack **motivation** to work hard and complete a college degree.*

- *Commitment:* a promise to do something

  *Sam must make a **commitment** to study at least two hours a night in order to pass his math class.*

3. Discuss these questions with a group of your classmates. Take notes on your answers.

- Do you have the motivation to reach your goals? Explain.

- What does it mean to make a commitment to succeed in your classes?

- What things do students do when they take responsibility for their learning?

Writing Sample

When students provide a writing sample at the beginning of a writing course, the instructor can find the students' strengths and weaknesses in writing.

Write one page on *one* of the following topics:

- How you take responsibility for your education

- What motivates you to go to school

- The commitments that you must make to be a successful student

  ### Example First Sentence

  I take responsibility for my education by attending classes and keeping up with all my homework.

READING FOR WRITING

Reading 1

Discuss these questions with your classmates before you read: Are you starting the semester with many responsibilities? If so, what are they? How can you make time for studies? Do you have a plan for your academic success?

The Most Organized Person

1   Paul Roberts was in my class several years ago, and he impressed me as the most organized person I had ever known. He always had his calendar with him; he took careful notes and read over them every day; and he never missed a deadline. Paul recognized that he had to prioritize[1] several components[2] in his life: his time, money, and social life. He had a regular schedule, which he followed exactly, that detailed on which day he would do laundry, on which day he would shop for groceries, and at what time he would exercise. Paul followed a carefully organized schedule so that he would have plenty of time for studying, reviewing his notes, and meeting with professors. Although he was not naturally outstanding academically, through these efforts Paul was able to keep his grades among the highest in the class.

2   His organization and his ability to stick to his priorities also allowed Paul to serve on the student council, to play on the men's basketball team, and to work fifteen hours a week. I have never known a student to be more disciplined about his work. One of the best things about his self-management style was that he always took time to have fun and to be with his friends. Paul noted in his calendar "sacred[3] days." These were days that were reserved[4] for him to have fun, to renew his spirit, to do nothing. Work was not on his "sacred day" agenda.[5] Paul had learned some of the most important time-management and organizational strategies at a very young age: *make a plan, stick to the plan, work hard, play hard, and reward yourself when you have performed well.*

---

[1]*prioritize:* put the things you must deal with in the order of their importance
[2]*components:* parts that make up a whole machine or system
[3]*sacred:* extremely important to someone
[4]*reserved:* kept for future need or use
[5]*agenda:* a list of subjects to discuss or tasks to do

Discussion and Analysis

In a group, do the activities and discuss the questions. Then write answers to questions 3, 4, and 5 on a separate piece of paper. Write your answers in complete sentences.

1. Underline the sentence that states the writer's main point about Paul.

2. Underline sentences that introduce the ways that Paul kept his grades high. Do you have some of the same organizational habits as Paul? Which ones? How do they help you succeed in school?

3. Which of his self-management techniques would *you* consider trying? Why?

4. Which techniques would not work for you? Why?

5. In the chart, record your own weekly activities. Then look at the chart, and on a separate piece of paper write two or three sentences to explain the activities that take up most of your time.

	Monday	*Tuesday*	*Wednesday*	*Thursday*	*Friday*	*Saturday*	*Sunday*
6:00							
7:00							
9:00							
11:00							
noon							
2:00							
4:00							
6:00							
8:00							
10:00							
11:00							
midnight							

Reading 2

Discuss these questions with your classmates before you read: How do you organize all of your daily tasks, or jobs, including school tasks? Do you write "to do" lists or keep a calendar? How do you find time to study?

My Keys to College Success

1   Several years ago, I began to volunteer[1] at my daughters' elementary school as a paraprofessional.[2] I began as a volunteer because I wanted to help my daughters and their school. To my surprise, I loved what I was doing. So I decided to return to college to major in elementary education. I had been out of school for some time, so I found it difficult to juggle[3] two children (ages twelve and nine), activities at work, my homework, helping with my daughters' homework, and trying to keep a neat home. All of this taught me the importance of two things: getting organized and learning how to get the most out of[4] my study time.

2   One of the hardest things I had to learn was that I had to become more selfish. I had to learn how to say no to some things if I wanted to have quality time with my children and time for my college education. I had to learn, as did my family and friends, that my study time was *my* time. They had to learn that I was not to be interrupted by anyone or anything short of[5] an emergency.

3   I also had to learn how to get organized. I did not have time to look for things. I learned to keep all the things I needed to study with in one place. With children in the house, that was not easy, but take it from me, it can be done. What a time-saver this turned out to be.

4   As tests, evaluations, papers, and assignments began to roll in, things began to get very hard. There were classes, children, home life, and even Math Lab hours that were prescribed[6] to me. It was only because I developed a study plan that I was able to make it. I wrote a list of things to do over the weekend, developed a regular study plan for the week, and learned how to prioritize.

5   These are the things that have helped me be successful in college.

Yolanda Agosto, Miami-Dade Community College

---

[1]*volunteer:* to offer to do something without expecting any reward
[2]*paraprofessional:* someone whose job is to help professionals
[3]*juggle:* try to fit two or more jobs, activities, etc. into your life
[4]*get the most out of:* get the most advantage that is possible from a situation
[5]*short of:* less than
[6]*prescribed:* stated officially what should be done in a particular situation

Discussion and Analysis   In a group, do the activities and discuss the questions. Then write answers to each question on a separate piece of paper. Write your answers in complete sentences.

1. What helped Yolanda succeed in college? Underline the sentence that introduces the ways she succeeded in college.

2. What specific things did she do to be a successful student? Underline these sentences.

3. Does her situation sound similar to or different from yours? Which parts of Yolanda's life are similar to yours? Which are different?

4. What types of day-to-day activities take up most of your time?

5. How do you schedule your time so that you allow enough time for school work?

6. Which of Yolanda's organizational and study habits do you find useful?

Journal Writing

A **journal** is a written record of feelings, ideas, and things that happen to you. Writing in a journal regularly gives you more practice in writing. When you write in your journal, don't worry about organization and grammar. Just concentrate on writing all your thoughts about the topic.

Write a one-page journal entry to describe your weekly activities. Describe your class schedule and other duties such as work or family obligations.

Language for Writing

Words to Know

1 Read the following list of phrases. Then read the sentences from Readings 1 and 2. From the list, choose a phrase with the same or similar meaning as the boldfaced words. The reading and paragraph numbers are given so that you can look back at how the word was used. The first one is done for you.

---

parts that make up a whole system or machine

made someone feel respect

put things you must do in order of importance, so that you deal with the most important items first

sets of plans and skills used in order to gain success or achieve a goal

someone whose job is to help a professional do his/her work

to offer to do something without expecting any reward

the act or process of controlling and organizing time

---

1. Paul . . . **impressed** me as the most organized person I had ever known. (Reading 1, paragraph 1)

   made someone feel respect

2. Paul recognized that he had to **prioritize** several **components** in his life: his time, money, and social life. (Reading 1, paragraph 1)

   _____

3. Paul had learned some of the most important **time-management** and organizational **strategies** at a very young age. (Reading 1, paragraph 2)

   _____

4. . . . I began to **volunteer** at my daughters' elementary school as a **paraprofessional.** (Reading 2, paragraph 1)

   _____

2 Think of someone you know who is very busy and successful. On a separate piece of paper, write complete sentences to answer the questions. Discuss your answers with your classmates.

1. What qualities **impress** you the most about this person?
2. How does the person **prioritize** his or her daily tasks?
3. Which **components** of this person's everyday life take up the most time?
4. What is one **time-management strategy** that works for him or her?
5. What kind of **volunteer** work could this person do well? Why?

Words with Multiple Meanings

In your dictionary, you may notice that definitions are numbered. The number 1 identifies the most common meaning. However, many words in English have more than one meaning. When you want to understand an unfamiliar word with multiple meanings, use the other words around it to determine which meaning the word has in a particular sentence.

1 Read the sentences and pay attention to the boldfaced words. Each boldfaced word has multiple meanings, numbered below. Circle the meaning that best fits the sentence.

1. Paul noted in his calendar "**sacred** days." These were days that were **reserved** for him to have fun, to **renew** his **spirit,** to do nothing. Work was not on his "sacred day" agenda. (Reading 1, paragraph 2)

sacred **1** relating to a god or religion and believed to be holy; **2** extremely important to someone

reserved **1** kept separate so that it can be used for a particular person or purpose, such as a seat on an airplane or a parking space; **2** unwilling to express emotions or talk about problems

renew **1** to arrange for a contract, official document, etc. to continue; **2** to begin to do something again; **3** to give someone new strength

spirit **1** the qualities that make someone live the way he or she does and that are often believed to continue to exist after death; **2** a living thing without a physical body, such as an angel or ghost; **3** courage and determination

2. I had been out of school for some time, so I found it difficult to **juggle** two children (ages twelve and nine), activities at work, my homework, helping with my daughters' homework, and trying to keep a neat home. (Reading 2, paragraph 1)

juggle **1** to keep three or more objects moving through the air by throwing and catching them very quickly; **2** to try to fit two or more jobs, activities, etc. into a schedule

3. There were classes, children, home life, and even Math Lab hours that were **prescribed** to me. (Reading 2, paragraph 4)

> **prescribe**   **1** say what medicine or treatment a sick person should have; **2** state officially what should be done in a particular situation

2 Complete these sentences.

1. On my "**sacred** days," I like to _____.

2. My days off are **reserved** for _____.

3. One way I **renew** my spirit is _____.

4. Every day, I **juggle** _____.

5. Some of the **prescribed** activities that I must do are _____

_____.

Words Often Used in Combination

Many words are commonly used together in English. Notice these two common *verb + noun* pairs:

VERB   ┌─NOUN─┐
She never **missed a deadline.**

VERB   ┌─NOUN─┐
She **followed a schedule.**

1 Work with a partner. Circle words in the list that you think are commonly used with the boldfaced word in the sentence. Read the sentence aloud to help you decide which words go together. More than one answer is possible. Compare your answers with those of another pair of students.

1. I _____ **a plan** whenever I have to do an important task.

   do   (make)   (stick to)   schedule

2. A successful student _____ **goals.**

   has   reaches   sets   puts

3. Can you **achieve** _____?

   success   your dreams   a great student   your thoughts

4. It's essential to **take** _____.

   notes in class   time to study   breaks from work   a meeting

5. Do you **prepare for** _____?

    a test   an objective   your classes   an unexpected event

6. Do you **do** your _____ every night?

    assignments   schedule   homework   plans

2 Write six sentences about your education, career, and personal goals. Use word pairs or groups from Exercise 1.

    Example

    I want to **achieve my dream** to become a doctor.

Academic Words

Certain words are commonly found in every type of academic writing, from history textbooks to science articles. Studying these words will help you succeed academically. Start an academic word list in your notebook and record and study unfamiliar words.

1 Study the following academic word list and the example sentences. Check (✔) the academic words you already know.

❑ **academic**   A positive attitude about learning will help you gain **academic** success.

❑ **achieve**   You can **achieve** your goals if you stay organized and work hard.

❑ **establish**   Before you choose what to study, you should **establish** your goals.

❑ **goals**   Is earning a degree one of your personal **goals**?

❑ **motivation**   One **motivation** for getting a good job is the need to support a family.

❑ **priority**   If you want to be a professional, make education a **priority** in your life.

❑ **strategies**   Successful students develop **strategies** for getting good grades.

2 Test your comprehension by matching one of the definitions to an academic word from the list in Exercise 1. Write the word on the line.

1. _____ educational

2. _____ reason

3. _____ succeed in getting

4. _____ start, set up

5. _____ most important activity

6. _____ something you hope to achieve in the future

7. _____ plans or skills used to succeed or achieve a goal

3 If you have difficulty matching any word from Exercise 1 to its definition in Exercise 2, put it in the academic word list in your notebook. Write its definition and a sentence using the word.

WRITING

Assignment

Write a paragraph describing two or three strategies a student can use to be academically successful. To write your paragraph, follow the steps of the writing process.

The Writing Process

Writing consists of steps that you may need to repeat as you write, rethink, and rewrite:

- Getting ideas
- Organizing your ideas
- Writing your first draft
- Revising to improve content and organization
- Editing for language errors

THE WRITING PROCESS

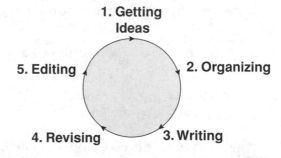

1. Getting Ideas

2. Organizing

3. Writing

4. Revising

5. Editing

STEP 1

Getting Ideas

Freewriting

There are several ways to get ideas for writing. One method is *freewriting*, or writing whatever comes into your mind about a topic in order to get ideas. When you freewrite, you write without stopping. You don't stop to correct your grammar or spelling; you let your ideas flow onto the page.

1 Freewrite for five to ten minutes about ways that a student can be successful. Think about ways that a student can organize time, study, do homework, prepare for tests or major assignments, and so on. Include your own ideas about other ways to succeed in school. Use your own experience to develop your ideas.

2 Read over your freewriting. Did you write about two or three ways to be a successful student? Did you include details about these ways? Did you tell about your own experiences that relate to academic success? Underline those sentences. Cross out the ideas that do not fit your writing topic, as the writer did in the example below.

~~I have a hard time studying, but~~ I think <u>a good student needs to find time to study.</u> ~~Sometimes my boss calls me and asks me to work until midnight. Then I have to go to school the next morning.~~ <u>I usually arrive early before class. That gives me time to study.</u> ~~I can't study at home. I can't concentrate. There's always some housework to do. So I have to go to school.~~ <u>I study at a desk in the study lounge, the library, or a quiet hallway. I try to study every morning. I should study about an hour or two every day for each class. It's also important to go to class. I try to go to class every day</u>. . . .

STEP 2

Organizing

Basic Elements of a Paragraph

Most writing in English is organized into paragraphs. A paragraph is a small unit of writing that contains information about one idea. A good paragraph follows this pattern:

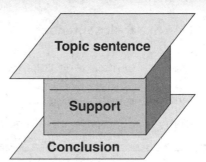

Topic sentence

Support

Conclusion

- Introduce the topic and give your opinion or idea about it in a **topic sentence.**
- Develop the topic with **supporting sentences** containing facts, details, or examples.
- **Conclude** with a sentence that refers to the topic.

Read the following paragraph. Work with a partner to identify its main elements. Circle the *topic sentence*, underline the *supporting sentences*, and circle the *concluding sentence*.

Academic Advisors

Academic advisors can help students with educational issues. The main job of academic advisors is to help students find out about classes, choose courses, and explore and select a major. For example, if a student is interested in computer science but doesn't know which majors or careers exist in this field, he or she can discuss these topics with the advisor. An academic advisor can also help students locate other offices and departments in a school. It may be difficult for new students to know where to go for help with personal issues or for information about student loans or work-study jobs on campus. Generally, a student meets his or her advisor at least once a semester. Students should make appointments to talk to their academic advisors any time they need help with academic problems.

Topic Sentence and Controlling Idea

An effective topic sentence does two things:

- It introduces the **topic** of a paragraph.

- It contains a **controlling idea** that tells the writer's opinion, attitude, or idea about the topic. The idea can be a fact, but it must be unique or interesting.

Effective topic sentence:

┌─────── Topic ───────┐ + ┌─────── Controlling Idea ───────┐
Many students attend college   **to prepare for a career that interests them.**

Ineffective topic sentence:

Many students attend college. (A simple fact, no controlling idea)

1 Read the following sentences. Decide if each is an effective topic sentence for a paragraph. For each effective topic sentence, underline the topic and circle the controlling idea. Rewrite the ineffective sentences to make them good topic sentences, adding or changing words as necessary. Then compare your revised sentences with a classmate's. The first one is done for you.

┌──── Topic ────┐
1. <u>Two-year colleges</u> give associate's degrees. (No controlling idea)

   Revised topic sentence:

   ┌──── Topic ────┐   ┌─ Controlling Idea ─┐
   <u>Two-year colleges</u> have (several advantages)

2. My life is very busy because of family, work, and school obligations.

3. My college's registered nursing program prepares students well for the state nursing examination.

4. Being a responsible student requires time, effort, and confidence.

5. Grants, loans, and scholarships are the three best ways to cut the cost of a college education.

6. Computer networking is a degree program at my university.

7. My friend is majoring in accounting.

8. Students have greater chances to succeed if they form study groups and use teachers and computers as resources.

9. The college computer lab has many computers with Internet access.

10. There are several advantages to having a job and taking classes at the same time.

2 Read over the freewriting you did in Step 1. Write a sentence that introduces your topic: ways that a student can be successful.

   Examples

   Keeping up with assignments and attending class regularly will help a student succeed academically.

   Students can use several strategies to perform well in their classes.

Major Points

One logical way to organize a paragraph is to explain the major points that support your idea. State all the points in the topic sentence. Then develop each point into a sentence. Look at this example:

Topic sentence:

┌──────Topic──────┐ + ┌──────────Controlling Idea──────────┐
Being a successful student   **takes motivation, organization, and discipline.**

Major points:

a. First, you must be motivated to learn and do well in your studies.

b. Moreover, you have to organize your time.

c. Last, you must be disciplined to work hard.

These sentences show the framework of ideas for a paragraph. The major points develop the topic sentence by presenting *ways* that a student can be *successful*.

1 Read each topic sentence and its major points. For each topic sentence, write one or more supporting points to logically develop the main idea.

1. **Topic sentence:**   Students should develop three habits that will help them succeed in college.

   Major points: a. First, students should set priorities.

   b. Second, they should schedule their time carefully.

   c. _____

2. **Topic sentence:**   There are two main reasons that I want a college degree.

   Major points: a. _____

   b. Most important, I want to get a good job.

3. **Topic sentence:**   Passing a test is easy if students use these strategies.

   Major points: a. First, start studying weeks before the test.

   b. _____

   c. _____

4. **Topic sentence:**   Before choosing a college, students should consider two major factors.

   Major points: a. _____

   b. _____

5. **Topic sentence:**   Studying in a group has three important benefits.

   Major points: a. _____

   b. _____

   c. _____

2 Read over your freewriting (Step 1) and the topic sentence you wrote (page 13). Write two or three major point sentences to develop the topic sentence. Show your sentences to your instructor or one of your classmates.

STEP 3

Writing the First Draft

Using your topic sentence and your major point sentences, write the first draft of your paragraph about strategies a student can use to be academically successful.

- Begin with the topic sentence.

- Organize the paragraph by major points:

    First, present and explain the first point.

    Next, present and explain the next point.

    If you include a third point, present and explain it.

- Write a concluding sentence that includes your topic and gives a final opinion about it.

STEP 4

Revising

1 Exchange drafts with a partner. Read each other's paragraphs and answer these questions.

- Is there an effective topic sentence that introduces ways to succeed academically?

- Is the paragraph organized with major points that describe the writer's strategies for being a successful student?

- Does the writer use his or her own experience as support?

- Is there a concluding sentence?

2 Examine the illustration.

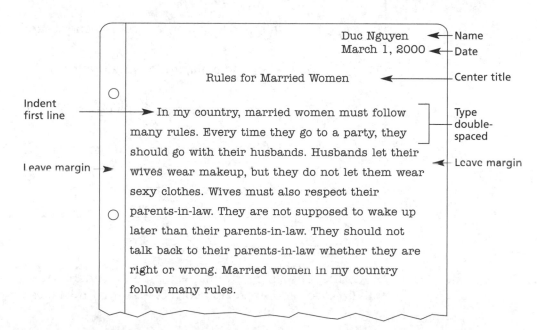

A paragraph should have these features:

- Title (a phrase that tells or suggests the topic of the paragraph)
- Indentation of the first line of the paragraph
- Margins on the left and right
- Name and date

3 Check your partner's paragraph. Does it contain all the features? If not, point out the problems to your partner.

4 Discuss your partner's comments. Take notes on any revisions you need to make. Write a second draft of your paragraph.

STEP 5

Editing

PRE-TEST

Read the following items. If they are complete and correct sentences, write **C**. Rewrite the other items to make complete and correct sentences. Make all necessary changes. There may be more than one way to correct the items. The first one is done for you.

_____ 1.   I ~~taking~~ *am taking* two classes this semester.

_____ 2.   I work 40 hours a week. Because I have to pay my bills.

_____ 3.   I a serious student, I come to every class.

_____ 4.   When I finish my ESL classes, I plan to take classes in my major.

_____ 5.   In my college have a cafeteria and several snack areas.

_____ 6.   Choosing a major is an important decision.

_____ 7.   my college has many buildings, so easy to get lost

_____ 8.   I not study every day, I work too many hours.

Have your instructor check your answers.

Grammar

Study the following grammar explanations and do the activities. They will help you recognize and correct grammar mistakes in your writing.

Complete Sentences

The sentence is the basic unit of writing in English. A sentence expresses a complete thought and has a subject and a complete verb. Study the following examples.

SUBJECT   VERB
Marcel understands the importance of attending class regularly.

┌──────SUBJECT──────┐   VERB
Shu, Tony, and Ana studied together after class.

The subject of a sentence may be

- a single noun   **Beatriz** works in the registration office.
- a noun phrase   **The computer lab** has more than 150 computers.
- a pronoun   **They** arrive at class on time every day.
- two or more nouns,   **Asaph and Weilun** went to the bookstore.
  noun phrases, or   **My boyfriend and I** study together.
  pronouns
- an *-ing* verb   **Preparing for a test** takes time.

The verb of a sentence

- must be complete or include all necessary verb parts
  Incomplete: She working in the lab.
  Complete: She **is working** in the lab.
- can consist of more than one verb
  Samboeurn **works, studies,** and **takes care of** his children.

Think about typical activities that a successful student does, such as homework, studying, writing, reading, and preparing for examinations. Write four to six sentences that explain these activities. Be sure that each sentence expresses a complete thought and consists of a subject and a complete verb.

1. *A successful student writes assignments on a calendar and reviews the calendar often.*

2. _____

   _____

3. _____

   _____

4. _____

   _____

DO IT YOURSELF

For more practice:

Complete
  sentences, 210
Sentence
  combining, 214

5. _____

   _____

6. _____

   _____

Sentence Boundaries

Use punctuation and capitalization correctly to mark sentence boundaries. A sentence *boundary* is the place where one sentence ends and the next one begins.

- End a complete sentence with a period (.), a question mark (?), or an exclamation point (!).

- Begin the next sentence with a capital letter.

   Notice the sentence boundaries in the writing below:

   You have to learn to deal with failure to be motivated. **H**ave you ever given up on something too quickly or gotten discouraged and quit? **C**an you think of a time when you were unfair to yourself because you didn't stay with something long enough? **O**vercoming failure makes victory much more rewarding. **M**otivated people know that losing is a part of winning.

- Be careful to avoid using a comma to end a complete thought. This is called a *comma splice*.

   COMMA SPLICE

   Incorrect: Difficult situations make you tougher, they build your strength.

   Correct: Difficult situations make you tougher. They build your strength.

- Be sure not to let a *dependent clause* stand alone. A dependent clause is a group of words that has a subject and verb and begins with a connecting word like *because, when, if, even though,* or *since.* A dependent clause must be connected to an independent clause as part of a complete sentence.

   DEPENDENT CLAUSE

   Incorrect: No one can set a goal for you. Because only you know what you want.

   Correct: No one can set a goal for you because only you know what you want.

   DEPENDENT CLAUSE

   Incorrect: When I started college. I wasn't sure about my major.

   Correct: When I started college, I wasn't sure about my major.

1 Look for sentence boundary mistakes in the following paragraph. If you find a mistake, correct it. The first one is done for you.

Being rich is a big dream for most people⊙ I would say that for me it is not really important, but I would not mind being rich. Because I want to help all the poor people around the world. I feel very sorry for all the poor people who are starving to death. I'm mad at the rich people who don't even give a quarter to them. A basketball player has millions, but he needs a kidney to survive, are his millions going to save him? I don't think so. All I want is a enough money to have a decent house and a comfortable life I don't care about money a normal life is good enough for me.

Vladimir Tabaku, Albania

2 Read the following paragraph. Look for each complete sentence: subject, complete verb, and complete thought. Then insert the correct sentence end punctuation and capital letter at the beginning of the new sentence. The first sentence is corrected for you.

C   C

¢ollege can be one of the most exciting times of your life⊙ ¢ertainly college brings stressful times, happy times, tearful times, and life-altering times college can also lead to a more rewarding future the book *Understanding* (1999) reports that men with a bachelor's degree earn US$21,984 more than male high school dropouts women with a bachelor's degree earn US$17,527 more than female dropouts this does not mean that the only reason for attending college is to make more money this is a secondary reason many other considerations are as important as money to a person's decision to attend college among the reasons are knowledge, sports, and parental pressure are any of these your reasons for attending college

DO IT YOURSELF
For more practice:
Comma Splices, 261
Sentence
    combining, 214

Writing the Final Draft

Use the checklist to edit your paragraph on strategies that a student can use to be academically successful. Then write your final draft.

Editing Checklist

❑ Do all the sentences express a complete thought and have a subject and a complete verb?

❑ Do all the complete sentences end with a period, a question mark, or an exclamation point?

Your instructor will grade your paper for its content, organization, and language using the evaluation sheet for this chapter on page 200. Read over the evaluation sheet. Then reread and edit your paper as necessary before you turn in the final draft. Turn in the first draft of your paper with the final draft.

On Your Own

More Writing Practice

Write a paragraph about one of the following topics.

REMEMBER Freewrite about your topic before you begin your first draft. In that draft, include all the basic elements of a paragraph: a topic sentence, supporting sentences, and, if desired, a conclusion. After you finish, read over your paragraph and edit it.

---

1. **Academic Resources**

   Describe the resources that you have to help you succeed academically. What resources does your school provide? How can you use them? What resources do you have at home or in your community? What new resources can you use that you haven't used before?

2. **A Good Listener**

   Describe your listening strategies in school. Are you a good listener? Do you pay close attention when the professor speaks in class? Do you understand the most important ideas? Do you take notes? What do you do with the notes after class? What do you do if you don't understand something?

3. **Test-Taking Strategies**

Describe your test-taking strategies. What do you do before the test? Do you study days before the test or only the night before? What do you study? Do you study alone or in a group? During the test, what do you do to make sure that you perform well? Do you read the directions carefully? Do you check your answers afterwards?

Chapter Goals   Take credit for achieving the learning goals for Chapter 1. Check (✔) all of the goals that you have achieved. If you are having problems with one of these goals, get extra practice by writing another composition on one of the topics on page 14, or do the additional exercises in the appropriate Do It Yourself section in the back of the book. Then talk to your instructor about your writing.

Chapter Goals Checklist

❑ Write a topic sentence with a controlling idea.

❑ Organize a paragraph with major points.

❑ Start an academic word list.

❑ Recognize and write complete sentences.

❑ Mark sentence boundaries correctly.

CHAPTER 2

Life Choices

Chapter Goals

- Develop paragraphs.
- Add specific details to your writing.
- Vary adverbs used in writing.
- Recognize and use basic sentence patterns.
- Use present tense verbs appropriately.
- Keep a personal spelling list.

Approaching the Topic

In Chapter 1, you explored the responsibilities of academic study. Students face another challenge: choosing paths to take after completing school. In this chapter, you will read and write about decisions relating to career, education, lifestyle, and other important areas.

Discuss these questions with your classmates.

1. Are you facing a decision about your future? If so, explain. Have you already made a decision about your future? If so, explain.

2. *Criteria* are the "facts or standards used to help judge or decide something." What are the *criteria* you use or used in choosing a career?

3. Have you decided where to live in the future? If so, explain your decision. If not, explain what factors might influence your decision.

READING FOR WRITING

Reading 1

Discuss this question with your classmates before you read: What are the most important things to consider when choosing a future career? Money? Job satisfaction?

My Career Dilemma

Right now I am trying to decide whether to get a degree in dentistry or nursing. One reason I might choose dentistry is that I have experience in it, and I love the field. I was a dentist in Warsaw for three years. I find dentistry very satisfying, challenging, and interesting. I always liked science as a child, and I enjoy studying and working with teeth. However, getting a dental degree here will take a long time. I had my university transcript[1] from Poland translated and evaluated. Most of my courses will be accepted in the United States, but I must redo all of the courses and training that are directly connected to dentistry. I am already 28, so I do not want to wait four years to begin a career in the United States. Becoming a nurse would take about 1½ years. Another factor that may make me choose nursing is the high cost of dental school. Getting a dental degree at a state university in my city will cost me about US$25,000. I can get a loan, but I cannot qualify for a federal grant because my husband earns too much money. A nursing program would cost about US$7,500. As you can see, I have a real dilemma[2] about which career to choose. My heart tells me to continue dentistry, but my head says to study nursing. I still have some time to decide, so I hope that I can make the best choice for my future.

Wieslawa Kaczaj, Poland

---

[1]*transcript:* an official document that has a list of the classes you took as a student and the grades you received
[2]*dilemma:* a situation in which you have to make a difficult choice between two actions

Discussion and Analysis

In a group, do the activities and discuss the questions. Then write answers to questions 4 and 5 on a separate piece of paper. Write your answers in complete sentences.

1. Underline the topic sentence of Reading 1.

2. What is the writer's main reason for choosing a dental career? Underline the sentence that introduces this reason.

3. What are the "cons"—the reasons against the writer choosing a dental career? Underline the sentences that introduce the cons.

4. Which career do you think the writer should choose? Why?

5. Do you have a career dilemma? If so, explain.

Reading 2

Discuss these questions with your classmates before you read: What are the most important factors you consider in choosing a place to live? Have you thought of moving to a different town or city? If so, what are the reasons?

A Move to Toronto

Toronto, Canada

Since I left my home country, I have considered cities where my family and I might live. For several reasons, we recently decided to move from Atlanta to Toronto, Canada. First of all, moving to Toronto makes sense because of the economic situation in Canada. The Canadian government is trying to attract foreign professionals. With my Ukrainian accounting degree and experience, I can easily get a job in Canada as an accountant. My wife also has an education degree from the Ukraine, so she can get a teaching job. Another reason that we decided to move is because my wife's parents live in Toronto. There is a large Ukrainian population in Atlanta, but it's not the same as family. We miss living close to our family, especially since we want our daughter to know her grandparents. My wife also wants to be able to take care of her parents as they grow older. Finally, we want to move to Toronto because the atmosphere there is similar to our home city of Kiev. In Toronto, the climate and the atmosphere are more European, like Kiev. The winters actually have snow, and there are many evergreen trees. Toronto has sidewalk cafes, street markets, and small shops, just like Kiev. In contrast, Atlanta's summers are hot and the city is spread out over a large area, so we must own two cars. Moving to Toronto will be like starting over again, so it will take some time to adjust. Nevertheless, we feel that there are many good reasons to make the move. Our new home will give us professional opportunities, closeness to family, and a European atmosphere.

Sergey Yeminskaya, Ukraine

Discussion and Analysis

In a group, do the activities and discuss the questions. Then write your answer to each question on a separate piece of paper. Write your answer in complete sentences.

1. Underline the sentence that introduces the writer's ideas about a place to live.

2. What are the major points, or reasons, for the writer's decision? Underline the sentences that introduce the major points.

3. Identify the supporting sentences for each major point. Write **1** above the sentences that support the first reason for moving, **2** above the sentences that support the second reason, and **3** above the sentences that support the third reason.

4. Do you think the writer had good reasons for moving? Have you ever made such a big move or thought about making one? Explain.

Journal Writing

In making decisions, is it generally better for people to follow their hearts or their heads? Write a one-page journal entry to describe situations when it is better to decide something based on emotions (your heart) and situations when it is better to decide something by following reason and logic (your head).

Language for Writing

Career versus Discipline Words

Notice the two boldfaced words in the following sentences. Which word describes a career or job? Which one describes a discipline, field, or subject of study?

> I am not certain if I will enjoy being a **nurse.**
>
> **Nursing** is a medical profession.

Look at the words on page 26 that describe a career or job and the words used to describe the discipline, or subject of study.

Career words	Discipline words
nurse	nursing
dentist	dentistry
engineer	engineering
computer scientist	computer science
computer programmer	computer programming
biologist	biology
pharmacist	pharmacy
accountant	accounting

1. Work with a partner. Add to the list. Write names of careers or jobs and the related discipline. Share your list with your classmates.

2. Write two sentences to describe a career or careers that you have considered. Then write two more sentences to describe disciplines or subjects that you have studied or plan to study to achieve those careers.

   Examples

   I want to become a **radiologist.**

   I plan to study **radiology** at the university.

Words Used Together

1 Look at the verbs on the left and the noun phrases on the right. Which verbs can be used with which nouns? Match the noun phrases on the right with the appropriate verbs on the left. Some verbs can be used with more than one noun phrase. Share your answers with your classmate. The first one has been done for you.

Verbs	+	Nouns
1. get _a, f_		a. a degree
2. pursue _____		b. a career
3. achieve _____		c. a salary
4. seek _____		d. a university
5. enter _____		e. a profession
6. earn _____		f. a job
7. choose _____		g. a program

2 Write five sentences about your future plans on a separate piece of paper. In each sentence, use one of the verb + noun combinations above.

Examples

I hope to **pursue a degree in engineering.**

It's difficult to **choose a major.**

Variety in Adverbs

Study how the boldfaced *adverbs* in the following sentences describe *adjectives*:

ADVERB + ADJECTIVE

In some ways, life is **very** easy for us.   *How "easy"?*   ***very*** easy

We have a **fairly** good life in Atlanta.   *How "good"?*   ***fairly*** good

Vary the adverbs in your writing. Do not overuse words like *very.* Here are some adverbs with similar meanings to use in place of *very* and *fairly:*

very	*fairly*
extremely	somewhat
remarkably	reasonably
especially	moderately
quite	adequately

Complete the following sentences to make them true for you. Fill in the blanks with one of the adverbs in the list. Circle one of the two adjectives provided to describe your situation.

Example

My writing in English is _____*fairly*_____ good/(weak).

1. I have (*a*/*an*) _____ *satisfactory*/*unsatisfactory* life.
2. The place where I live is _____ (*pleasant*/*unpleasant*).
3. My present city is _____ (*similar to*/*different from*) my hometown.
4. Right now my life is _____ (*easy*/*difficult*).
5. My future career plans are _____ (*clear*/*unclear*) in my mind.
6. I am _____ (*satisfied*/*dissatisfied*) with my career choice.
7. I am _____ (*certain*/*uncertain*) about where I will be living five years from now.
8. It is _____ (*hard*/*simple*) to make future choices.

Academic Words

1 Study the following academic word list and the example sentences. Check (✔) the academic words that you already know.

❑ **federal**   The **federal** government of Canada is located in Ottawa.

❑ **consequences**   The **consequences** of your choice will be felt for a long time.

❑ **criteria**   What **criteria** do you use in choosing a career?

❑ **urban**   Do you prefer **urban** life or country life?

❑ **evaluate**   When you are considering a move to a new city, **evaluate** the cost of the move.

❑ **nevertheless**   He needs money. **Nevertheless,** he plans to quit his job.

❑ **investigate**   If you love the arts, you should **investigate** a city's cultural resources before moving there.

❑ **procedure**   The **procedure** for choosing a career starts with discovering your interests.

❑ **range**   A wide **range** of degree and certificate programs exists today.

2 Test your comprehension by matching one of the following definitions to an academic word from the list in Exercise 1. Write the word on the line.

1. _____ number   6. _____ process

2. _____ effects   7. _____ city

3. _____ however   8. _____ judge

4. _____ national   9. _____ principles

5. _____ explore

3 If you have difficulty matching any word from Exercise 1 to its definition in Exercise 2, put it in the academic word list in your notebook. Write its definition and a sentence using the word.

WRITING

Assignment

Write a paragraph about an area of your life in which you need to make or have already made an important choice. Examples are choices about a move, a career, a living situation, marriage, parenthood, and so on. Give two or three reasons for making a certain choice. To write your paragraph, follow the steps for writing.

STEP 1

Getting Ideas

> ### Brainstorming and Listing
>
> One way to get ideas for your writing is to *brainstorm.* Brainstorming means discussing a subject with a group of people or thinking by yourself to get ideas. When you brainstorm ideas, you may take notes or make lists of your ideas. *Listing* helps you to record ideas to use later in your writing.

1 With a group of your classmates, brainstorm topic ideas. Discuss different areas of your life in which you must make or have already made an important choice. Choose one area to discuss.

2 Once you have selected a topic, think about the criteria for making the choice. A good way to brainstorm ideas about a choice is to make a list of "pros" (reasons in favor of something) and "cons" (reasons against something). Read the sample list.

A Move to Miami

Pros	Cons
Many family members there	Hot weather, hurricanes
Low cost of housing	Lots of crime
No state or city income taxes	Lower salaries
Large Hispanic community	

---

3 Now make your own list of pros and cons that you should consider in making your choice. If you are writing about an important past decision, make a list of pros and cons that helped you to make the decision.

4 Circle three items from your pros and cons list that you want to include in your paragraph. You may want to write about all pros, all cons, or a mixture of both. These circled items will be the reasons, or major points, in your paragraph.

STEP 2

Organizing

1 Write a topic sentence for your paragraph. In this sentence, introduce the choice and state the reasons for your choice in a general or a specific way.

Examples

┌── REASONS ──┐   ┌── CHOICE ──┐
There are **several factors** that may convince me to **move to Miami.**

┌──────── CHOICE ────────┐   ┌── REASONS ──┐
Miami seems like **a good place to relocate** because of my **family ties, the low cost of living, and the Hispanic community** there.

2 Organize your paragraph so that each of the two or three major supporting points gives one reason for the future or past decision. If you mentioned the reasons specifically in your topic sentence, be sure to follow the same order in your paragraph, as the following topic sentence and major supporting point sentences illustrate.

Topic sentence:

Miami seems like a good place for me to relocate because of my

Reason 1   Reason 2   Reason 3

family ties, the **low cost** of living, and the **Hispanic community** there.

Major point 1:

First, I have many **family** members in Miami.

Major point 2:

Another good thing about Miami is its **low cost** of living.

Major point 3:

Finally, Miami has a large **Hispanic community.**

3 Write sentences like the examples to introduce each of your major points.

Paragraph Development

As you have learned, a paragraph has a certain structure. The first sentence—the topic sentence—often presents the main idea and includes the major points. Then each major point is developed with supporting sentences that contain details, facts, and examples. Generally, a well-developed paragraph contains *at least two* supporting sentences for each major point.

A Well-Developed Paragraph

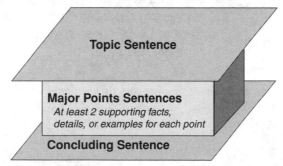

Topic Sentence

Major Points Sentences
At least 2 supporting facts, details, or examples for each point

Concluding Sentence

The number of sentences in a well-developed paragraph depends on the topic. The drawing above shows how a paragraph could be developed with eight or more sentences: a *topic sentence,* two *major points* sentences, and two or more facts, details, or examples to develop each major point, plus a *concluding sentence.*

1 Study the two paragraphs. In each paragraph, underline the *topic sentence, major points* sentences, and *concluding sentence*. How are the two paragraphs different? Which one do you prefer? Why?

--- **Living Independently** ---

My classmate Aminata Nioke recently moved out of her parents' home after considering several factors. First of all, she had saved enough money from her job. She works part time and studies full time. Second, she has a friend who would make a suitable roommate. Her friend Sara has a steady job. She also gets along well with Aminata. Most important, she wanted more freedom. She felt that she would be able to come and go as she pleased if she lived independently. It was a difficult decision, but in the end, Aminata feels that she made the right choice.

--- **Living Independently** ---

My classmate Aminata Nioke recently moved our of her parents' home after considering several factors. First of all, she had saved enough money from her job. Now she works twenty hours per week as a grocery store cashier and studies full time, but last summer she worked full time and saved US$2,000. She calculated that an apartment with a roommate would cost her about US$600 per month. Second, she has a friend who would make a suitable roommate. Aminata needed a roommate who could pay her share of the bills. Her friend Sara has a steady job in a dry cleaning shop. Also, Aminata is a very good-natured person, but she didn't want a roommate who was messy or noisy. The two friends also get along well and have known each other for two years. Aminata says that Sara is cheerful, neat, and quiet. Most important, Aminata wanted more freedom. She felt that she could do as she pleased if she lived independently. Now that she has her own apartment, she can come home late, eat meals whenever she wants, and invite her friends over. It was a difficult decision, but in the end, Aminata feels that she made the right choice.

2 Read the sentences on page 32. Then put the sentences in the correct order to make a well-organized and well-developed paragraph. Write **1** next to the first sentence, **2** next to the second sentence, and so on. The first one is done for you. Compare your answers with your classmates.

Thinking About Dropping Out

_____ 1. Her family needs money because her younger sister wants to enter a private nursing school.

_____ 2. She is serious about her education, but several issues are making it difficult to continue.

_____ 3. If Almaz quits school for a year, she can work full time and send money home to Ethiopia.

__1__ 4. My friend Almaz is thinking about dropping out of college temporarily. (*Topic sentence*)

_____ 5. Almaz's first issue is that she is so busy.

_____ 6. In the end, Almaz must decide whether delaying her own education is the right way to solve these problems.

_____ 7. Another factor that may convince Almaz to drop out of school is her family's finances.

_____ 8. Working part time and studying full time takes all her time and energy.

_____ 9. In fact, she has missed a lot of English classes, and she has trouble keeping up with her reading and writing.

_____ 10. She wants to study for two years and then get a job in a doctor's office.

Adding Specific Details

As you develop your ideas, include specific details. *Details* are single facts or pieces of information about something. They make your writing more interesting and effective. Notice how a writer might add specific details to drafts of a paragraph.

First draft:

My friend works full time. She takes two classes.

Second draft:

My friend *Almaz Haile* works full time *at Dunkin Donuts.* She takes two *ESL* classes.

Third draft:

My friend Almaz Haile works *forty hours per week as a cashier* at Dunkin Donuts. She takes two ESL classes *in reading and writing.*

Study these ways of going from a general topic to more specific detail.

- Add names of places, people, or things.

   My friend → My friend *Almaz Haile*

- Add dates and numbers.

  works full time → works *forty hours per week*

- Add sensory details that tell what you *see, hear, smell,* or *feel.*

  summers → *hot, humid* summers

  an apartment → a *bright, sunny* apartment

- Add an adverb.

  She might drop out. → She might drop out *temporarily.*

1 Read the revised paragraph "Thinking About Dropping Out." The author improved this paragraph by adding more specific details. Compare the revised paragraph with the original paragraph from Exercise 2 on pages 31–32. Underline the specific details that were added. Above each line write what type of details the writer added. Compare your answers with a partner's. The first one is done for you.

--- **Revised Draft: Thinking About Dropping Out** ---
Name

My friend Almaz <u>Haile</u> is thinking about dropping out of Mission College temporarily. She is serious about her education, but several issues are making it difficult to continue. She wants to study for two years and then get a job as a medical records clerk in a doctor's office. Almaz's first issue is that she is too busy. Working 25 hours per week and studying full time takes all her time and energy. Due to fatigue, she has missed more than five English classes in 10 weeks, and she has trouble keeping up with reading her novel and writing paragraphs and journals. When she comes to class, her eyes often look red, and she sometimes falls asleep in the back row. Another factor that may convince Almaz to drop out of school is her family's finances. Her family needs money because her 18-year-old sister Tekia wants to enter a private nursing school in Addas Ababa, Ethiopia. If Almaz quits school for a year, she can work 40 to 50 hours per week and send at least US$400 per month home to Ethiopia. In the end, Almaz must decide whether delaying her own education is the right way to solve these problems.

2 Work with your partner. Read the following paragraph. Discuss where you might add more supporting sentences. On a separate piece of paper, rewrite the paragraph together. Make up appropriate supporting details, facts, or examples to develop the paragraph. Add details to existing sentences, or add more sentences with details where they are needed.

My Classmate's Decision

My classmate was looking forward to returning to his home, but recently he decided to remain in the United States to get a bachelor's degree. He has two main reasons for making this choice. First of all, he thought he could get a better job if he studied here. He had a job in his home country. He thought he could get an even higher position in a better corporation if he had a college degree from the United States. Another reason he decided to stay here and study was to improve his English. English will help him in many areas of life. He is taking English classes now. He also got a job at a place where he has to use English. Now he is pleased with his decision to obtain a college degree here. It will take hard work, but he made the right choice to remain here.

---

3 Share your revised draft of the paragraph "My Classmate's Decision" in a group.

STEP 3

Writing the First Draft

Using your lists (Step 1) and your topic sentence and major points sentences (Step 2), write the first draft of your paragraph about an important choice or decision. Organize your paragraph in the following way:

- Begin with a topic sentence to state the choice or decision that you will make or have made, and the reasons for it.

- In each major point sentence, present one reason for the choice or decision. Develop each major point with supporting sentences containing details, facts, or examples.

- In your concluding sentence, refer to your main idea. Conclude your paragraph in a logical way, for example, by making a prediction or stating a result.

STEP 4

Revising

Exchange drafts with a partner. Read each other's paragraphs and answer the following questions.

❑   Does the paragraph begin with a sentence that states the topic (an important choice or decision) and the major points for making it?

❑   Is the paragraph organized with sentences that support each major point given for the choice or decision?

❑   Should the writer add more supporting sentences? If so, make notes in the margin of the paragraph.

❑   Does the writer include enough specific details, facts, or examples in the supporting sentences? If not, make notes in the margin of the paragraph.

Discuss your partner's comments. Take notes on any revisions you need to make. Write a second draft of your paragraph.

STEP 5

Editing

Use the following explanations and activities to help you edit your writing.

PRE-TEST

Test your knowledge.

Complete the sentences with any appropriate nouns, verbs, adjectives, or adverbs. There is more than one way to complete the items. Make sure your sentences are complete. Also, use verbs correctly. The first one is done for you.

1. I _____ *never have* _____ enough time.

2. There are _____ in my college.

3. Right now _____ about my future.

4. _____ a clock on the desk in her bedroom.

5. _____ not easy to choose a major.

6. Making a decision _____ .

7. _____ at midnight tonight.

8. The rain _____ at the moment.

9. Sometimes my life seems _____ .

10. This semester _____ classes.

Have your instructor check your answers.

Grammar

Study the following grammar explanations and do the activities. They will help you recognize and correct grammar mistakes in your writing.

Basic Sentence Patterns

Words in sentences follow a specific order. Understanding several basic sentence patterns will help you use the correct word order in your sentences.

Study the word order in these common sentence patterns. Each of the example sentences below is a *simple sentence* because it has one main part, or clause, with a subject and verb.

- **Pattern 1: Subject + action verb + (object + adverb)**

  These sentences must have a subject and verb. They may have an object or adverb.

  ┌Subject┐ ┌───Verb───┐
  Jenny doesn't work.

  ┌────Subject────┐ ┌Verb┐ ┌Adverb┐
  The college library closes at 11 p.m.

  ┌───Subject───┐ ┌Verb┐ ┌─Object─┐ ┌────Adverb────┐
  The professor gave the lecture in the auditorium.

- **Pattern 2: Subject + linking verb + complement**

  ┌Complement (Noun)┐
  Nora is a serious student.

  Complement
  ┌(Adjective)┐
  The vocabulary words seem difficult.

  Complement
  ┌(Adverb)┐
  The test papers are on the desk.

- **Pattern 3: *There is* and *there are* sentences (*There is* + singular noun or *There are* + plural noun)**

  ┌──Singular Noun──┐
  There is a great opportunity to advance at the pharmaceutical company.

  ┌──Plural Noun──┐
  There are many nursing jobs in my city.

- **Pattern 4: *It is* sentences (*It is* + adjective or *It is* + noun or noun phrase)**

  ┌Adjective┐
  It is difficult to move to a new place.

  ┌─Noun─┐   ┌─Noun─┐
  It is 10:30 a.m.   **It is** a nice day.

1 Complete the sentences with an appropriate word or words. Which pattern does your sentence follow? Write the sentence pattern number next to each sentence. Share your answers with your classmates.

Pattern

_____ 1. _____ have many resources for students.

_____ 2. The library is a _____.

_____ 3. _____ has organizations like the Chinese Students Association, the Latin American Students Organization, and the Haitian Students Club.

_____ 4. The school catalog _____.

_____ 5. _____ is open twenty-four hours a day.

_____ 6. Health clinics provide _____.

_____ 7. There are _____ in the financial aid office.

_____ 8. _____ has weight rooms, a swimming pool, indoor tracks, basketball courts, and racquetball courts for students.

_____ 9. The child-care center _____.

_____ 10. It is _____ at a large college.

DO IT YOURSELF
For more practice:

Basic sentence
   patterns, 213
Sentence
   combining, 214

2 Write *two* sentences using each of the four sentence patterns presented on page 36. Write about your future plans and decisions—your education, your career, your family plans, and so on. Compare your sentences with a partner's.

Example

Sentence Pattern 1: *I plan to transfer to a four-year university.*

Using Present Tense Verbs Appropriately

English has two main verb tenses for writing or speaking about present time actions.

- **Simple present tense verbs** are used to write about regular activities, habitual action, facts, beliefs, and ownership.

   I **have** a real dilemma about which career to choose.

   We **miss** living close to our family, especially since we **want** our daughter to know her grandparents.

- **Present progressive verbs** (-*ing* verbs) may be used to write about actions that occur for a limited period of time.

I **am facing** a difficult choice right now about my future career.

My heart **is telling** me to continue dentistry, but my head **is saying** I should study nursing.

Some present tense verbs are not used in the progressive form. See page 219 for a list of verbs that are not commonly used in the progressive form.

Example

Incorrect: My wife **is wanting** to be able to take care of her parents . . .

Correct: My wife **wants** to be able to take care of her parents as they grow older.

1 Complete the following paragraph. Use the simple present or present progressive forms of the verbs in parentheses. Compare your answers with a partner's. The first one is done for you.

───────────────── **Leaving Home** ─────────────────

My friend Martina ___is considering___ (*consider*) where she wants to attend college. She _____ (*try*) to decide whether to leave her home in Missouri and study at the University of New Orleans. For one thing, Martina _____ (*be*) tired of living in her hometown. She has lived in Kansas City, Missouri, all her life. Whenever she _____ (*travel*), she always _____ (*enjoy*) the new sights around her. Martina's aunt _____ (*live*) in New Orleans, and Martina _____ (*love*) the city. Another reason for studying out of state _____ (*be*) so that she can be independent. She _____ (*work*) right now and _____ (*pay*) for many of her expenses, but she also _____ (*want*) to have her own apartment or house so that she can go where she _____ (*like*) and do what she _____ (*please*). However, one thing that _____ (*hold*) her back is her friends. Martina _____ (*know*) that she will miss her good friends if she moves. They _____ (*not, have*) a lot of money, so they might not be able to visit her often. If she chooses to stay in Missouri, she can study at a local university and see her friends often. At the same time, she _____ (*think*) about the positive changes that will occur if she moves away from home.

2 Write complete sentences using the phrases provided. Add time words and other information to make the sentences true for you at the present time. Use simple present or present progressive tense verbs. Share your sentences with a classmate. The first one is done as an example.

1. live on my own _Right now I am not living on my own._
2. have a job _____
3. own a car _____
4. like my city (or town) _____
5. think about moving _____
6. want to change my _____
7. do well in my classes _____
8. spend time with friends _____
9. attend college full time _____
10. feel satisfied with my _____

DO IT YOURSELF
For more practice:

Present tense
  verbs, 217
Non-progressive
  verbs, 219

Writing the Final Draft

Use the checklist to edit your paragraph on an important choice or decision. Then write your final draft.

> ### Editing Checklist
> ❏ Are present tense verbs used correctly?
> ❏ Are sentence patterns used correctly?
> ❏ Is there a variety of adverbs?

Your instructor will grade your paper for its content, organization, and language using the evaluation sheet for this chapter on page 201. Read over the evaluation sheet. Then reread and edit your paper as necessary before you turn in the final draft.

Sharing Your Writing

Exchange drafts with a partner. Read each other's paragraphs about an important choice or decision. Then write a letter of advice to your partner. Tell him or her which choice is better. Support your opinion with examples from your experience, facts, or other details. Use the format shown on page 40 to write your letter:

November 1, 2003

Dear Wieslawa,

~~~~~~~~~~~~~~~~~~~~~~~~~~~~~~~~~~~~~~~
~~~~~~~~~~~~~~~~~~~~~~~~~~~~~~~~~~~~~~~
~~~~~~~~~~~~~~~~~~~~~~~~~~~~~~~~~~~~~~~
~~~~~~~~~~~~~~~~~~~~~~~~~~~~~~~~~~~~~~~
~~~~~~~~~~~~~~~~~~~~~~~~~~~~~~~~~~~~~~~
~~~~~~~~~~~~~~~~~~~~~~~~~~~~~~~~~~~~~~~.

Sincerely,

Your name

On Your Own

Personal Spelling List

The spelling of some English words can be confusing. There are some reasons for this: The pronunciation of some words has changed when the spelling has not, and English has always borrowed words from other languages. To help you remember the correct spelling of difficult words, keep a spelling list.

The following exercises will help you practice the spelling of vowel sounds in different words. For example, the underlined parts of the following words are all pronounced like the *ee* in *feet*, but they have different spellings. Dictionaries give the pronunciation of words. The *ee* sound is usually marked /i/.

> **r<u>ea</u>lize**   **bel<u>ie</u>ve**   **rec<u>ei</u>ve**

1 Read the boldfaced words in the following list. Write a sentence using each word. The first one is done for you.

Words with the *ee* sound
(Most dictionaries mark this sound /i/.)

1. **ach<u>ie</u>ve** *I want to achieve my goals.*

2. **r<u>ea</u>son** _____

3. **<u>e</u>valuate** _____

4. **s<u>ee</u>k** _____

Words with the *i* sound, as in *give*

(Most dictionaries mark this sound /ɪ/.)

5. **d<u>i</u>fficult** _____

6. **t<u>y</u>pical** _____

7. **s<u>i</u>gnify** _____

Words with the *ay* sound, as in *take*

(Most dictionaries mark this sound /eɪ/.)

8. **m<u>a</u>jor** _____

9. **g<u>ai</u>n** _____

10. **n<u>ei</u>ghborhood** _____

2 Next, test each other on the correct spelling of each word. Take turns calling out each word and asking your partner to spell it.

3 Write the words that you misspelled in Exercises 1 and 2 in your personal spelling list. Put the list in a special place in your notebook. Now read through all the writing that you did for Chapters 1 and 2. Add words that you misspelled to your list.

More Writing Practice

Write a paragraph about one of the following topics.

REMEMBER Brainstorm ideas and take notes before you begin to write. Begin with a sentence that states your topic and your main idea. Organize your paragraph by stating major points. Support the major points with sentences that include details, facts, or examples. Add a concluding sentence to refer to the main idea. After you finish, revise and edit your paragraph.

1. **My Future Home**

   Write a paragraph about the home that you want to have in the future. Organize the description of the home with logical major points. For example, describe the features of the home, its location, who will live there, and any other information you want to include. Include details. Explain why you want things this way.

2. **My Life in Ten Years**

   Write a paragraph about the life you want to live in ten years. Describe each area of your life in the major points. What job will you have? Who will you live with? Where will you live? What will you do in your free time?

3. **An Important Decision**

   Write a paragraph about a friend or family member who made an important decision in his or her life. In your paragraph, describe briefly what the decision was. In the major points, give reasons why you think this was a good or bad decision.

Chapter Goals   Take credit for achieving the learning goals in Chapter 2. Check (✔) all of the goals that you have achieved. If you are having problems with one of these goals, get extra practice by writing another paragraph on one of the topics on pages 41–42, or do the additional language exercises in the appropriate Do It Yourself section in the back of the book. Then talk to your instructor about your writing.

Chapter Goals Checklist

❑ Develop paragraphs.

❑ Add specific details to your writing.

❑ Vary adverbs used in writing.

❑ Recognize and use basic sentence patterns.

❑ Use present tense verbs appropriately.

❑ Keep a personal spelling list.

CHAPTER 3

My Culture, Your Culture

Chapter Goals

- Recognize the main parts of an essay.
- Use a graphic organizer to organize your writing.
- Recognize parts of speech and use common word endings.
- Combine simple sentences to make compound and complex sentences.

Approaching the Topic

Today's modern world is truly "a global village." People of different cultures no longer live separately but mix with each other on a regular basis. In Chapter 3, you can explore the *components*, or parts, of culture and share aspects of your own culture.

Discuss these questions with your classmates.

1. Look at the photograph above. What cultures do you think are represented in this group? Do people of these cultures live in your community?

2. In what areas of your life do you interact with people of different cultures?

3. Give one example of a component of culture that distinguishes you (marks you) as someone who is from a different culture.

READING FOR WRITING

Reading 1

Discuss this question with a group of your classmates before you read: The first reading describes the way people show relationships in Turkey. In your native culture, what are the main ways that people show their relationships with others? For example, do they kiss, shake hands, walk arm in arm, stand close together or far apart?

Personal Communication in Turkey

Turkish people communicate their relationships with others through gestures,[1] physical distance, and types of greetings. First of all, people from Turkey often use gestures to communicate with each other. Placing the right hand over the heart means "hello" or "thank you." People make this kind of gesture when they pass an acquaintance or a stranger  along a street. Physical distance is another way that people communicate with each other in Turkey. Personal space defines how good or bad a friendship or relationship is between two people. Therefore, strangers stay somewhat distant from one another, and good friends stand very close to one another. Turkish people use physical closeness as a way of showing that they get along with and care for another person. Finally, there are several acceptable greetings in Turkey. When people say hello, it is very common for them to kiss the person's hand and then place their hand on the person's forehead. This respectful greeting is appropriate for elders such as grandparents. Greetings most often include a hug and a kiss on both cheeks. When these actions are not shown, it can mean that there are problems in the relationship. In conclusion, the Turkish culture has its own traditional style of communicating relationships.

[1]*gestures:* movements of the head, arm, or hand that show what you mean or how you feel

Discussion and Analysis In a group, do the activities and discuss the questions. Then write answers to question 5 on a separate piece of paper. Write your answers in complete sentences.

1. What is the writer's main point? Underline the topic sentence.
2. Underline the sentences that introduce each major supporting point (one part of the main idea of the topic sentence).
3. Highlight or circle the sentences that support each major supporting point. How many ideas does the writer use to support each point?
4. Underline the concluding sentence.
5. Which ways of communicating in Turkey are the same as in your native culture? Which ways are different?

Reading 2

Discuss these questions with a group of your classmates before you read: How do you identify people's cultures? In addition to language, what other behavior marks people as being from one culture?

What Makes Up Culture?

1   With people from diverse[1] cultures living side by side, how do you identify different cultures? Sometimes you can tell by the way people look and dress or by the way they speak. Other components of culture are not so visible. People may show their cultures by a gesture or a look or by a belief or value. According to sociologist David Popenoe, there are five main components of culture: *language, symbols, values, norms,* and *sanctions.*

2   Languages vary across cultures, of course, but you may be less aware that each culture has its own symbols. Symbols are items that stand for something. For example, to many Americans, the flag is an obvious symbol and it stands for honor, duty, patriotism, service, and freedom. Most people recognize the swastika[2] as the symbol of Nazi Germany. However, this widely used symbol represented good luck and prosperity to many ancient cultures of India, Pakistan, and South and Central America. Some common symbols may appear in more than one culture. For instance, *purple* signifies royalty in some cultures, and an *octagon sign* indicates "Stop!" in several countries.

3   Another important aspect[3] of culture is values and beliefs, which are typically based on family traditions and religion. What is unacceptable in one culture may be acceptable in another. Most young people in the United States would be unwilling to allow their parents to choose their future husband or wife, yet in many countries this practice[4] is still common. Some people in religious congregations, or groups, practice religion in a joyful way, often with singing, hand clapping, and music, while others practice in a more serious way with prayer and meditation. Funeral practices also differentiate[5] cultures. In Vietnam, for example, family members place items like food and clothing on the grave to assist the dead person after death. Many people in the Philippines believe that no one should clean house when a deceased person is lying in state, that is, being viewed before burial. The idea behind this norm is that the deceased person's spirit should not be disturbed. Like so much else, what people believe and value depends on the culture.

4   In addition, every culture has norms and sanctions. Norms are the rules for how a culture or society expects people to act, and sanctions are the ways in which society enforces[6] its norms. In China, for example, a woman is expected to remain indoors for one month after giving birth, and she is harshly criticized by friends and family members if she does not do so. When a society adopts[7] a set of norms that are considered as valuable, it typically seeks a way to enforce these norms through formal laws. In every society there are people who do not follow the rules. A person in the United States who breaks the law may be required to do community service, sent to jail, and in some states, put to death, depending on the crime. The punishment for stealing in some Middle Eastern cultures may be public or private flogging.[8] Norms and sanctions vary widely from culture to culture.

5   People are born into a culture, and many of the beliefs and values that they have are passed down from one generation to another. Learning about cultures can help people understand and appreciate their own culture as well as gain valuable lessons from other cultures.

---

[1]*diverse:* very different from each other
[2]*swastika:* a cross with the ends of the arms extended at right angles all in the same direction
[3]*aspect:* one of the parts or features of a situation, idea, problem, etc.
[4]*practice:* something that people do often and in a particular way
[5]*differentiate:* to make one thing different from another
[6]*enforces:* makes people obey a rule or law
[7]*adopts:* formally approves and accepts something
[8]*flogging:* whipping

Discussion and Analysis

In a group, do the activities and discuss the questions. Then write answers to questions 2–6 on a separate piece of paper. Write your answers in complete sentences.

1. What is the main idea of this essay? Underline the main idea sentence.
2. Each major point of the main idea sentence appears as one paragraph in the essay. Is this is a logical way to organize the writing. Why?
3. Name a symbol from your culture. What does this symbol mean?
4. Name a value of the culture in which you were raised. Is this value still important to you? Why or why not?
5. What is a norm in your culture? Why do you think it is a norm? Why is it important?
6. Give an example of a sanction in your culture. Why do you think it is a sanction?

Journal Writing

In your journal, describe the culture or cultures in your neighborhood. Using the knowledge that you have, describe the different cultures, ethnic groups, and religions that coexist (live together) in your neighborhood. Do your neighbors come from different cultures or only one culture? Are they of different ethnicities or religions? How do you fit into the community? Are you culturally different from or similar to your neighbors?

Language for Writing

Prepositions

Prepositions are words that are used in phrases before nouns or pronouns to show place, time, direction, and other meanings. Notice the boldfaced prepositions in the following example sentence.

> Males **in** the United States may wear long hair to show that they are rebelling **against** some traditions **of** their society.

Test your knowledge of prepositions by using one of the prepositions in the list in each blank space in the following sentences. Then find the sentences in Readings 1 and 2 to check your answers. There may be more than one correct answer for some sentences.

across	in	through	by	along	into
from	with	during	of	to	between

1. First of all, people _____ Turkey often use gestures.
2. Turkish people communicate their relationships _____ others _____ gestures.
3. People make this kind of gesture when they pass an acquaintance or a stranger _____ a street.

4. Personal space defines how good or bad a friendship or relationship is _____ two people.

5. Finally, there are several acceptable greetings _____ Turkey.

6. Gestures, physical closeness, and greetings reflect the traditions and values _____ the Turkish culture.

7. Languages vary _____ cultures.

8. _____ many Americans, the flag stands for honor.

9. People are born _____ a culture.

Word Families: Parts of Speech

Words belong to "families" consisting of all or some of the following "members" or parts of speech: *noun, verb, adjective,* and *adverb.* Reading 2 contains words in the *symbol* family of words. Notice in the following chart that each part of speech has a different word ending.

Noun	*symbol*	A gold band worn on a finger of the left hand is a **symbol** of marriage in many cultures.
Verb	*symbolize*	In parts of India, the mustache **symbolizes** manliness.
Adjective	*symbolic*	Holding hands is a **symbolic** gesture. It means that two people have a very close relationship.
Adverb	*symbolically*	In U.S. culture, a restating of marriage vows does not mean that a couple is legally getting married again. It means that they are **symbolically** renewing their commitment to each other.

Complete the following paragraph by choosing the correct member of the word family. Pay attention to the word endings. Use a dictionary to help you. The first one is done for you.

─────── **Hospitality in Azerbaijan** ───────

Foreigners who happen to visit Azerbaijan are always amazed by the

hospitality and _____*friendliness*_____ of the Azerbaijanis. This
                    1. friendly / friendliness

hospitality comes from an old _____ of welcoming
                              2. tradition / traditional

strangers and sharing meals and shelter with them. Guests are always

welcome in Azerbaijan and are treated to the best food _____
3. available / availability

in the house. However, it is customary to let a host know in advance before

coming to his house because the cuisine in Azerbaijan is very sophisticated

and many dishes require much _____. At a dinner
4. prepare / preparation

party, the hostess is usually very busy serving _____
5. vary / various

dishes and beverages while the host _____ his guests
6. honors / honorable

with long toasts, a tradition in many of the mountain regions of the

Caucasus. In their turn, the guests are always welcome to

_____ toasts in honor of the host and his family.
7. propose / proposal

Azerbaijani _____ is indeed unique, and surprising to
8. hospitable / hospitality

many _____.
9. visit / visitors

Using Words from Reading

Complete the following sentences to practice using the boldfaced words
and phrases from the chapter readings. Check how the words are used in
the readings, or use a dictionary to help you.

1. One important **component** of any culture is _____.

2. In my culture, _____ **indicates** _____.

3. **It is common** for married women to _____ in my culture.

4. In the country where I live now, it is **unacceptable** for children to _____
   _____.

5. Many beliefs are **based on** family traditions. In my family, my parents
   believe _____.

6. Cultures often have **superstitions.** One example from the
   _____ (insert name of culture) culture is _____
   _____.

7. It is **appropriate** for elderly people in my culture to live _____
   _____.

Academic Words

1 Study the list of common academic words from Chapter 3 and the sentences in which they are used. Check (✔) the words that you already know.

❏ **accompany** It is necessary for a man to **accompany** a woman in public places in some Middle Eastern cultures.

❏ **traditions** What are the formal **traditions** in a wedding ceremony in your culture?

❏ **diverse** Living in a culturally **diverse** community can be both challenging and interesting.

❏ **differentiate** The wearing of certain kinds of traditional clothing may **differentiate** one culture from another.

❏ **aware** In today's "global village," people are becoming more **aware** of other cultures.

❏ **enforce** A culture often **enforces** its rules of behavior through formal laws.

❏ **aspect** Another **aspect** of culture relates to food and eating habits.

❏ **visible** Symbols and gestures are **visible** components of culture.

2 Test your comprehension of the academic words in Chapter 3 by matching one of the following definitions to each boldfaced word in Exercise 1. Write the word on the line.

1. _____ able to be seen

2. _____ part

3. _____ make people obey a rule or law

4. _____ realizing that something is true or exists

5. _____ very different

6. _____ beliefs or customs that have existed for a long time

7. _____ go somewhere with someone

8. _____ make one thing different from another

3 If you have difficulty matching any word from Exercise 1 to its definition in Exercise 2, put it in the academic word list in your notebook. Write its definition and a sentence using the word.

WRITING

Assignment

Write an essay about one component of a culture, such as eating, raising children, or superstitions. For your major points, choose interesting or uncommon aspects of your topic. Write about a culture that you know. To write your essay, follow the steps of the writing process.

Getting Ideas

1 Review the definitions of *culture* and *component*.

culture   the art, beliefs, behavior, ideas, etc. of a particular society or group of people: *the culture of ancient Greece*

component   one of several parts that make up a whole machine or system; *stereo components*

2 Work with a group of your classmates. Discuss components of culture that you might want to write about. Think about different areas of "art, beliefs, behavior, and ideas" in a culture. The following chart lists a few components of culture. List other cultural components.

> *Components of Culture*
>
> • *Clothing*
> • *Food*
> • *Dating "rules"*
> • *Wise sayings*
> •
> •

3 Reread the Writing Assignment above. Examples of possible topics and major points for this assignment are shown on page 52. Which of the topics focus on one component of culture? Mark these with a check (✔). Which topics focus on more than one component of culture? Mark these with an **X** and circle the extra component(s).

Cultural Component	*Major Points*
_____ 1. Past roles of women in China	Female children undervalued Females undereducated Divorce unacceptable for women
_____ 2. Indian traditions	Namaskar, a popular greeting Burning oil for special occasions Necklace worn by brides
_____ 3. Special rice dishes in Puerto Rico	Everyday white rice and beans Chicken and rice Rice dish for special occasions
_____ 4. Pre-wedding customs in Vietnam	Choosing a husband or wife Using a fortuneteller to check choice of husband or wife Engagement Day party
_____ 5. Tabaski holiday in Mali	Sacrificing a sheep Money gifts The big party

Share your list with your classmates.

4 Brainstorm writing topics about one component of a culture that you know well. Think of **two or three** ideas or aspects that fall into the component of culture. For example, under the component of *wedding customs*, you might write about two or three special things that people in one culture do when a couple marries. Tell your ideas to the members of your group to find out which ideas are the most interesting or uncommon to your classmates.

5 Choose two or three aspects of the component of a culture that you will write about. Write a main idea sentence to express these ideas. In your sentence, name the culture that you will write about and the aspects of the cultural component that you will describe.

Example

In the Scottish culture, whisky, haggis, and shortbread are popular foods.

6 Share your main idea sentence with your group and the rest of your class.

Organizing

Parts of an Essay

An **essay** is a multiparagraph composition on a single topic. Like a paragraph, it has three basic elements: *introduction, body (support),* and *conclusion.* In an essay, each of these parts is expanded into a separate paragraph. In essays about detailed subjects, the body usually has several paragraphs.

The following graphic illustrates the similar organizational patterns of a paragraph and a five-paragraph essay.

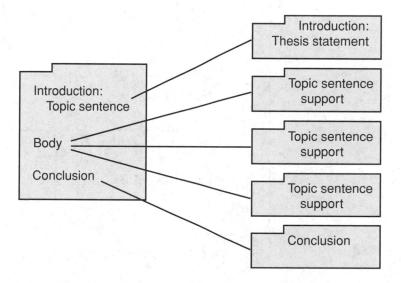

In the paragraph, the introduction begins with a topic sentence. The body contains the major points. The conclusion may have one or more sentences.

A five-paragraph essay has these main parts:

- The introduction paragraph includes the **thesis statement,** which expresses the topic and the writer's attitude, opinion, or idea about the topic. This sentence may also state the major points that will be presented in the essay. The introduction paragraph also includes other sentences to introduce the topic.

- Each **body paragraph** begins with a topic sentence and supports one major point. There are three body paragraphs.

- The **conclusion** is a paragraph by itself. It brings together the important ideas of the essay and makes a final statement about the thesis.

1 Scan the paragraph "Personal Communication in Turkey" on page 44 to identify its basic elements. Fill in the box with the *topic sentence, major point sentences,* and *concluding sentence.* The first major point sentence is provided for you.

Topic sentence: _____

_____

_____

Major point 1: *First of all, people from Turkey*

often use gestures to communicate with each

other.

B
O Major point 2: _____
D
Y _____

_____

Major point 3: _____

_____

_____

Concluding sentence: _____

_____

_____

2 The essay "What Makes Up Culture?" on pages 45–46 follows the same basic organization plan. In the boxes, write the essay's *thesis statement,* the *topic sentences* for each major point paragraph, and the *concluding sentence.* Each box represents one paragraph.

Introduction

Thesis statement: _____

_____

_____

Major point 1

Topic sentence: _____

_____

_____

Support

Major point 2

Topic sentence: _____

_____

_____

Support

Major point 3

Topic sentence: _____

_____

_____

Support

Conclusion

Thesis statement: _____

_____

_____

B
O
D
Y

Graphic Organizer

A *graphic organizer* is a drawing or map that is used to organize ideas in a text. It's called *graphic* because you can visualize the main ideas. It's an *organizer* because it shows the order of ideas and relationships among them. You can use a graphic organizer to help you organize ideas for your writing.

In the sample that follows, the writer made a "map" of the ideas she planned to put in the five paragraphs of her essay. She wrote a few words to show the main idea of the *thesis statement,* the *topic sentences* introducing each major supporting point, the *support* for each body paragraph, and the *conclusion.* Each box represents a paragraph.

Sayings of Benjamin Franklin

Introduction

Thesis statement idea:

Sayings by American statesman and philosopher Benjamin Franklin

Some sayings reflect U.S. values today

Major point 1: Franklin's sayings on money
—"Waste not, want not."
—"A penny saved is a penny earned."

Major point 2: Franklin's sayings on behavior
—"The early bird gets the worm."
—"Early to bed and early to rise makes a man healthy, wealthy, and wise."

Major point 3: Franklin's sayings on relationships
—"Keep your eyes wide open before marriage and half-shut after marriage."
—"Fish and visitors stink after three days."
—"Three can keep a secret if two are dead."

Conclusion

Restate thesis statement:

Importance: Franklin's sayings reflect U.S. values still popular today, over 200 years later.

B
O
D
Y

1 Discuss these questions with a group of your classmates.

1. What would be an appropriate complete thesis statement for this essay on sayings of Benjamin Franklin? Write the sentence next to the introduction paragraph box on page 56.

2. What is the writer's first major supporting point? What facts and details will she include? What is the writer's second major point? What are the facts and details? What is the third major point? What facts and details will be in this paragraph?

3. What will the writer include in the conclusion paragraph?

2 On page 52, you brainstormed ideas for an essay on a component of culture. Now organize your ideas with a graphic organizer like the one on page 56.

1. In the first box, write your thesis statement. You will include this statement in your introduction paragraph.

2. Draw three boxes for your body paragraphs. In each box, list one major point. Each major point will be an aspect of the cultural component that you are writing about. Include notes that will support each major point.

3. Draw a box for the conclusion paragraph. Put notes about the importance of the component of culture that you wrote about here.

3 Develop your thesis statement. Make sure that the thesis statement identifies the culture that you are writing about and the component of the culture that you will describe. Then write topic sentences for the body paragraphs in your essay. Put these sentences inside the appropriate box in your graphic organizer. Study these examples for the "Sayings of Benjamin Franklin" essay:

Example thesis statement: Benjamin Franklin wrote many wise sayings that reflect the values and customs of U.S. culture.

Example topic sentence: First, he wrote many sayings that showed how Americans value money.

STEP 3

Writing the First Draft

Write the first draft of your essay using your graphic organizer.

1. Begin with your thesis statement.

2. Develop your essay with body paragraphs. Remember that each body paragraph should present one major point.

   ■ Begin with the notes that you wrote to introduce the major point. Develop them into a topic sentence.

   ■ Include facts, details, and/or examples to tell more about the point.

   ■ Do this for each major point.

3. Write a conclusion that relates to your main idea and explains the importance of the component of culture that you described.

STEP 4

Revising

Exchange drafts with a partner. Read each other's essays and answer these questions.

❑ Does the introduction paragraph introduce one component of one culture?

❑ Does it have a thesis statement that identifies the culture and the component of that culture that the writer will describe?

❑ Does each body paragraph begin with a topic sentence?

❑ Does each body paragraph tell about one aspect of the cultural component?

❑ Is there a conclusion? Does it relate to the thesis statement?

❑ Does the conclusion also explain the importance of the cultural component described?

Discuss your partner's comments. Take notes on any revisions you need to make. Write a second draft of your essay.

STEP 5

Editing

PRE-TEST

Combine each pair of sentences into one sentence. Add logical connecting words (such as *and, or, but, when, because*), and use appropriate punctuation. Be sure to write complete sentences.

Japanese Food Customs

1. Miso soup is one of the most popular dishes in Japan. It originated in Korea.

   _____

2. I was a child. I ate miso soup.

   _____

3. Sushi is made with vinegar. It's very sour.

   _____

4. I don't make my own sushi. It's very difficult to prepare.

   _____

5. You want to have good sushi. You must go to a restaurant.

   _____

6. People think using chopsticks is wasteful. Chopsticks are made of left-over wood.

   _____

7. People don't drink sake alone. The custom is for someone else to serve you your sake.

   _____

Have your instructor check your answers.

Grammar

Study the following grammar explanations and do the activities. They will help you recognize and correct grammar mistakes in your writing.

Sentence Combining

Study the following pairs of sentences. Which ones you do you prefer? Why?

1. a. In Algeria, the official government language is Arabic. Many officials use French.

1. b. In Algeria, the offical government language is Arabic, but many officials use French.

2. a. The culture of the United States is undergoing rapid change. Its population is getting older.

2. b. The culture of the United States is undergoing rapid change because its population is getting older.

In each pair, the second sentence is more effective because it logically combines the ideas of two simple sentences into one longer sentence. Look at each sentence (b), and underline the word in each sentence that *logically* connects the two ideas in the two simple sentences.

To combine simple sentences into a longer sentence, follow these patterns:

- **Compound sentence:** Add a *coordinating conjunction* such as *for, and, nor, but, or, yet,* and *so* between two simple sentences. Notice that you put a comma before the coordinating conjunctions when you write a *compound sentence.* See page 214 for a more complete explanation of these conjunctions.

> **Simple sentence 1, + coordinating conjunction + simple sentence 2**

  Simple sentence 1: In India, the mustache was once very popular.
  Simple sentence 2: Nowadays, male Indian actors are usually clean-shaven.

  Compound sentence: In India, the mustache was once very popular, **but** nowadays male Indian actors are usually clean-shaven.

- **Complex sentence:** Combine two simple sentences with subordinating conjunctions like *when, because, although,* and *if.*

> **Main sentence + subordinating conjunction + dependent clause**

Simple sentence 1: Many French Canadian families have big family New Year's celebrations.

Simple sentence 2: The New Year is an important holiday in French Canada.

Complex sentence:

┌───────────────────────MAIN CLAUSE───────────────────────┐
Many French Canadian families have big family New Year's celebrations

┌──────────────────────── DEPENDENT CLAUSE────────────────────────┐
because the New Year is an important holiday in French Canada.

Simple sentence 1: There is a death in the family.

Simple sentence 2: Many Chinese wear a piece of cloth pinned to their sleeves.

Complex Sentence:

┌──────────DEPENDENT CLAUSE──────────┐ ┌──────────MAIN CLAUSE──────────┐
When there is a death in the family, many Chinese wear a piece of cloth pinned to their sleeves.

Complex sentences have at least two *clauses,* or groups of words containing a subject and a verb. The *dependent clause* "depends" on the main clause to make it complete. See page xx for a more complete explanation of subordinating conjunctions.

1 Complete the following sentences by adding a coordinating conjunction (*for, and, nor, but, or, so, yet*). Choose a conjunction that logically combines the ideas in the two parts of the sentence. Vary your choices. Compare your answers with a classmate's. The first one is done for you.

Curanderismo

1. *Curanderismo,* the art of folk healing, is practiced in Mexico, Central America, and South America, _____*but*_____ it is also popular in other Spanish-speaking cultures, including the southwestern United States.

2. *Curanderismo* has been influenced by many ancient cultures from Greece to the Middle East to Native America, _____ it has been shaped by present-day spiritual beliefs and by scientific medicine.

3. People who practice folk medicine in some Hispanic cultures recognize several types of healers. The *yerbero* (herbalist), the *partera* (midwife), and the *sabador* (masseur) are common healers, _____ the *curandero* is the only healer who has the skill to treat *mal puesto,* or illness caused by witchcraft.

4. *Curanderos* treat people with physical illnesses, _____ they also treat the physical symptoms that patients believe come from supernatural causes.

5. *Curanderos* can be male, _____ they can be female.

6. Some Hispanics believe that the *curandero* has been given a gift from God to heal the sick, _____ he or she can fight the evil powers that cause illness.

7. The *curandero* may prescribe an herbal remedy, _____ he or she may conduct a religious ceremony.

2 Combine the sentence pairs that follow by making complex sentences. Choose a subordinating conjunction that logically combines the two sentences. Refer to the list of subordinating conjunctions on page 214-215. Write your sentences on the lines. Compare your answers with a classmate's. The first one is done for you.

Women and Village Life in Korea

1. Korean women today hold government and business occupations.
   In traditional Korean society, women had set roles.
   Although Korean women today hold government and business positions,
   in traditional society, women had set roles.

2. In the past, women got married.
   They went to live in their husbands' houses.
   _____
   _____

3. They were expected to stay at home.
   They had to raise their children, keep house, and prepare meals.
   _____
   _____

4. Women lived in farming villages.
   They also worked in the fields.
   _____
   _____

5. A young wife had to obey her mother-in-law.
   In traditional Korean society, the mother-in-law was very important.
   _____
   _____

DO IT YOURSELF
For more practice:
Sentence
   combining, 214

3 Combine the pairs of simple sentences in Exercise 2 to make compound sentences. Choose a coordinating conjunction that logically combines the two sentences. Refer to the list of coordinating conjunctions on page 59. Write your sentences on a separate piece of paper. The first one is done for you.

Example

1. Korean women today hold government and business occupations, **but** in traditional Korean society, women had set roles.

Writing the Final Draft

Use the checklist to edit your essay on a component of culture. Then write your final draft.

Editing Checklist

❏ Are word endings used correctly?

❏ Are compound and complex sentences written correctly?

❏ Are sentences complete? Do they have correct punctuation?

Your instructor will grade your paper for its content, organization, and language using the evaluation sheet for this chapter on page 202. Read over the evaluation sheet. Then reread and edit your paper as necessary before you turn in the final draft.

On Your Own

More Writing Practice

Write an essay about one of the following topics.

REMEMBER Brainstorm ideas before you begin to write. Include a thesis statement in the introduction. Begin each body paragraph with a major point sentence. Add details, facts, or examples to support each point. Add a conclusion paragraph to restate the main idea. After you finish, revise and edit your essay.

1. **Cultural Difficulties**

Write an essay about two or three aspects of a new culture that you find (or found) difficult to accept or learn. Write about the culture of a country where you live now (or lived or visited in the past). Describe each cultural aspect. Why are (or were) these aspects difficult for you? In your conclusion, explain the results of your difficulties.

2. **How to Adapt to a New Culture**

   Write an essay about two or three ways to adapt, or change your behavior or ideas, in order to succeed in a new culture. Write about the culture in which you now live, if it is different from your own culture, or write about a new culture in which you lived in the past. Use your experience, facts, or knowledge to explain each way to adapt.

3. **Family Values**

   Write an essay about two or three values that you learned from your family. Describe each value. Explain why they are important. Use your experience, facts, or knowledge to support your ideas.

Chapter Goals   Take credit for achieving the learning goals for Chapter 3. Check (✔) all of the goals that you have achieved. If you are having problems with one of these goals, get extra practice by writing another composition on one of the topics above, or do the additional language exercises in the appropriate Do It Yourself section at the back of the book. Then talk to your instructor about your writing.

Chapter Goals Checklist

❏ Recognize the main parts of an essay.

❏ Use a graphic organizer to organize your writing.

❏ Recognize parts of speech and use common word endings.

❏ Combine simple sentences to make compound and complex sentences.

CHAPTER 4

Birth Order, Gender, and Personality

Chapter Goals

- Write an introduction paragraph.
- Write an effective thesis statement.
- Recognize and use person suffixes.
- Make subjects and verbs agree in number.
- Recognize and use gerunds and infinitives.
- Choose between similar words correctly.

Approaching the Topic

In Chapter 1, you examined the challenges of academia. A successful family is another of life's challenges. In this chapter, you will read and write about how people's personalities and relationships with family members may be determined by birth order and gender (being female or male).

Discuss these questions with your classmates.

1. Do you have any brothers or sisters, or are you an only child? If you have siblings, how would you describe your childhood relationships with them? Your present relationships?

2. Think back on your childhood. Do you think that your birth order—being the oldest, middle, youngest, or only child—affected your personality? In what ways?

3. How did or does your gender affect your relationship with your family members?

READING FOR WRITING

Reading 1

Discuss these questions with your classmates before you read: Think about one of your siblings or friends. What is the person's birth order: oldest, middle, youngest, or only child? What are two or three words that you would use to describe him or her?

Birth Order Test

Are you an only child? The oldest child? A middle child? The youngest? Recently, researchers have begun to study the personalities of people in relation to their birth order. Their studies suggest that there may be a connection between the way people act and the position they hold in a family.

Test this theory by taking the following "birth order test." Read the personal descriptions. Which of the descriptions best describe the firstborn (**A**), middle born (**B**), youngest child (**C**), or only child (**D**)? Write the appropriate letter next to each description.

_____ 1. My husband's workshop is an absolute mess, but whenever he wants to find something, he knows exactly which pile it's in. That's *his* area, so he doesn't want me to arrange anything.

_____ 2. As a child, my sister was a pleasing girl who liked to show off her talents and was good at getting what she wanted. Today, she's a top salesperson in her company and is highly successful.

_____ 3. My brother, Al, was nicknamed Albert Einstein because he was so good in math and science. He's an engineer now, and he's a real perfectionist.[1]

_____ 4. My friend is a bit of a individualist.[2] She has a lot of friends but values her independence. A good mediator,[3] she'd rather "read" people than books. She's just the opposite of her only sister.

_____ 5. I'm able to get along better with older people than I do with people my age. Some people think I'm self-centered.

[1]*perfectionist:* someone who is not satisfied with anything unless it is completely perfect
[2]*individualist:* a person who wants to do things his or her own way without being influenced by others
[3]*mediator:* a person who tries to help two groups stop arguing and make an agreement

Answers

___A___ 1. According to research, firstborn children take charge of situations and command respect. They like to do things right and have everything under control. Firstborns set goals and reach them. They are also likely to read a lot.

___C___ 2. Youngest children are likeable, fun to be around, and people oriented,[1] according to research. They can be stubborn, but also caring and lovable. Researchers say last-born children appear relaxed and sincere. Other traits of the "baby of the family" are intelligence and affectionate behavior. The last-born child is an attention seeker and a people person who blames others and loves surprises.

___A___ 3. Firstborn characteristics include dependable, well organized, hard working, critical, serious, and studious. The firstborn is a natural leader and list maker who doesn't like surprises but loves computers.

___B___ 4. Research shows that middle children are often unspoiled and realistic[2] because they didn't grow up as the center of their parents' attention. They are independent thinkers who are willing to take risks and do things differently. Middle children know how to get along with others and can see issues from both sides. They are also trustworthy[3] and loyal friends, researchers say. Other middle-child characteristics are independent, loyal to peers, and secretive. A middle child has many friends and avoids conflict.[4]

___D___ 5. Only children have many of the same characteristics as firstborns. Only-child qualities include very careful, self-motivated, and fearful. The only child is a little adult by age 7 and a high achiever. He or she uses *very*, *extremely*, *exactly* a lot, can't bear to fail, and has very high expectations for himself or herself.

---

[1]*people oriented:* friendly, sociable, enjoying the company of others
[2]*realistic:* practical and sensible
[3]*trustworthy:* able to be trusted or depended on
[4]*conflict:* disagreement between people, groups, etc.

Discussion and Analysis

In a group, do the activities and discuss the questions. Then write answers to each question on a separate piece of paper. Write your answers in complete sentences.

1. Were your answers to the test correct? Did any of the answers surprise you? Why or why not?

2. Does the reading accurately describe the personality of your family members and/or friends, considering their birth order? Discuss one or two people whose personalities match or do not match the descriptions in the reading, considering their birth order.

3. Does the reading describe your own birth order personality accurately? Why or why not?

Reading 2

Discuss these questions with your classmates before you read: In the next reading, a writer recalls his memories of being the only male child in a family. Do you know someone who is the only male or female in a family? Has gender affected that person's role and relationships in the family?

A Family of Women

1   I have seven older sisters. They can be loud and bossy, so when we have family gatherings, I sometimes escape outside with my brothers-in-law. However, when I think back on my childhood, I have only pleasant memories. Being the only male child and the youngest in a family full of  women had some important positive effects on my life.

2   First, being the only son made me stand out in the family, especially to my father. My father truly enjoyed being around his "girls"—my mother and sisters—but I realize now that because he had only one son, he paid more attention to me. He, my sisters, and I passed the summers at my grandfather's house swimming, fishing, and hiking. If I had had brothers, my father might have let us go our ways unnoticed. However, because I was the only son, he often did special things with me.

3   As I was growing up, I learned to value the company of my sisters. They were my models since they were older than I. My eldest sister, Beatrice, was the one who taught me to ride a bicycle, and my older sisters Angela and Maria often helped me with math. More important, my sisters welcomed me as a playmate, even though I was younger. My three youngest sisters—Rosa, Frederica, and Paulina—included me in their sports and games. All my sisters made me feel so loved that I truly enjoyed and sought[1] their company. I really grew to enjoy living in a house full of women.

4   Finally, having so many female siblings[2] affected my relationships with women in general. Because I was close to my sisters, I had the experience of understanding females and knowing how to communicate with them. From my sisters, I learned to respect and admire women's intelligence and understand the difficulties of their roles[3] in society. When I was a teenager, my second-oldest sister, Sara, advised me about how to ask girls out. As a result, I think I was better at dating than my male friends. I think my sisters' influence also helped me become a happily married man today.

5   My wife, Anna, recently presented me with our second daughter, and when the baby arrived, Anna was worried that I would be disappointed. I looked at her and said, "Thank you so much. I really mean it," so she knew I did. All my sisters were pleased by my reaction. If I have a son, even if he is the youngest, I only hope that he will have a happy childhood like I did.

Benjamin Soliz, Peru

---

[1]*sought:* past tense of *seek; seek:* to try to find or get something
[2]*siblings:* brothers and sisters
[3]*roles:* positions, jobs, or functions people have in a particular situation

Discussion and Analysis

In a group, do the activities and discuss the questions. Then write answers to each question on a separate piece of paper. Write your answers in complete sentences.

1. What is the writer's main point about growing up in "a family of women"? Underline the sentence that tells his main idea.

2. Underline each sentence that introduces an effect of the writer's being the only male child in his family.

3. Does the writer use details, facts, or examples to support his ideas? If so, underline the sentences with these ideas.

4. Is the writer's story similar to or different from relationships in your own family or in another family that you know well? In what ways?

Journal Writing

Write a one-page journal entry to answer this question: Do you agree with Benjamin that being the only male child in a family of female children has mainly positive effects, or do you think it might have mainly negative effects? If you know a family with only one son or one daughter among siblings of the opposite gender, support your opinions by describing the relationships in this family. If not, support your opinions with your own knowledge or by using Benjamin's family as an example.

Language for Writing

Birth Order Expressions

Here are common expressions to describe a person's birth order:

- the firstborn (child), the oldest or eldest (child)
- the middle child, the child in the middle
- the youngest (child), the last-born (child), the baby in the family
- an/the only child
- younger/older sibling/brother/sister/child
- the second-oldest/youngest child

Write five sentences about people you know (siblings or friends). Use one of the birth order expressions in the list to describe each person's birth order.

> **Example**
>
> Eileen is **the eldest child** in her family.
> John is **the second-youngest child** in his family.

Words to Know

1 *Adjectives* to describe people are printed in boldfaced type in the following list. Circle the synonyms for each adjective. Use a dictionary, if necessary. Compare your answers with your classmates' answers.

1. **charming**   (appealing)   (delightful)   unattractive
2. **self-centered**   generous   selfish   egotistic
3. **likeable**   bad-tempered   lovable   good-natured
4. **people oriented** sociable   friendly   unfriendly
6. **unspoiled**   pampered   overprotected   unselfish
7. **secretive**   open   uncommunicative   reserved
8. **self-motivated** self-starting   independent   inactive

2 Think of three people you know. Write one sentence to introduce each person and state an important quality or behavior that he or she has. Using words from Exercise 1 or other words that you know, describe the person's behavior. Then write one or two more sentences to describe a specific action that shows that he or she has this quality or behavior.

Examples

My friend Suzanne is very **self-motivated.** If she has a class project to do, she always starts to work on it right away. The first thing she does is make a list of tasks and a schedule for doing them. She always hands in her class projects on time, because she never waits until the last minute.

My brother Tom is a very **diplomatic** person. He knows how to avoid uncomfortable situations. If he doesn't want to go out with a girl, he thanks her politely and tells her about his busy schedule.

"Person" Suffixes

Three common *noun suffixes,* or endings, that identify a person are *-er, -or,* and *-ist.* These suffixes indicate "a person or thing that does something." Notice the boldfaced nouns in the sentences that follow.

Ana, the firstborn, leads her siblings. She is a natural **leader.**

Joseph, an only child, keeps his desk in a perfect order. He is a **perfectionist.**

Complete the sentences with one of the nouns from the list. If necessary, add *-s* to the noun.

researcher	list maker	individualist
achiever	mediator	attention seeker

_____ have studied the connection between a person's
_1._

birth position and his or her qualities. Studies show that the typical firstborn

child is a(n) _____ who likes to organize his or her tasks. The
_2._

middle child can be called a(n) _____ because he or she can
_3._

get along with different types of people and solve disagreements. The child

in the middle is also a(n) _____ who likes to do things his or
_4._

her own way. The youngest child may be a(n) _____ who
_5._

wants everyone to notice him or her. Finally, studies show that the only child

may also be a high _____ who has high personal expectations.
_6._

Academic Words

1 Study the following academic word list and the example sentences.
Check (✔) the academic words that you already know.

❑ **benefit**   One **benefit** of being the youngest child is having more
        freedom.

❑ **challenge**   Getting along with your siblings is sometimes a
        challenge.

❑ **environment**   Every child needs a healthy family **environment.**

❑ **gender**   Does **gender** have an effect on a person's position in a
        family?

❑ **issue**   Child rearing is an important **issue** in today's world.

❑ **research**   Scientific **research** shows a connection between birth
        order and personality.

❑ **role**   The eldest son has an important **role** in many cultures.

❑ **structure**   Children need a strong family **structure** to feel secure.

2 Test your comprehension by matching one of the following definitions to
an academic word from the list in Exercise 1. Write the word on the line.

1. _____ job   5. _____ advantage

2. _____ surroundings   6. _____ studies

3. _____ topic   7. _____ sex

4. _____ organization   8. _____ difficulty

3 If you have difficulty matching any word from Exercise 1 to its definition in Exercise 2, put it in the academic word list in your notebook. Write its definition and a sentence using the word.

WRITING

Assignment

Write an essay to describe three ways that your birth order and gender have affected your personality and/or relationships. To write your essay, follow the writing steps.

STEP 1

Getting Ideas

1 Find one or more classmates whose birth order is the same or similar to yours. Brainstorm ideas for your writing by discussing the following questions.

- How do you feel about your birth order?

- How does/did gender affect your family role?

- What makes/made you feel this way?

- What examples from the past or present support your opinion?

Take notes that relate to your birth order and gender.

2 Look over your notes. What is your main point about birth order and gender? Underline comments that relate to your main point. Cross out comments that are not useful.

3 Write a sentence that states your main point about your birth order or gender, whichever is important to your main idea. This will be your thesis statement, the main idea sentence of your essay.

Example

Being the youngest one in the family had both advantages and disadvantages.

As the only girl of the family, I was at times spoiled but also bullied and ignored by my brothers.

STEP 2

Organizing

Introduction Paragraph

The first paragraph of your essay should introduce the topic, catch a reader's interest, and present the thesis statement. There are many ways to begin an essay. Here are a few suggested types of introductions.

The Funnel

To use the "funnel" approach, begin with a general statement about the topic and then lead into the more specific thesis statement. Don't begin with a sentence that's too general. Include a key word in the first sentence, and repeat the idea in the thesis statement. Read this example of a funnel introduction. Find the repeated key word(s) or ideas(s).

> Friends are friends, but there are no groups of people who have closer ties than siblings. In fact, psychologists say that sibling relationships are likely to last longer than any other personal bond. Brother and sister relationships outlast marriages, survive the death of parents, and withstand quarrels that would sink any friendship. Indeed, researchers found in a recent survey of 650 adults that most brothers and sisters showed mutual support, longing for each other's company when they are apart, and positive competition in their relationships.

Shared Experience

To use the "shared experience" approach, begin with a sentence that makes the reader feel involved in the topic. Use words like *we, everyone, you,* or *all of us* in the first sentence. Throughout the introduction, continue to use more words that engage the reader: *us, our, we, you,* or *your.* These sentences should lead into the thesis statement, which expresses your specific opinion or idea about the topic. Read this example.

> If you ever dream of being a famous scientist who makes a revolutionary discovery, you may be surprised to hear that birth order may be the key to your fame. A recent study analyzed 4,000 scientists from Copernicus through the twentieth century. Who would you guess were the most revolutionary scientists: firstborns or later-born children? In truth, most firstborn scientists supported traditional scientific ideas while later-born children like Charles Darwin grew up to make radical scientific discoveries. Therefore, if you are a later-born child, you may have the three essential characteristics that you need to be a successful scientist: open-mindedness, intellectual flexibility, and a noncompetitive attitude.

The Turnabout

Opposing view

Your view

To use the "turnabout" approach, begin with a statement or statements contrary to your thesis statement, especially if this is the most popular opinion about the topic. Then introduce the opposite view (your own opinion) with words of contrast like *however, on the other hand,* or *in fact.* State your opinion in the thesis statement. Here is a sample turnabout introduction.

> Traditionally, a man and woman who want to spend their lives together are expected to marry. Marriage is a commitment recognized by a government and/or a religious institution. When a couple lives together without marriage (called cohabitation), many people believe it is morally wrong. Many people also assume that a couple who cohabitate without marriage may be unwilling to make a long-term commitment. However, cohabitation without marriage is often preferable to marriage for several important reasons.

1 Read the following introductory paragraphs. Underline the word or words in the first sentence that also appear in the thesis statement.

1. Why do some siblings remain close while others drift apart? You may guess that it's due to their age or their childhood relationships. Or perhaps you think that brothers remain closer than a brother and sister do. A recent survey on sibling relationships produced some surprising findings. In fact, black and Hispanic siblings are closer than white siblings, siblings in large families remain closer than those in smaller families, and sisters are more likely than brothers to keep up close relationships.

2. Most people know a family like this: Two children have the same parents, grow up in the same house, and share many of the same experiences, and yet they are surprisingly different. Although it may not seem logical, people can differ as much from their siblings as they do from their friends. Psychologists say that the differences are caused by three important factors: genetics, birth order, and parental relations.

3. Humans are not alone in having to deal with the ups and downs of sibling relationships. According to a growing amount of scientific research, ape and monkey siblings also demonstrate the emotions that are well known to any human brother or sister. Like humans, apes and monkeys display cooperation, competition, and generosity toward their siblings.

2 What type or types of introductory paragraphs are the three paragraphs in Exercise 1? Reread the first paragraph of "A Family of Women" on page 67. What type or types of introductory paragraph does the writer use?

Thesis Statement

The *thesis statement* expresses the main topic of the essay. Like the topic sentence, it should also give your opinion about the topic. The *thesis* differs from the topic sentence, however, because it expresses the main idea of the entire essay, not just one paragraph. In basic essay writing, the thesis statement appears at the end of the introductory paragraph.

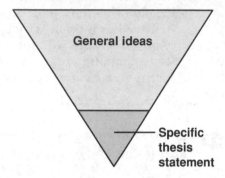

Here are some important points to remember when you write the thesis statement:

- A thesis statement must be a complete sentence.

  Not a thesis statement: The advantages of being an only child.

  Thesis statement: Being the only child has several advantages.

- A thesis statement should not simply announce the topic; rather, it should express your attitude, opinion, or idea about the topic.

  Not a thesis statement: I am going to write about how the oldest son enjoys many privileges.

  Thesis statement: The oldest son enjoys many privileges.

- A thesis statement should express an opinion, not a fact.

  Not a thesis statement: Nurturing a child means feeding and taking care of it.

  Thesis statement: Parents must be firm, kind, and patient in order to nurture a child.

- A thesis statement may express more than one idea about a topic, but these ideas should be consistent.

  Not a thesis statement: My friend Elaine is friendly, and she has three children.

  Thesis statement: My friend Elaine is a friendly, cheerful, and kind person.

- A thesis statement is most often not a question.

  Not a thesis statement: What are the advantages of being single?

  Thesis statement: Being single means that you have a peaceful, private, and independent life.

1 Read the following sentences. Decide if each is a correct thesis statement. On a separate piece of paper, rewrite the incorrect sentences to make them good thesis statements. Add or change words as necessary.

1. I would like to discuss the negative effects of divorce.

2. Women in my home country usually marry at the age of 20.

3. Getting along well with my older siblings requires maturity, a sense of humor, and love.

4. The best way to raise my children.

5. U.S. families have become substantially smaller in the last fifty years.

6. In this essay, I am going to describe three effects of being the oldest male child in a family.

7. Parents should teach their children to respect their elders, be honest, and work hard.

8. My friend Paul, an only child, is an independent, self-starting, and self-critical person.

9. The responsibilities of children to their parents.

10. What are the effects of growing up as an only child?

2 With a partner, brainstorm ideas for essays on the general topics that follow. On the lines, write a possible thesis statement for each one.

Example

working mothers
Working mothers lead very busy lives.

1. a small family

_____

_____

2. an ideal friend

_____

_____

3. my bad habits

_____

_____

4. single parents

_____

_____

5. family values

_____

_____

6. cohabitation before marriage

_____

_____

7. divorce

_____

_____

8. a large family

_____

_____

STEP 3

Writing the First Draft

Using your brainstorming notes (Step 1) and your work from organizing ideas and sentences (Step 2), write the first draft of your essay on birth order and gender.

- Introduce the topic in the introduction paragraph. State your opinion about your birth order/gender role in the thesis statement.

- Develop your opinion in three body paragraphs. Begin each paragraph with a topic sentence that introduces one major point (one part of your opinion about your birth order/gender role). Support each major point with details, examples, and facts.

- Conclude by restating your main idea.

STEP 4

Revising

Exchange drafts with a partner. Read each other's paragraphs and answer these questions.

- ❏ Does the introduction paragraph introduce the topic and catch the reader's interest?
- ❏ Does it have an effective thesis statement?
- ❏ Does each body paragraph begin with a topic sentence introducing a major point?
- ❏ Is there a conclusion paragraph?

Discuss your partner's comments. Take notes on any revisions you need to make. Write a second draft of your paper.

STEP 5

Editing

PRE-TEST

Circle the appropriate verb form to complete the sentences.

1. Everyone in my family _help/helps_ with work around the house.

2. The people in my family _enjoy/enjoys_ each other's company.

3. Being the parent of five children _take/takes_ a lot of energy.

4. Joseph _don't have/doesn't have_ any family in the area.

5. One of my best friends _live/lives_ in San Francisco.

6. Do you enjoy _to be/being_ the oldest child, or would you rather be the youngest one in your family?

7. She wants _to become/becoming_ more independent.

8. It is difficult for parents _to teach/teaching_ their children well.

9. _To keep/Keeping_ the house in order is difficult during school vacations.

10. I learned how to cook by _watch/watching_ my mother.

Have your instructor check your answers.

Grammar

Study the grammar explanations on page 78 and do the exercises. These will help you recognize and correct grammar mistakes in your writing.

Subject-Verb Agreement

Study the sentences that follow. Notice how the subjects and verbs differ in each sentence.

```
    ┌──────SUBJECT──────┐┌VERB┐
    My sisters and I  live in the same city.
```

```
    ┌──────────SUBJECT──────────┐ ┌VERB┐
    My oldest brother, Mark,  lives in Colorado.
```

In the first sentence, the subject is the noun phrase *my sisters and I.* The subject is plural, so the plural form of the verb, *live,* is used. In the second sentence, the subject is the noun phrase *my oldest brother, Mark.* The subject is singular, so it takes a singular form of the verb, *lives.*

Subject-verb agreement can prove troublesome in sentences with the following features.

■ The subject is a third-person singular noun or a pronoun that stands for a third-person singular noun. Third-person singular pronouns include *he/she/it* and words that end in *-body, -one,* and *-thing.*

   My uncle lives in California. **He** owns a dry cleaning business.

   Everyone in my family depends on me.

■ The subject is a gerund, which is always singular.

   Being the oldest child was sometimes difficult.

■ The subject is a noun phrase containing a head noun and a descriptive phrase.

```
        HEAD NOUN                    VERB
    The papers on my brother's desk were disorganized.
```

```
        COMPLETE SUBJECT          VERB
    The papers on my brother's desk were disorganized.
```

```
            HEAD NOUN              VERB
    The strongest bond in most societies is among family members.
```

```
        COMPLETE SUBJECT          VERB
    The strongest bond in most societies is among family members.
```

The verb must agree in number with the head noun, not with other nouns in the descriptive phrase.

■ The sentence has two subjects.

   Richard and Regina have four children.

■ The sentence begins with *There is* or *There are.*

   There are four people in my family.

   There was a big mess in my little sister's room.

Edit the following paragraph for errors in subject-verb agreement. Find the subjects and verbs of each sentence. Change the verb if it does not agree in number with the subject. Some sentences are correct. The first one is done for you.

Family Values

Parents should teach their children to be hard-working, kind, and

respectful. First, parents ~~needs~~ *need* to teach their children to work hard.

Working hard is a great way to bring money into the home. If you have

money, it is easy to support a family. If a parent teach the children to

work hard, the children will never have a problem supporting

themselves. Second, kindness is an important value. A mother and father

teaches their children to be kind by showing kindness to them. When

you is kind, people will be kind to you, too. Third, parents has to teach

their children to be respectful to others. Being respectful to friends,

family members, and coworkers shows that you are a person with good

character. A person who give respect receive respect. These are the most

important values that a parent has to teach children when they is young.

Ylli Merzani, Albania

DO IT YOURSELF
For more practice:
Subject-verb
  agreement, 220
Simple present
  tense verbs, 217

Gerunds and Infinitives

Gerunds and infinitives are verbs that function like nouns. Gerunds (-*ing* verbs) and infinitives (*to* + verb) can serve as subjects or objects in sentences.

Being the youngest child is not easy.	gerund = subject of sentence
I want **to have** more freedom.	infinitive = object of sentence

Gerunds

- Gerunds can be subjects or subject complements. Notice that a gerund subject is singular.

Cooking is my mother's favorite pastime.	**gerund** = subject
My father's hobby is **fishing.**	**gerund** = subject complement

- Gerunds can also be objects of certain verbs like *avoid, consider, enjoy,* and *keep.* See page 236 for a list of more verbs that take gerunds as objects.

  My brother enjoys **going** out with his friends.   gerund = object of verb *enjoy*

- Gerunds can be objects of prepositions.

  My sister Vicki is good at **drawing.**   gerund = object of preposition *at*

  We save money by **eating** at home.   gerund = object of preposition *by*

- Form the negative gerund by adding *not.*

  Not eating chocolate is sometimes hard for me.

Infinitives

- Infinitives are not commonly used as subjects of sentences. We usually use *it* as the subject and put the infinitive at the end of the sentence.

  Raising children is not easy.   =   It's not easy **to raise** children.

- Infinitives are used as the objects of certain verbs like *decide, hope, learn, plan,* and *want.* See page 236 for a list of more verbs that take infinitives as objects.

  My brother has **decided to go** to pharmacy school.
  He **plans to study** at Temple University.

  Some of these verbs follow the pattern **verb + object + infinitive.**

  I **asked my brother Stephen to carry** my heavy packages.

- Form the negative infinitive by adding *not.*

  My parents told my friends **not to call** our house after 10 p.m.

Common Problems

- Don't confuse gerunds with progressive verbs.

  GERUND
  Talking on the telephone is Nora's favorite pastime.

  PROGRESSIVE VERB
  She **is talking** on the phone right now.

- Never change an infinitive ending, even when the subject or the time changes.

  Incorrect: My aunt Elizabeth loves to goes shopping.
  Correct: My aunt Elizabeth loves **to go** shopping.
  Incorrect: My cousin and I wanted to visited the museum yesterday, but it was closed.
  Correct: My cousin and I wanted **to visit** the museum yesterday, but it was closed.

1 Underline the gerunds and infinitives in the first part of the essay "Solving Family Problems." The first one is underlined for you.

Solving Family Problems

What makes one family able to get along while another is always in conflict? A new study of how families really work reveals three important ways <u>to solve</u> family problems.

Task One: Family Contracts

A family needs a set of rules to run smoothly. The parents should make the rules clear by spelling out who does what and when. They should include everything from Mom's agreeing not to be angry when she is under stress to teenage Jim's getting home by 10 p.m. on weeknights. The parents should invite the children to discuss the rules and suggest changes to them.

---

2 Read the rest of the "Solving Family Problems" essay. Complete the sentences using gerunds and infinitives and any other logical words. Share your writing with a group of your classmates.

Task Two: Family Meeting

When the family's rules do not work well, everyone in the family should come to a family meeting. They should be ready

_____ their feelings. Children shouldn't be afraid of
     1.

_____ difficult questions, and parents should not be
     2.

worried about _____ honest answers. It's important for
     3.

everyone _____ to each other. After everyone has spoken,
     4.

the parents go off _____. Meanwhile, the children go off
     5.

separately _____. Then the family meets again.
     6.

_____ a family meeting is an important part of
     7.

_____ family problems.
     8.

Task Three: Sharing Feelings

The family must schedule time every day when they can all be together, and each family member should talk for a brief period of time—five to ten minutes—about whatever happened during the day.

_____ time to talk and listen to each other is important in a
 9.

family. It's especially important _____ things that made
 10.

each family member angry, hurt, or frustrated. Each should give the

other a chance _____ his or her feelings by
 11.

_____ quietly. In this way, family members learn
 12.

_____.
 13.

_____ family problems is not easy, but it can be done
 14.

with a little work. Every family should consider _____
 15.

family contracts and meetings as a way _____ the family
 16.

_____.
 17.

DO IT YOURSELF
For more practice:
Gerunds, 234
Infinitives, 235

Writing the Final Draft

Use the checklist to edit your essay on birth order and gender. Then write your final draft.

Editing Checklist

❏ Are people suffixes used correctly?

❏ Do subjects and verbs agree in number?

❏ Are gerunds and infinitives used correctly?

Your instructor will grade your paper for its content, organization, and language using the evaluation sheet for this chapter on page 203. Read over the evaluation sheet. Then reread and edit your paper as necessary before you turn in the final draft.

On Your Own

Choosing Between Similar Words

As your vocabulary grows, you will find that English has many words with similar pronunciation and spelling. It's easy to confuse similar words, as this student did:

> My mother doesn't lesson to me.

The incorrect word is *lesson*. The word *lesson* is spelled and sounds almost the same as *listen*, which is the correct word needed in this sentence.

Be sure that the word you use is the word you mean.

1 Work with a partner. Study the pairs of words and read how each word is used in a sentence. Then read each sentence to your partner. Ask your partner to cover the page and write down the word you have used. Switch roles, and check each other's words.

1. though/thought
   a. Even **though** I didn't finish the exam, I still got a good grade.
   b. I **thought** about our conversation for a long time.

2. they're/their
   a. Those children are happy because **they're** playing together.
   b. The students picked up **their** books.

3. live/leave
   a. I **live** in an apartment.
   b. If you **leave** work early, let me know.

4. felt/fell
   a. I **felt** sick today.
   b. He **fell** down and broke his leg.

5. along/alone
   a. There are many shops **along** the road.
   b. I don't like being **alone.**

6. he's/his
   a. Do you see that man? **He's** my neighbor.
   b. **His** father is a doctor.

7. think/thing
   a. I **think** you are nice.
   b. You did a nice **thing.**

8. sit/seat
   a. Please **sit** down.
   b. Your **seat** is in the front row.

9. than/then
   a. Peaches taste better **than** lemons.
   b. First, we will go to the park. **Then** we will have a picnic.

10. thought/taught   a. I **thought** that I was sick, so I went to the doctor.

                                             b. The teacher was absent. Who **taught** her class?

11. bought / brought   a. I **bought** a new backpack last week.

                                             b. Sam **brought** his cousin to class today.

12. quite / quiet   a. I need a **quiet** place to study.

                                             b. I'm going to sleep. I'm **quite** tired.

2 Write any words that you misused in your Personal Spelling List. Write the word and the sentence in which it is used.

3 Look over the writing that you have done in Chapters 3 and 4. Find the words that you misspelled. Add these words to your spelling list.

4 Work with a partner. Study the words on your spelling list. Test each other on the spelling of each word. Ask your instructor to help you pronounce the words, if necessary.

More Writing Practice

Write an essay about one of the following topics.

REMEMBER Gather ideas before you write your first draft. In that draft, include an introduction with a thesis statement. Begin each body paragraph with a major point sentence. Add details, facts, or examples to support each point. Add a conclusion paragraph to restate the main idea. After you finish, revise and edit your essay.

---

1. _____'s Birth Order

   Write an essay explaining how birth order and/or gender has affected the personality of a friend or sibling. In the thesis statement, state three of the person's characteristics and relate the person's qualities to his or her birth order and/or gender. Include examples to illustrate that the person has the qualities.

2. **My Best Qualities**

   Write an essay about two or three of your best qualities. Explain the qualities and give examples to show that you have them.

3. **An Ideal Friend**

   Write a paragraph about the qualities you look for in an ideal friend. What are the most important qualities in a friend? Why do you appreciate these qualities? Give examples of specific actions that illustrate the qualities that you value.

Chapter Goals   Take credit for achieving the learning goals for Chapter 4. Check (✔) all of the goal(s) that you have achieved. If you are having problems with one of these goals, get extra practice by writing another essay on one of the topics on page 84, or do the additional language exercises in the appropriate Do It Yourself section at the back of the book. Then talk to your instructor about your writing.

Chapter Goals Checklist

❑ Write an introduction paragraph.

❑ Write an effective thesis statement.

❑ Recognize and use person suffixes.

❑ Make subjects and verbs agree in number.

❑ Recognize and use gerunds and infinitives.

❑ Choose between similar words correctly.

Two Sides of Technology

Chapter Goals

- Use an outline to organize an essay.
- Use examples to support an opinion.
- Write a summary of a reading.
- Recognize and use adjective endings.
- Use present and past tense verbs together.
- Use articles appropriately.

Approaching the Topic

Today's technology has both benefits and drawbacks. The saying "You can't live with it, and you can't live without it" may well describe the ways we interact with technology. In Chapter 5, you can examine both positive and negative sides of technology.

1. The photograph above shows *technological devices*.

   - *Technological* means that these items were developed through the knowledge and methods gained from science and industry.
   - *Devices* are tools or machines used for special purposes.

   Which of these technological devices do you consider the most important in your life? Why?

2. Do technological devices sometimes create problems for you? How? Give examples of the disadvantages of technological devices.

READING FOR WRITING

Reading 1

Discuss these questions with your classmates before you read: What is your opinion of cell phones? Do you own one? Do you think they are beneficial? Are they problematic?

Living with Cell Phones

1   In today's technology-driven world, the cell phone has emerged as a great success. If you have any doubt about the popularity of "cells," just look around you. In buildings, parking lots, stores, vehicles, and on the street, nearly everyone is carrying a cell. However, the popularity of cell phones is also the problem with cell phones.

2   Of course, no one can deny that cell phones are very useful. Parents and children carry them around so that they can keep track of[1] each other. Friends use cell phones to chat with each other on the spur of the moment.[2] In emergencies, people use cell phones to call tow trucks, taxis, or ambulances or notify others that they are running late. Users soon discover that their cell phones are so useful that they cannot go anywhere without them.

3   The fact that cell phones are in everyone's pocket, purse, and hand means that the din[3] of ringing phones and conversation has invaded public spaces. Cell phones ring in restaurants, cinemas, and libraries. In stores, shoppers talk long and loudly, asking their family members what size or color clothing they want. People even carry on long conversations about personal topics with friends and lovers where everyone around them can hear. Recently I was sitting in chemistry class, listening closely to the professor's lecture, and "ring" went my classmate's cell phone. All this noise is disrupting[4] the peace.

4   However, the most significant[5] disadvantage of cell phones is that so many people drive and talk simultaneously.[6] Increasingly, drivers take to the roads and pull out their phones—on highways and on busy streets. It stands to reason that drivers are distracted[7] when they drive and talk. In fact, in 1997, the *New England Journal of Medicine* reported that motorists

who use cell phones are four times more likely to crash. A three-year study in Oklahoma found that accidents connected with cell phone use were nine times more likely to result in deaths. Japan, Australia, and numerous other countries have banned the use of hand-held cell phones while driving.

5   Clearly, cell phones are helpful devices. Still, as long as people use them irresponsibly,[8] they will cause problems, particularly when their users don't think about others around them. In public, cell phone users often disturb other people with the noise they make; on the road, they put pedestrians and other drivers in danger. People shouldn't throw away their cell phones, but they should get into the habit of using them more considerately and carefully.

---

[1]*keep track of:* follow the movements of
[2]*on the spur of the moment:* without planning ahead of time
[3]*din:* noise
[4]*disrupting:* stopping a situation, event, etc. from continuing in its usual way
[5]*significant:* noticeable or important
[6]*simultaneously:* at the same time
[7]*distracted:* not able to think clearly because something takes your attention away from what you are doing
[8]*irresponsibly:* doing things carelessly without thinking about the possible results

Discussion and Analysis

In a group, do the activities and discuss the questions. Then write answers to each question on a separate piece of paper. Write your answers in complete sentences.

1. What is the writer's opinion about cell phones? Underline the thesis statement.

2. What advantage of cell phones does the writer present? Underline the sentence that introduces this major point.

3. What disadvantages of cell phones does the writer present? Underline the sentences that introduce these major points.

4. What examples, facts, or details does the writer include to tell more about each major point?

5. What kind of information does the writer include in the conclusion?

6. Do you agree with the writer's opinion? Why or why not? Write a quick response to the writer stating whether you agree or disagree with his ideas.

Reading 2

Discuss these questions with your classmates before you read: Do you know how a CD (compact disc) burner works? Do you buy music CDs? Do you listen to music on the Internet? Do you use CDs for other purposes?

The Pros and Cons of CD Burners

1   Music lovers of all ages are "burning" their own compact discs these days on home computers. It's tempting to want to make a CD rather than pay for one at a music store. Computer manufacturers are encouraging this practice by offering CD recorders, or "burners," as standard equipment. However, there are disadvantages along with benefits when you use a CD burner to record music.

2   First, the major disadvantage of burning music CDs is that it can be illegal. Until recently, Internet users traded tens of millions of songs on a Web site called Napster. Then major music companies, which blamed online piracy[1] for a drop in CD sales, took Napster to court for violating copyright[2] laws. In July 2001, the site was shut down. Before this event, the Napster phenomenon[3] had caused an explosion in music file-sharing on the Internet. New services still allow Internet users to trade all types of copyrighted materials—from songs to video games and movies. However, in most cases, these sites do not get permission from the copyright holders to reproduce or copy the materials. Only a few artists who hope to make their names better known have agreed to allow their music to be copied from free music sites.

3   In addition to the legal issues it raises, burning music files from free music sites also has technical drawbacks. The main difficulty comes from the fact that files are shared from one user to another. When a user connects to a file-sharing site, he or she requests a song. The site's central server[4] lists all the songs that are available from other users connected to the server at that time. A user can download[5] a music file only while the user who has that file on his or her computer remains connected to the site. It takes about five minutes to download just one song, so downloads are commonly interrupted when the user whose files are being copied disconnects from the site. Unfortunately, the music lover may find that he or she has only copied parts of songs.

4   There are, in fact, legal music sites available on the Internet, but they have drawbacks, too. As with file-sharing sites, music from these sites can be listened to, downloaded onto a computer, or copied onto a CD. One site advertises that all of its music is legally licensed from music companies or artists. However, the main limitation of these sites is that the user can copy only songs available from the site's music library. Also, the service is not free. A user pays a monthly fee of about US$10 to US$25 to access the site's library.

5   Music lovers who want to use their CD burners have two choices. They can get free music files that may be imperfect and illegal, or they can pay for their files but have limited choices and more expenses.

---

[1]*piracy:* illegally copying and selling other people's work
[2]*Copyright* laws give the creator control over his or her original work. Copyrighted materials may not be reproduced, published, or copied without the copyright holder's permission.
[3]*phenomenon:* something that happens or exists in society, science, or nature that is unusual or difficult to understand
[4]*server:* in computer language, the main computer on a network that controls all the others
[5]*download:* to move information from one computer to another using a *modem,* a piece of electronic equipment that allows information from one computer to be sent along telephone wires to another computer

Discussion and Analysis   In a group, do the activities and discuss the questions. Then write answers to each question on a separate piece of paper. Write your answers in complete sentences.

1. What is the writer's opinion about CD burners? Underline the thesis statement.

2. Underline the sentences that introduce each major point (the disadvantages of CD burners).

3. What examples, details, or facts does the writer use to support each major point?

4. What type of information does the writer include in the conclusion?

5. Do you agree with the writer's major points? Why or why not?

Journal Writing   The name *Luddites* is still used today to refer to people who don't like the changes caused by technology. The name comes from workers who revolted against the startup of cloth factories in England in the 1800s, led by an imaginary hero, General Ned Ludd. Are you a Luddite, someone who doesn't accept new technology? Or are you a "techie," someone who likes new technology? Write a journal entry about your attitude toward technology.

Language for Writing

Word Families: Adjective Endings

Learning the most common adjective endings will help you to use adjectives correctly in your writing. Study the endings of the following adjectives.

care**ful**	practi**cal**	danger**ous**	surpris**ed**
expens**ive**	relax**ing**	proble**matic**	effici**ent**

1 Complete the words in the paragraph with the appropriate adjective endings. Use a dictionary to help you. The first one is done for you.

DVDs or Videocassettes?

There are advantages and disadvantages to watching films on digital versatile discs (DVDs). First, DVDs are very easy to use. You can move to different tracks on a DVD just like on a CD. This may be very use *ful*_____ to you if you enjoy watching one very excit_____ or
   1.   2.
romant_____ scene of a movie over and over. If you try to search for
     3.
an interest_____ scene with a videocassette tape, you may become
          4.
impati_____. DVDs are also advantage_____ because they are
    5.   6.
small. If you have limit_____ space, you will appreciate the fact that
          7.
a DVD requires one-third the space of a videocassette tape. However,
DVDs have one bas_____ disadvantage. They are more
          8.
expens_____ than videocassettes. Many DVDs costs more than
    9.
USD$20, so it may be more economic_____ to rent a movie DVD
                                    10.
than to buy one unless it's one of your person_____ favorites. In
                                       11.
conclusion, DVDs are more high-pric_____ than videocassette tapes,
                         12.
but they are still more conveni_____.
               13.

2 Write five sentences to describe technological devices. In each sentence, use one of the *adjectives* from the box or paragraph in Exercise 1.

Example

Using a microwave oven is an **efficient** way to cook food.

Advantage/Disadvantage Sentences

Here are some common sentence patterns for introducing an advantage or disadvantage.

Pattern 1

SUBJECT   VERB
An advantage of using the Internet is its convenience.
└─────────Topic─────────┘ └──Advantage──┘

Pattern 2

SUBJECT   VERB   SUBJECT-VERB
One advantage of palm pilots is that you can keep data in a small space.
└─────────Topic─────────┘ └──────────Advantage──────────┘

Pattern 3

HEAD NOUN + DESCRIPTIVE PHRASE   VERB
One of the disadvantages of the Internet is that people can track your activities.
└─────────Topic─────────┘ └──────Disadvantage──────┘

Note: The subject consists of a head noun (*One*) plus a descriptive phrase (*of the disadvantages of the Internet*). In the descriptive phrase, the noun that follows *of the* is always plural. The head noun in the noun phrase is *one*, so the verb is singular.

Complete the *advantage/disadvantage* sentences below. For the last two, write your own *advantage/disadvantage* sentence about one technological device.

1. One of the benefits of DVDs _____

   _____.

2. _____ is that you can thaw frozen food in minutes.

3. _____ is its speed.

4. Another disadvantage of audiocassettes is _____.

   _____.

5. One of the advantages of using e-mail _____.

6. _____ is that they are convenient.

7. Another advantage of cell phones is that _____.

8. An important benefit of microwave ovens is _____

   _____.

9. _____

   _____.

10. _____

    _____.

Academic Words

1 Study the following academic word list and the example sentences. Check (✔) the academic words that you already know.

❑	**consumer**	A smart **consumer** spends money wisely.
❑	**contribution**	Seat belts have made a major **contribution** to automobile safety.
❑	**devices**	Cell phones are popular technological **devices.**
❑	**format**	The digital versatile disc is one **format** for viewing films.
❑	**interact**	We **interact** more and more with computers and less and less with people.
❑	**constant**	We have **constant** problems with our car, so we plan to sell it.
❑	**method**	The electric scooter is an interesting **method** of transportation.
❑	**simultaneously**	The on-screen TV schedule lets you view a program and scan the schedule **simultaneously.**

2 Test your comprehension by matching one of the definitions below to an academic word from the list in Exercise 1. Write the word on the line.

1. _____ means, way
2. _____ size, shape, design
3. _____ at the same time
4. _____ continuous
5. _____ buyer
6. _____ something given
7. _____ tools, machines
8. _____ communicate

3 If you have difficulty matching any word from Exercise 1 to its definition in Exercise 2, put it in the academic word list in your notebook. Write its definition and a sentence using the word.

WRITING

Assignment

Write an essay that presents three advantages and/or disadvantages of one technological device. To write your essay, follow the writing steps.

STEP 1

Getting Ideas

1 Select a technological device to write about. Think of technological tools used at work, home, or in your daily life in general.

2 Once you have decided on a topic, list the advantages (pros) and disadvantages (cons) of this device, as the graphic organizer below illustrates.

Hand-Held Computer

Pros	Cons
– Keeps track of appointments	– "Pen" is awkward to use
– Keeps personal information	– Easy to forget or misplace
– Lets me check e-mail	– Expensive
– Lets me do calculations	
– Lets me write short notes	

3 Decide whether you want to write about the advantages or disadvantages of the device, or both advantages and disadvantages. Circle ideas from the list that you want to include in your paragraph.

STEP 2

Organizing

Outlining

An *outline* gives the main ideas or facts about something without all the details. It helps you organize your writing because it lists the main ideas in the order that they will appear in your essay. Look at the following outline of Reading 2 on pages 89–90. Each Roman numeral represents one paragraph.

The Pros and Cons of CD Burners

 I. **Introduction:** Introduce the topic and present your thesis statement.

   Example thesis statement: There are disadvantages along with benefits when you use a CD burner to record music.

II. Body Paragraph 1: State the first major supporting point in your topic sentence.

> **Example topic sentence:** First, the major disadvantage of burning music CDs is that it can be illegal.

> **A.** Give a first supporting point (details, examples, or facts) about this idea.
> **B.** Give a second supporting point.

III. Body Paragraph 2: State the second major supporting point in your topic sentence.

> **Example topic sentence:** In addition to the legal issues it raises, burning music files from free music sites also has technical drawbacks.

> **A.** Give a first supporting point.
> **B.** Give a second supporting point.

IV. Body Paragraph 3: State the third major supporting point in your topic sentence.

> **Example topic sentence:** There are, in fact, legal music sites available on the Internet, but they have drawbacks, too.

> **A.** Give a first supporting point.
> **B.** Give a second supporting point.

V. Conclusion: Include the thesis or your major points and a final opinion or statement about the importance of the topic.

1 Look back over the lists that you made on page 94. Write a thesis statement that introduces the topic (the technological device) and contains a controlling idea (advantages and/or disadvantages).

Examples

My hand-held computer has helped me organize my life in several useful ways.

Three important benefits of my hand-held computer are that I can record appointments, store personal data, and write notes or lists.

Using a hand-held computer has both advantages and disadvantages.

2 Use the sample outline on page 94 and above to guide you in making your own outline for this assignment. As in the sample outline, write your thesis statement and body paragraph topic sentences in complete sentences.

Examples as Support

As you learned in Chapter 2, you should develop paragraphs with details, facts, or examples. Examples can be used to show why an opinion is true. They also add interest to your writing. For instance, in Reading 1, the writer presented three *disadvantages* of cell phones. To support one of the points, the writer used an example, highlighted here:

> The fact that cell phones are in everyone's pocket, purse, and hand means that the din of ringing phones and conversation has invaded public spaces. . . . Recently I was sitting in chemistry class, listening closely to the professor's lecture, and "ring" went my classmate's cell phone.

This example is a brief story with *specific* details that *shows* that something is true. Examples are the most effective when they include *specific* information about one *specific* instance. Include specific details about *when* and *where* the story took place, *who* was involved, and *what* happened.

1 Work with a partner. Develop the paragraph that follows by adding supporting sentences that contain examples. The examples may also have specific details or facts in them. Rewrite your paragraph on a separate piece of paper. Share your sentences in a group.

Air Conditioning in Summer

Having air conditioning in the summertime keeps you comfortable, but it also has distinct disadvantages. First, you stay cool indoors, but the minute you go outside, you feel *really* hot. Your body becomes so accustomed to the ice-cold air that when you go outside, you feel that it's hotter than it really is. _____

_____

_____

_____

Another disadvantage of air conditioning in the summer is that you need two sets of clothing. _____

_____

_____

_____

On summer days, I often wonder if it wouldn't be better just to turn off the air conditioners and live in a one-temperature world.

2 Work with your partner. Read the following outline. Each body paragraph starts with a topic sentence that states one of the writer's major points about the topic of music. Under each topic sentence, write two examples to support each point. Include *specific* information in the sentences about each example. The first one is done for you.

The Benefits of Music

I. Introduction

Thesis statement: Music benefits people in several important ways.

II. Topic sentence: First of all, music makes exercise more enjoyable.

Example 1 *For example, in the workout room of my college gymnasium, students play fast music to keep them motivated while they are running on treadmills or riding stationary bicycles.*

Example 2 *Aerobic exercise programs on television also use lively music to keep the pace fast. People move their arms and legs quickly to follow the rhythm of the music.*

III. Topic sentence: Also, music can cheer people up when they are feeling down.

Example 1 _____
_____

Example 2 _____
_____

IV. Topic sentence: Finally, music helps some people do their work.

Example 1 _____
_____

Example 2 _____
_____

V. Conclusion

3 Read over the outline about a technological device that you wrote on page 195. Under each body paragraph topic sentence, list two examples that you could add to support the opinion in the topic sentence. Then write at least one complete sentence for each example. Follow the outline format used in Exercise 2.

Conclusion Paragraph

The conclusion paragraph brings an essay to a logical close. It may have a sentence or sentences that include the main idea of the thesis statement. You can also conclude an essay in these ways: *make a prediction, tell a result,* or *make a recommendation.*

Generally, the type or types of conclusion you use depends on your writing assignment. Here are some common ways to conclude an essay.

- **Refer to the main idea.** This type of conclusion reminds the reader of the main idea of the thesis statement or sums up the major points of the essay. It should not repeat the main idea in the exact words of the thesis statement. The concluding sentence or sentences may come close in thought to the idea in the thesis statement.

    Thesis statement: There are several important advantages to a digital camera.

    Conclusion: In conclusion, using a digital camera is an outstanding way to take pictures.

- **Make a prediction.** This type of conclusion makes a future prediction about the topic.

    Thesis statement: Technology has influenced music in several unique ways.

    Conclusion: In the future, technology may create even more diverse forms of music.

- **Tell a result.** This type of conclusion states a result or results of a problem, a situation, or a process that is presented in an essay.

    Thesis statement: In fact, the technology of television sets has improved in major ways.

    Conclusion: As a result of the improvements in the television set, this device has become an essential part of our daily lives.

- **Make a recommendation.** This type of conclusion gives the writer's advice, recommendation, or suggestions about a problem or a situation. It works well with essay topics in which the writer wishes to state a strong opinion.

    Thesis statement: The most popular automobiles of the twenty-first century are bigger, more expensive, and equipped with more distractions than ever before.

    Conclusion: Car manufacturers should make an effort to make the automobile a more practical means of transportation for future generations.

Read the essay "The Way We Listen to Music." Underline the thesis statement. Add a logical conclusion paragraph of at least two sentences. Compare your conclusion paragraph with your classmates'. Discuss which type of conclusion would be the most logical for this essay topic.

The Way We Listen to Music

1   In the twentieth century, the means for listening to music advanced from record players to tape decks to disc players. In the new millennium, music listening has evolved to the point that people can even listen to and record music digitally on their computers. In fact, today's music delivery systems are less bulky, less fragile, and less expensive.

2   First of all, the size of music listening devices has decreased considerably. In the 1960s, a high-fidelity record player was a large piece of wooden furniture with a lid that opened to a turntable and controls. The speakers were built into the wooden cabinet. The "hi-fi" played three sizes of vinyl records at three speeds, and it also had a radio built in. In the following decades, people listened to music on eight-track tapes about the size of a videotape, inserted into a "deck." Audiocassettes replaced eight-track tapes and could be played on smaller players. Now thin compact discs (CDs) can be played on players as small and thin as a salad plate. In this decade, technology and music enthusiasts are using mini-CDs with progressively smaller machines to play them on. An "MP3" music file is played on a player that is smaller than a deck of cards. The new millennium has produced more compact ways to enjoy music.

3   Music devices are also more durable now than they were. The motors on record players of the 1960s and earlier burned up and had to be replaced if they were overused. Also, needles that were used to play records and the plastic and metal "arms" that held the needles often broke. Likewise, the once popular eight-track and audiocassette tape players were problematic because tapes often got stuck in the players, which destroyed the tapes. Compact disc players and MP3 players of today are less easily broken because they contain fewer fragile parts. The CDs and mini-CDs themselves are thicker and harder, so they're also more durable than vinyl records or tape. And MP3 players that don't require discs have even fewer breakage problems. Clearly, as technology has advanced, the music delivery devices have become longer lasting.

4   Most important, music listening devices have decreased substantially in price. The "hi-fi" of the 1960s cost about $2,000 to $3,000 in current U.S. dollars, whereas today a person can buy a decent stereo system with a multitude of components—compact disc player, cassette player/recorder, and AM-FM radio—for less than US$100. Even stereo systems that play five compact discs automatically and have remote controls can be purchased for under US$200. Furthermore, the computer has contributed to the drop in the cost of music listening devices. Nowadays, it has become very popular to download music onto a computer from free music sites. Many people copy downloaded songs onto an MP3 player, which costs about US$100 and eliminates the need for purchasing CDs or tapes. Clearly, the equipment for playing music is much more affordable today.

5   _____

_____

_____

STEP 3

Writing the First Draft

Using your revised outline about a technological device that you wrote on page 98, write the first draft of your essay.

- In the introduction paragraph, include sentences to introduce the topic and catch the reader's interest. End this paragraph with your thesis statement.

- Begin each body paragraph with a topic sentence to introduce each advantage or disadvantage (a major point). Support each point with at least two examples. Include specific information in the examples.

- Add a conclusion paragraph that includes your main idea and gives other information to logically close the essay, such as telling a result, making a prediction, or giving a recommendation.

STEP 4

Revising

Exchange drafts with a partner. Read each other's essays and answer these questions.

- ❑ Does the introduction paragraph include a thesis statement that presents the advantages or disadvantages of one technological device?
- ❑ Does each body paragraph begin with a topic sentence that presents one major point (an advantage or disadvantage)? Is the paragraph supported with examples, facts, or details?
- ❑ Does the conclusion paragraph relate to the main idea? Does it include other information to close the essay in a logical way?

Discuss your partner's comments. Take notes on any revisions you need to make. Write the second draft of your essay.

Sharing Your Writing

After you have revised your essay, discuss with your partner the main ideas of his or her essay. Then write a brief summary of your partner's essay.

Summary Writing

A *summary* is a short statement or report that gives the main information about an event, plan, or report. You can use a summary to tell others the main information about what was spoken or written. You can also write a summary for yourself to help you remember important ideas in a reading.

A good summary has the following characteristics:

- It identifies the source being summarized.
- It presents all the main ideas and major points—not all the details—in the original text.
- It is shorter than the original.
- It does not change the meaning of the original text.
- It does not contain the writer's opinions about the original text.

1 Read the following brief summaries of Reading 1, "Living with Cell Phones." Work with your partner. Discuss which is the best summary. Share your answer with your classmates.

1. The essay "Living with Cell Phones" says that there are many benefits to using cell phones. People can call others anytime or any place. They can talk to them when there is an emergency. People even use cell phones in libraries. However, cell phones make noise.

2. The essay "Living with Cell Phones" says that cell phones are useful, but they can cause some problems. One problem is the noise. People talk on the phones and disturb others. Another problem is using cell phones while driving. The writer believes it may be dangerous. According to the writer, people should use cell phones responsibly.

3. The essay "Living with Cell Phones" says that using cell phones while driving can distract drivers. They may have accidents. I agree with the author. I believe people should pull over and stop driving if they want to talk on their cell phones.

2 Write a brief summary of your partner's essay. Be sure to identify the essay by its title and author. Include the main idea and major points but not all the ideas. Write the summary in your own words, if possible. Do not include your opinion. After you have finished, share your summary with your partner. Ask him or her if you have accurately stated the main information in the original essay.

STEP 5

Editing

PRE-TEST

1. Correct the five verb errors in the paragraph.

A telephone answering machine allows me to miss calls when I am busy. If I don't have time to talk to someone, I can let the machine take a message and then call the person back later. I remembered one particular time when I make bread. My hands are full of dough and the telephone started to ring. I don't want to pick up the receiver because my fingers were sticky. I let the answering machine take the call, and I continue my work. Then I called the person back later.

2. Complete the sentences with an appropriate article: *a, an, the,* or ∅ (no article).

With _____ answering machine, I can also screen my telephone
        1.
calls. If I let _____ machine pick up _____ call, I can listen to
                 2.   3.
part of _____ message and decide if I want to talk to _____
              4.   5.
person or not. For example, if my best friend calls, I listen to _____
                                                                            6.
message and pick up the call. However, I may not want to talk to

_____ old boyfriend or _____ nosy neighbor. _____
      7.   8.   9.
answering machine also helps me to avoid _____ calls from
                                                         10.
_____ telemarketers who want to sell me something. Generally, if
      11.
_____ telemarketer calls _____ home and _____ machine
      12.   13.   14.
answers, he or she will hang up and try another number.

Have your instructor check your answers.

Grammar

Study the following grammar explanations and do the activities. They will help you recognize and correct grammar mistakes in your writing.

Using Present and Past Tense Verbs Together

Study how verbs in the present and past tense are used together in the passage that follows.

First of all, microwave ovens **help** you to prepare last-minute meals. They **thaw** frozen food as well as **cook** food in a hurry. Recently I **realized** how much I **depend** on my microwave oven when I **had** unexpected dinner guests. I **used** the microwave to thaw frozen fish in five minutes. Then I **grilled** the fish in the oven while four potatoes **baked** in the microwave for fifteen minutes. The whole meal **took** less than thirty minutes to prepare, thanks to the microwave.

The passage illustrates that simple present tense verbs (*help, thaw, cook, depend*) are most commonly used to state present actions, situations, or conditions. Simple past tense verbs (*realized, had, used, grilled, baked, took*) are most commonly used to state past actions, situations, or conditions.

Review simple past tense and other less common past tense verbs on pages 222–223.

Complete the essay by adding simple present or simple past tense forms of the verbs in parentheses. Share your answers with a group of your classmates.

Tools for Washing Clothes

Since ancient times, people have used various methods and machines for washing clothes. From washing laundry in a river to using computerized electric washing machines, the methods for cleaning clothes _____*share*_____ (*share*) some common characteristics.

First of all, most clothes-washing techniques _____ (*involve*) moving fabric through water. For example, sea voyagers of the past

_____ (*wash*) their clothes by placing the dirty laundry in a cloth bag and throwing it overboard, letting the ship drag the bag along in the water. In his 1962 novel *Travels with Charley*, American writer John Steinbeck _____ (*offer*) a similar method. He _____ (*put*) his dirty laundry in a bucket of soapy water in the back of his motor home. Then he simply _____ (*let*) the motion of the vehicle clean his clothes as he _____ (*drive*) down the road. Modern-day washing machines _____ (*work*) on the same principle. They _____ (*push*) water through the fabric of the clothes.

Second, many washing tools and methods _____ (*imitate*) the movement of human hands. The first commercial tool for washing clothes _____ (*was*) the washboard, which _____ (*come*) along in 1797. People all over the world still _____ (*use*) it today. A washboard _____ (*allow*) a person to clean clothes simply by rubbing them along the board with the hand. A later tool for washing clothes, the "dolly," _____ (*be*) not much more than a broom with four "fingers" at the bottom to move the clothes around in a bucket. Similarly, today's electric washing machines _____ (*have*) paddles that operate like hands and _____ (*stir*) the clothes in the water.

Third, many washing machines _____ (*have*) a similar design. Handles or paddles _____ (*move*) the clothing through water contained in a large drum or bucket. Mr. H. Sidgier of Great Britain _____ (*design*) the first washing machine in 1782. It _____ (*consist*) of a tublike wooden cage with rods and a handle for turning. Modern-day washing machines generally _____ (*run*) on electric motors, but they also

_____ (*have*) large drums in which you _____

DO IT YOURSELF
For more practice:
Present tense
    verbs, 217
Past tense
    verbs, 222
Using present and
    past tense verbs
    together, 226

(*place*) the dirty clothes and paddles that _____ (*move*) the

laundry in a circular or back-and-forth motion in water.

In sum, the methods for washing clothes have changed over time.

However, even the washing machines of today _____

(*continue*) to display the same characteristics of early washing methods

and tools.

Articles and Noun Phrases

An *article* (*a/an/the*) is a word that is used before a noun to show if it is a particular example of something or a general example. The charts that follow introduce the rules for article use. See page 241 for more rules.

Rules for Article Use: Count Nouns

Example	Meaning	Use
An economical way to travel is to use **a bicycle.**	The articles *a* and *an* indicate a **general** *way* and a **general** *bicycle*.	Use *a* and *an* only with singular count nouns. Use *an* if the noun or adjective before the noun begins with a vowel.
I saw **the new bicycle** that you bought recently.	The article *the* indicates a **specific** *bicycle*.	Sometimes specific nouns with *the* are followed by words that specify which one it is.
Calculators are valuable tools.	The absence of an article before the noun *calculators* indicates that the writer is talking about *calculators* in **general.**	Use no article when you write or talk about general plural count nouns.
A calculator is a valuable tool. **The calculator** is a valuable tool.	These sentences tell about the **general** characteristics of all *calculators*.	To show the general characteristics of a group, use a singular noun with the articles *a, an,* or *the* or a plural noun with no article.

Example	Meaning	Use
The dictionary that you must buy for this class is the *Longman Dictionary of American English*. **The students** in the front row can work together as a group.	The article *the* indicates a **specific** *dictionary* and **specific** *students*.	Use *the* with both singular and plural count nouns.
The Internet is a useful tool for finding information. There are many satellites in **the sky**.	The article *the* indicates a specific item that is unique, or that the writer/reader both understand that there is only one of this item.	

Rules for Article Use: Non-Count Nouns

Example	Meaning and Use
Technology brings both benefits and drawbacks.	The absence of an article before the noun *technology* indicates that the writer is talking about *technology* in **general**.
The water in the refrigerator is cold.	The article *the* indicates **specific** *water*.
Note: The articles *a* and *an* cannot be used with non-count nouns.	

1 Work with a partner.

1. Underline the articles and nouns that follow them in the first two paragraphs of the following essay. Discuss the use of articles. The first two are done for you.

2. Then add appropriate articles (*a, an, the,* or ∅) in the blank spaces. Compare your answers with a partner's.

The AirBoard

The *AirBoard* is *an* interesting new *way* to travel. The vehicle is called a hovercraft because it hovers, or floats, three to four inches off the ground. At US$15,000, it may not be the vehicle for you. However, it has several interesting features.

First of all, you control its direction with your body. You ride it like a snowboard or a skateboard. You lean to the left or the right, and the AirBoard moves with you. It also has a hand throttle to control speed. The AirBoard can go up to 15 miles per hour. Experienced riders can do tricks with the AirBoard.

Also, it looks different from _____ average vehicle. It has _____ round saucer, about 6 feet (182 centimeters) in diameter and 2½ (76 centimeters) feet high. It weighs about 300 pounds (136 kilograms). You stand on _____ saucer, hold onto _____ rope connected to it, and ride standing up. Unlike _____ car or _____ motorcycle, you can either "park" it outside or use _____ wheeled cart to bring it inside.

Finally, it is easy to operate. You start it with _____ key. It has _____ battery-powered electric starter. _____ AirBoard runs on gasoline. It will go about one hour on _____ tank of gas. In addition, _____ engineers who made it are working on _____ electric model. _____ electric model should be even easier to operate because you can charge _____ battery at home and not worry about adding _____ gasoline.

_____ AirBoard may not be _____ best vehicle for everyone, but may appeal to _____ city residents who travel _____ short distances. It is _____ appealing new way to travel.

2 Write sentences using the following nouns. Pay attention to whether the noun is singular or plural, and use appropriate articles. Compare your sentences with a partner's.

Example

automobile

An automobile is a convenient means of transportation.

1. bicycles

_____

_____

2. students in the computer lab

_____

_____

3. technology

_____

_____

4. electronic dictionary

_____

_____

5. monthly fee for cell phones

_____

_____

6. telephone answering machine

_____

_____

7. Internet

_____

_____

8. microwave oven

_____

_____

9. motorcycles

_____

_____

10. express trains

_____

_____

DO IT YOURSELF
For more practice:
Count and non-count nouns, 240
Article usage, 241
Articles with proper nouns, 241

Writing the Final Draft

Use the checklist to edit your essay on a technological device. Then write your final draft.

> ### Editing Checklist
>
> ❑ Are adjective endings used correctly?
>
> ❑ Are present tense verbs used appropriately?
>
> ❑ Are past tense verbs used appropriately?
>
> ❑ Are articles used appropriately?

Your instructor will grade your paper for its content, organization, and language using the evaluation sheet for this chapter on page 204. Read over the evaluation sheet. Then reread and edit your paper as necessary before you turn in the final draft.

On Your Own

More Writing Practice

Write an essay about one of the following topics.

REMEMBER Gather ideas before writing. Organize your writing into introduction, body, and conclusion paragraphs. Add supporting examples, details, or facts. Include the main idea in the conclusion paragraph.

1. **The Pros and Cons of the Internet**
   Write an essay about the advantages and/or disadvantages of the Internet. Use your own experience and general knowledge to support your opinions.

2. **Benefits of Music**
   Write an essay describing the benefits of music in your life. Does music relax you or stimulate you? Does it help you study, sleep, or do work? Explain how you use music in your life.

3. **One Means of Transportation**
   Write an essay about the advantages and/or disadvantages of one means, or method, of transportation, such as bus, train, car, or plane. Use facts and your own experience to support your opinions.

Chapter Goals   Take credit for achieving the learning goals in Chapter 5. Check (✔) all of the goals that you have achieved. If you are having problems with one of these goals, get extra practice by writing another essay on one of the topics on page 109, or do the additional language exercises in the appropriate Do It Yourself section at the back of the book. Then talk to your instructor about your writing.

Chapter Goals Checklist

❑ Use an outline to organize an essay.

❑ Use examples to support an opinion.

❑ Write a summary of a reading.

❑ Recognize and use adjective endings.

❑ Use present and past tense verbs together.

❑ Use articles appropriately.

Energy Revolution

Chapter Goals

- Recognize and use noun endings.
- Use clustering to gather ideas for writing.
- Outline a problem-solution essay.
- Use transitions.
- Use present perfect tense verbs appropriately.
- Avoid comma splices.

Approaching the Topic

There is a revolution occurring in the ways that we use natural resources to produce energy. Debates are ongoing about how people can conserve petroleum, gas, coal, trees, and water and use alternative energy resources. In Chapter 6, you will explore the topic of energy and the way people use it.

1. Look at the photo above. What energy resource or resources are being used in this situation? Do you know any alternative sources that might be used in place of the usual energy resource?

2. Think about all the things that you do in a typical day. Which activities require a natural resource such as fuel, water, or products made from wood? When and where do you use the resources?

3. What do you think are the major issues related to natural resources? What are your opinions about these issues?

READING FOR WRITING

Reading 1

Discuss these questions with your classmates before you read: The world has limited supplies of *natural resources* like petroleum, gas, coal, trees, and water. What are people already doing to reduce the use of natural resources? What can people do to conserve energy in buildings and homes?

Green Building

1   The world's energy needs are increasing while the supply of natural resources is diminishing.[1] Governments, businesses, and individuals have made some effort to reduce their energy usage, but we must do more. Since buildings have a tremendous[2] impact[3] on energy and the environment, one solution to the energy crisis is to use *green building*. Green building means designing, constructing, and using homes and buildings in energy-efficient ways. The principles[4] of green building call for a safer environment, intelligent use of materials, and energy conservation.

2   First, buildings and homes should create a safe environment for people and nature. Surprisingly, many homes and buildings today use synthetic[5] materials that may cause illness. Green building requires the use of safe materials. For example, green builders use cellulose insulation[6] in place of fiberglass insulation because fiberglass may create toxic[7] dust. Green building also demands that paints and carpets contain no lead[8] or dangerous dyes. Green building construction seeks to minimize damage to the environment. For example, in Harrisburg, Pennsylvania, the state Department of Environmental Protection built its headquarters on top of a former landfill.[9] This site was chosen because it would not harm plants or animals.

3   Next, green buildings should use recycled[10] and recyclable materials. The Pennsylvania Department of Environmental Protection offices have interior walls made of agricultural waste and recycled paper and floor tiles made of recycled glass. The partitions, walls that separate office spaces inside the building, are made from recycled soda bottles. Similarly,

steel is a recommended product in green building because it contains 70 percent recycled material and can be reused. Considering that 90 percent of the products consumed by Americans becomes waste in less than a year, reusing materials is essential in building construction, according to U.S. government studies.

4   Most important, buildings must conserve energy and water. Green building practices help builders conserve nonrenewable energy and use more renewable energy.[11] For example, in Alameda County, California, officials instruct homeowners on how to install solar panels on roofs to collect the sun's energy. The energy is stored in batteries to meet nighttime energy needs or collected by the public utility, which gives homeowners reduced utility bills. Alameda County's Green Building Guidelines also urge new residents to use solar water-heating systems. Using south-facing windows alone can store enough solar heat to reduce heating requirements by 30 to 50 percent. Green building guidelines also require builders to seal leaks, increase insulation, and utilize energy-saving lighting, appliances, and furnaces.[12] "Gray water," or reused water, is recycled for watering gardens. Low-flush toilets and low-flow showers and faucets are also used. All these practices are designed to conserve energy and water.

5   In sum, green building seeks to make the construction of homes and buildings part of the solution to energy shortages and environmental issues, rather than part of the problem. If we use green building, our environment will be safer and natural resources will last longer, giving scientists and engineers time to develop alternative energy sources such as wind power, water power, and solar energy.

[1]*diminishing:* becoming smaller or less important

[2]*tremendous:* very great in amount, power, size, etc.

[3]*impact:* the effect that an event or situation has on someone or something

[4]*principles:* moral rules or sets of ideas that make you behave in a particular way

[5]*synthetic:* made by combining several different substances; not natural, artificial

[6]*Insulation* is material used to cover or protect something so that electricity, sound, heat, etc. cannot get in or out. *Cellulose* insulation is made from recycled newspaper; *fiberglass* insulation is a synthetic product.

[7]*toxic:* poisonous

[8]*lead:* type of metal

[9]*landfill:* a place where waste is buried in large amounts

[10]*Recycled* objects or materials have been put through a special process so that they can be used again.

[11]*Renewable* energy is energy that can be replaced by natural processes so that it is never used up, like wind or solar power; opposite: *nonrenewable*.

[12]*furnaces:* large containers with fire inside, used for producing power or heat

Discussion and Analysis   In a group, do the activities and discuss the questions. Then write answers to each question on a separate piece of paper. Write your answers in complete sentences.

1. What is the writer's main idea? Underline the thesis statement.
2. What problem or problems are presented in the first paragraph?
3. What are the writer's solutions to the problem(s)? Underline the three sentences that introduce each solution.
4. Does green building seem like an effective strategy for solving the energy shortage problem? Why?
5. Does green building seem like an effective way to protect the environment? Why?
6. What other ideas do you have for making a home or building more energy efficient and environmentally safe? Explain.

Reading 2

Discuss this topic with your classmates before you read: *Wind farms*, like the one shown in the photograph, produce energy in an alternative way. Their source of energy is the wind, not the burning of the usual energy sources: petroleum, natural gas, and coal. What are some other alternative energy sources?

Limitations of Alternative Energy

1   Windmill "farms" dot the countryside of Great Britain, a visible sign of the revolution in energy production. In Europe and across the globe, governments are relying more on wind power and other alternative energy sources, less on oil and gas. However, the change is occurring slowly, due to serious limitations of alternative energy.

2   One major problem with alternative energy has been called the "not in my backyard" syndrome[1] (NIMBYism). Many people support alternative energy, but they don't want to see it in their local areas. Europe, which leads the world in its use of wind power, provides one example. Many British citizens have protested that wind power is noisy and disrupts television and radio reception. Residents have also complained that wind farms spoil the rural landscape. One solution to these dilemmas has been to locate the wind farms offshore. In Scotland, a proposed wind farm of 120 turbines[2] in the shallow waters of the North Sea may supply 5 percent

of Great Britain's renewable[3] energy needs. Likewise, Ireland approved plans in 2002 to build the world's largest wind farm with 200 offshore turbines that will generate about 10 percent of the country's energy needs.

3   Another problem with so-called green energy is its effect on the environment. Hydroelectric[4] plants don't burn anything and don't create air pollution, so they are considered "clean." Nevertheless, environmentalists argue that water power plants damage land, plants, and animals. In hydroelectric plants, the force of the water in rivers or ocean tides is used to turn blades of a turbine and generate electricity. The World Wildlife Fund reports that many fish are sucked into the plants' pipes and are killed or injured. "Many people think hydroelectric power is clean," says Kate Kempton of Sierra Club Canada. "In fact, big hydro projects flood wetlands and forests, and the vegetation rots under water, releasing methane—a gas that causes global warming."[5] One solution to the environmental problems has been for governments to require environmental studies before a new water power plant is authorized. In Uganda, a proposal to build a hydroelectric plant on the Nile River in 2002 was denied by the World Bank until the government was able to guarantee that steps would be taken to protect animals and plants.

4   Of all the problems, however, the greatest obstacle to using alternative energy sources is cost. Even the least expensive alternative energy sources cost three times more than fossil fuels, researchers report. In 2002, solar power cost four times as much as natural gas power. Alternative energy supporters urge governments to give tax breaks and loans to "green" energy producers. In Sacramento, California, the local government has encouraged its residents to install solar power panels on homes by paying half the cost. Companies have also begun to construct solar panels with cheaper materials. Solar power and wind power cost more, in part, because the energy output is not steady. Scientists and engineers are exploring ways to store solar and wind energy for times when the sun or wind is not strong, making these energy sources more productive.

5   Each of these renewable energy sources has practical limits. Nonetheless, countries continue to explore ways to increase their effectiveness—and, thus, decrease the world's dependence on limited, nonrenewable energy sources. Despite the problems, the development and use of alternative energy sources continues to rise.

---

[1]*syndrome:* a set of physical or mental conditions that show that a particular problem exists

[2]*turbines:* engines that work when the pressure from liquid, steam, or wind moves a special wheel inside

[3]*renewable:* able to be replaced by natural processes so that it is never used up

[4]*hydroelectric:* using water power to produce electricity

[5]*global warming:* an increase in the world's temperature, caused by an increase of carbon dioxide around the earth

Discussion and Analysis

In a group, do the activities and discuss the questions. Then write answers to each question on a separate piece of paper. Write your answers in complete sentences.

1. What is the main idea of this essay? Underline the thesis statement.
2. Underline the topic sentences of the body paragraphs.
3. Complete this sentence: Each body paragraph presents one _____ about alternative energy.
4. Underline the words in the conclusion that relate to the main idea.
5. Which of the problems presented in the essay seems the most difficult to solve? Why?

Journal Writing

Write two journal entries to give your reactions to two important ideas about energy: one idea from Reading 1, the other from Reading 2. In your journal, copy one sentence from each reading that presents an important idea. Then write responses to the ideas. Support your opinions with your knowledge, experience, and facts.

Language for Writing

Word Families: Noun Endings

In Chapter 4, you learned that the noun endings -er, -or, and -ist indicate the "person or thing that does an action." Here are four more common noun endings:

-ance, -ence, -ense	-ment	-ess, -ness	-ion, -tion

1 Find examples of nouns with these endings in Readings 1 and 2. Write them in the chart. Then think of other examples of nouns with these endings, and write them in the chart. A few are provided for you. Use a dictionary to check meanings and spelling.

Noun Endings	Examples from Readings 1 and 2	Other Examples
1. -ance, -ence, -ense	dependence	conference
2. -ment	government	
3. -ess, -ness		process

Noun Endings	Examples from Readings 1 and 2	Other Examples
4. *-ion, -tion*		*deterioration*
5. *-ist*		
6. *-er, -or*	*reflector*	

2 Complete the words in the article by adding a noun ending from the box. Use a dictionary to check meanings and spelling. Share your answers with a partner.

-ance, -ence, -ense   *-ment*   *-ist*   *-ess, -ness*   *-ion, -tion*   *-er, -or*

Ireland's Shrinking Coast

Giant's Causeway—Northern Ireland

Templepatrick, Northern Ireland, Mar 25, 2002 (Associated Press)—Ireland is shrinking, a scient*ist*___ warned Monday at a
1.
confer_____ on the
2.
deteriora_____ of
3.
coastlines worldwide.

Andrew Cooper, direct_____ of the Coastal Research Group at
4.
the University of Ulster, said the sea was swallowing up about 750 acres

of Ireland each year, and warned that the proc_____ would quicken.
5.

He said global warming was likely to subject Ireland's shores,

particularly along the northern and western Atlantic coasts, to more

frequent and powerful storms, but the govern_____s of Northern
6.
Ireland and the Irish Republic were doing little to erect[1] sensible

coastline def_____s.
7.

"Manage_____ of the Irish coast, north and south, is conducted
8.
in a piecemeal[2] fashion," Cooper told about 160 coastline-

conserva_____ special_____s gathered at a Northern Ireland
9.   10.
hotel.

"The growing demands on the coast mean that urgent act_____
11.
is needed," he said, calling for "much closer cooperat_____ between
12.
planning, conserva_____, social, and develop_____ interests."
13.   14.

During the weeklong confer_____ scient_____s were visiting
15.   16.
Northern Ireland's Giant's Causeway, which features basalt cliffs and

rocks that have crystalized into hexagonal columns. Tourism officials have

been forced to close some of the Causeway's cliffside hiking trails because

of a growing risk of collapse.

Words to Know

As you have learned, associating unfamiliar words with familiar
synonyms can expand your vocabulary.

Study the boldfaced words in the phrases and sentences taken from Reading
2. Match each word in 1–5 with the lettered sentence on page 119 that
contains its synonym. Write the correct letter on the line. The first one is
done for you.

___e__ 1. . . . a visible sign of the **revolution** in energy production. (paragraph 1)

_____ 2. . . . energy **production.** (paragraph 1)

_____ 3. . . . a new water power plant is **authorized.** (paragraph 3)

_____ 4. Companies have also begun to **construct**. . . (paragraph 4)

_____ 5. **Nonetheless,** countries continue to explore. . . (paragraph 5)

---

[1]*erect:* build
[2]*piecemeal:* happening or done slowly in separate stages that are not planned or related

a. . . . Ireland approved plans in 2002. . . (paragraph 2)

b. . . . however, the greatest obstacle . . . (paragraph 4)

c. . . . the energy output is not steady. (paragraph 4)

d. . . . a proposal to build . . . (paragraph 3)

e. . . . the change is occurring slowly . . . (paragraph 1)

Academic Words

1 Study the following academic word list and the example sentences. Check (✔) the academic words that you already know.

❑ **diminishing**   The world's supply of natural resources is **diminishing.**

❑ **consumption**   Meanwhile, the **consumption** of energy is increasing.

❑ **alternative**   Environmentalists are interested in **alternative** energy sources.

❑ **switch**   Drivers can save energy if they **switch** to energy-efficient cars.

❑ **solar**   Many students use **solar** calculators.

❑ **investment**   Development of alternative energy requires a large **investment** in research.

❑ **generate**   Niagara Falls can **generate** hydroelectric power.

❑ **utilize**   Some countries **utilize** their natural resources to produce energy.

❑ **widespread**   In Europe, the **widespread** use of wind farms reduces dependence on petroleum products.

2 Test your comprehension by matching one of the following definitions to an academic word from the list in Exercise 1. Write the word on the line.

1. _____ to change

2. _____ to use

3. _____ to produce

4. _____ becoming smaller

5. _____ happening in many places

6. _____ the amount that is used

7. _____ different from what is usual

8. _____ powered by the sun

9. _____ money spent to get a profit or benefit later

3 If you have difficulty matching any word from Exercise 1 to its definition in Exercise 2, put it in the academic word list in your notebook. Write its definition and a sentence using the word.

WRITING

Assignment

Write a problem-solution essay that relates to natural resources. A problem-solution essay presents a problem or problems and its solutions. To write your essay, follow the steps of the writing process.

STEP 1

Getting Ideas

Problem-Solution Essay

A *problem-solution* essay is a type of *argumentative* essay. In writing, an *argument* is "a set of explanations you use to try to prove that something is right or wrong, or true or false," according to the *Longman Dictionary of American English.* A problem-solution essay presents a problem or problems and tries to persuade the reader to accept the writer's proposed solutions to the problem. Reread the first and second paragraphs of Reading 2, a problem-solution essay.

With a group of your classmates, brainstorm a list of topics that relate to energy and natural resources. In your list, include types of natural resources, energy sources, ways people use energy, ways people conserve energy, and other related ideas. Share your list with the rest of your class.

Clustering

A *cluster map* is a graphic organizer in which you write ideas about a topic in circles or boxes. A cluster map has the following features:

- The main topic appears in a circle or box in the center.
- Circles or boxes surrounding the central idea contain supporting ideas.
- Lines connect the central and supporting ideas.

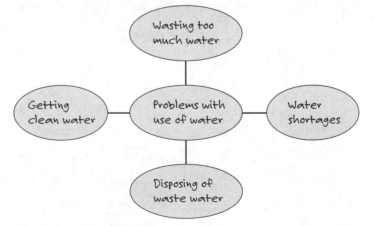

Notice how the writer organized ideas about problems with the use of one natural resource: *water.*

1 Read the list of energy-related topics. Choose one topic that interests you. Make a cluster map about it. In the center circle, write the topic. Write supporting ideas in the surrounding circles.

- Use of water

- Gas consumption

- Recycling programs

- Food production and consumption

- Composting

- Commuting

- Use of electricity

- Hydroelectric power

- Nuclear power

- Wind power

- Solar power

2 Find a group of your classmates who chose the same topic. Share your cluster maps. Write down ideas on your own map that seem useful for your topic, as the writer did in the map that follows. If necessary, cross out ideas on your map that are not useful.

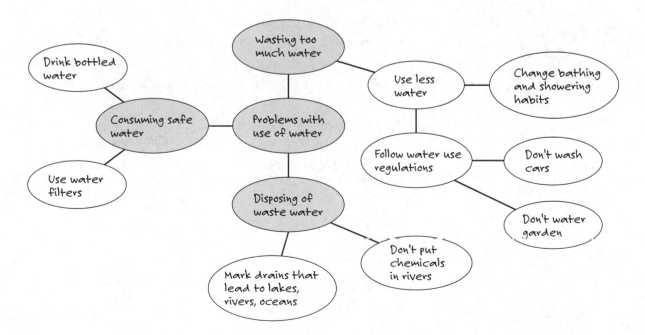

3 Share your cluster map with your entire class. Present and explain your cluster topics.

4 Make a cluster map for your own essay. Keep the topic you started with, or change your topic if you get new ideas from your classmates.

STEP 2

Organizing

Outlining a Problem-Solution Essay

Here are two suggested outlines for organizing a problem-solution essay. The plan that you choose will depend on your topic.

Outline A presents a problem in the first paragraph and introduces possible solutions. The two or three body paragraphs explain the solutions.

Outline A
Using Water Wisely

I. Introduction

Present the problem(s) and the situation.

Thesis Statement: State that your essay will present three solutions to the problem(s).

Example thesis statement: *There are three important solutions to avoiding water shortages.*

II. Body Paragraph 1: Solution 1

Topic Sentence: Introduce the first possible solution.

Example topic sentence: *One solution is to use less water.*

Support: Present facts, details, and examples to explain the solution.

III. Body Paragraph 2: Solution 2

Topic Sentence: Introduce the second possible solution.

Example topic sentence: *A second strategy is to reuse water.*

Support: Present facts, details, and examples to explain the solution.

IV. Body Paragraph 3: Solution 3 (if included)

Topic Sentence: Introduce the third possible solution.

Example topic sentence: *Above all, we must keep our water supplies clean so that more water is available.*

Support: Present facts, details, and examples to explain the solution.

V. Conclusion

Include the main idea of the thesis statement.

Offer predictions, results, or other recommendations related to the topic.

Outline B presents a topic and introduces problems related to the topic in the first paragraph. The two or three body paragraphs explain the problems and offer solutions.

Outline B
The Drawbacks of Hybrid Cars

I. **Introduction**

Introduce the topic and the situation.

Thesis Statement: State three major problems related to the topic.

Example thesis statement: *There are three major problems related to the use of "hybrid" (battery- and gasoline-powered) automobiles.*

II. **Body Paragraph 1: Problem 1**

A. Topic Sentence: Introduce the first problem.

Example topic sentence: *First of all, hybrid cars are expensive.*

Describe the first problem. Include facts, details, and examples about the problem.

B. Present possible solution(s). Include facts, details, and examples about the solution(s).

III. **Body Paragraph 2: Problem 2**

A. Topic Sentence: Introduce the second problem.

Example topic sentence: *Another problem is that the battery-powered motor does not work under some conditions.*

Describe the second problem. Include facts, details, and examples about the problem.

B. Present possible solution(s). Include facts, details, and examples about the solution(s).

IV. **Body Paragraph 3: Problem 3**

A. Topic Sentence: Introduce the third problem.

Example topic sentence: *Finally, the hybrid car still relies too heavily on gasoline power.*

Describe the third problem. Include facts, details, and examples about the problem.

B. Present possible solution(s). Include facts, details, and examples about the solution(s).

V. **Conclusion**

Include the main idea of the thesis statement.

Offer predictions, results, or other recommendations related to the topic.

1 Reread Readings 1 and 2. With a partner, discuss which outlines Reading 1 and Reading 2 follow. Share your answers with the rest of your class.

2 Using the cluster map that you made on page 121, write a thesis statement for your essay on a topic related to energy and natural resources. Turn in the cluster map and thesis statement to your instructor.

Example Thesis Statements

Solo commuters[1] should use alternative ways to travel.

Homeowners should look for areas of their homes where energy is wasted and make changes.

3 After your instructor approves your topic, make an outline for your essay, using one of the suggested outlines shown on pages 122–123. Have your instructor check your outline before you begin to write your paper.

Paragraph Development

As you have learned, a well-developed paragraph has major points and supporting facts, details, and examples.

---

1 Study the two paragraphs that follow. In each paragraph, underline the *topic sentence, major points,* and *concluding sentence.* How are the two paragraphs different? Which one do you prefer? Why? Discuss these questions in a group.

--- **Saving Paper** ---

One solution to the shortage of paper is to reuse it. First, newspapers have many uses after they are read. They can be used to line the floor when painting or cleaning. In addition, leftover computer paper also has many uses. Scraps of pages make good notepaper or shopping lists. Paper bags from the grocery store can also be reused. For example, they can be used for groceries again, and they can also carry lunches or line wastebaskets. Reusing paper before it's thrown away is a simple way to conserve paper.

---

[1]*solo commuters:* commuters who drive to work alone

Saving Paper

One solution to the shortage of paper is to reuse it. First, newspapers have many uses after they are read. Old newspaper sheets can be used to pack dishes or fill a box when mailing things. They can also be used to line the floor when painting or cleaning a room. In addition, leftover computer paper has many uses. The most obvious use is to print things out on both sides of the paper. Scraps of pages also make good notepaper or shopping lists. Paper bags can also be reused. Many grocery stores will give you a credit for reusing the bags. Students can cut the bags up and use them to cover books. They can also carry lunches or line wastebaskets. Reusing paper before it's thrown away is a simple way to conserve paper.

2 Read and analyze the paragraph. Identify the following elements: *topic sentence, major points, supporting ideas for each major point,* and the *concluding sentence.*

Conserving Electricity at Home

Using electricity wisely in the home can help conserve energy. First of all, people should not leave lights on when they are not needed. In addition, appliances and machines should be turned off throughout the house when they are not in use. It's not good to leave the television or radio playing while you are sleeping. People should pay attention to how much electricity they use in their homes.

3 With a partner, revise the paragraph. As you revise, think about these questions: Is the paragraph fully developed? Does it need more supporting facts, details, or examples? Add more supporting sentences where they are needed. Write your revised paragraph on a separate piece of paper. Share your revised paragraph in a group.

Transitions

Transitions are words or phrases that show relationships between ideas within a sentence, between sentences, within paragraphs, or between paragraphs. They make the ideas in your writing flow more smoothly.

Here are some common transitions and their meanings:

Transitions	Purpose
in addition, furthermore, also, moreover	To add an idea
first, second, next, then, last, finally	To show time order
however, in contrast, on the other hand	To contrast
as a result, therefore, consequently	To show result
in fact, indeed, clearly, certainly	To emphasize
for example, for instance, in particular	To show an example
in general, in short, generally	To generalize
in conclusion, in summary, in short, to conclude	To conclude

Examples

"Conservation energy," the practice of using less energy to do the same amount of work, is now the most popular alternative energy strategy. **Clearly,** conservation energy became popular because it has been supported by both government and industry in several important ways. **In fact,** the federal government strongly encourages it. In 2002, the U.S. government paid nearly US$9 billion in bonuses to companies and organizations that reduced energy use. **Moreover,** industries support conservation energy by developing energy-efficient appliances. **For example,** air conditioners now cool air more effectively yet use less energy.

1 Scan Reading 1. Circle the transitions that are used at the beginnings of body paragraphs and the conclusion paragraph. What other transitions could the writer have used? Write these transitions in the margins next to the words you circled. Share your answers with a partner.

2 Read the paragraph on page 127. Fill in the blanks with logical transitions from the list above. Compare your answers with those of your classmates.

Hybrid Automobiles

"Hybrid" cars are getting attention from carmakers and some consumers. _____, a growing number of automobile

1.

manufacturers are showing interest in selling these half-electric, half-gasoline powered automobiles. Toyota and Honda produced hybrid cars in 2002. _____, General Motors and Ford Motor Corporation

2.

planned to introduce hybrids. _____, celebrities drive them.

3.

_____, actor Leonardo di Caprio has two hybrids, and

4.

actress Cameron Diaz has one. Recently di Caprio bought three more hybrid cars for family members. Several U.S. congressional representatives have also purchased hybrids. The increase in availability and popularity may, _____, mean that drivers will be seeing more hybrid

5.

automobiles on the road in coming years.

STEP 3

Writing the First Draft

Using your cluster map (Step 1) and outline (Step 2), write the first draft of your problem-solution essay on a topic related to energy and natural resources. Follow your outline (Step 2), making sure that your essay contains five paragraphs.

STEP 4

Revising

Exchange drafts with a partner. Read each other's essays and answer these questions.

- ❑ Does the introduction present the problem or the situation related to the topic?
- ❑ Does the introduction include a thesis statement that tells the main idea of the essay?
- ❑ Are there two or three body paragraphs? Does each body paragraph describe one problem or one solution related to the topic?
- ❑ Are facts, details, and examples used to fully develop the ideas in the body paragraphs?
- ❑ Does the conclusion paragraph restate the thesis statement?

Discuss your partner's comments. Take notes on any revisions you need to make. Write a second draft of your paper.

STEP 5

Editing

PRE-TEST

1. Choose the appropriate verb forms to complete the paragraph.

Computer recycling centers like the Alameda County Computer
Resource Center (ACCRC) _____ widespread in
                                                        1. became / have become
recent years. The ACCRC _____ in operation
                                                 2. is / has been
since 1994. Its staff collects old and used computers from businesses and
individuals. Workers and volunteers test and repair the equipment and
then donate it to schools and individuals. Over the years, the center
_____ electronic devices ranging from
        3. has received / received
televisions and telephones to fax machines. The ACCRC
_____ the computers to schools in Cuba,
        4. redistributed / has redistributed
China, Ecuador, and Latvia—even Antarctica.

2. Read the paragraph. Correct any errors in punctuation and add
capital letters at the beginning of sentences, if necessary.

Recycling at home saves energy and resources. For instance,
when people recycle newspaper, it can be remade into new paper,
paper made from recycled paper uses about one-third less energy
than paper made from raw materials. It's also good to recycle glass
bottles and jars, it takes about one-third less energy to make glass
from recycled glass than glass made from raw materials, making
aluminum products from recycled aluminum uses 90 percent less
energy than products made from raw aluminum, consumers can
conserve resources by buying products that were made of recycled
products. Look for the recycle mark—three arrows that make a
triangle—on the package, the small efforts to recycle in the home
and to buy recycled items for the home can mean real savings in
energy and resources.

Have your instructor check your answers.

Grammar

Study the following grammar explanations and do the activities. They will help you recognize and correct grammar mistakes in your writing.

Present Perfect Tense

The present perfect tense is used to show a connection between the past and the present, as in this example from Reading 1:

> Governments, businesses, and individuals **have made** some effort to reduce their energy usage, but they must do more.

Here, the verb *have made* is used to state a past action, situation, or condition. The verb *must do* refers to a present action or situation.

Uses

- **Past to present action.** The present perfect is used to refer to indefinite past action that continues to the present.

  > *For the past ten years,* Denmark and Sweden **have led** the world in wind power production.

  > Niagara Falls **has generated** hydroelectric power *since 1883.*

  Common time markers:

  > *for* + a period of time. The *for* can usually be deleted.

  > *since* + a point in time (a clock time, a day, a date, or an event in the past expressed in a phrase or a clause)

- **Indefinite past.** The present perfect is also used to refer to indefinite, or unspecific, past time.

  > Europe **has**n't **reached** its alternative energy goals *yet.*

  > Brazil and Sri Lanka **have had** numerous power shortages *in the past* because of droughts.

  Common time markers:

already*	ever*	many times	recently
yet	never*	before	in the past
up to now	rarely*	often*	in recent years
always*	so far	just*	

*These time words usually appear between the two parts of the verb.

Time markers are not always necessary to show indefinite past time.

> Governments **have spent** billions of dollars on energy research.

> Engineers **have created** automobiles that run on hydrogen.

> ### Form
>
> The present perfect is made of *have* or *has* + the past participle. Add *-ed* to the base form to make the past participle form of regular verbs. Study irregular past participles on page 223.
>
> > **Regular:** The local government **has encouraged** its residents . . .
> > **Regular:** Many British citizens **have protested** that wind power is noisy . . .
> > **Irregular:** One solution . . . **has been** to locate the wind farms offshore.
> > **Irregular:** Companies **have** also **begun** to construct solar panels . . .

1 Read the timeline to learn about the history of a fossil fuel called *orimulsion* in Venezuela.

Development of Orimulsion in Venezuela

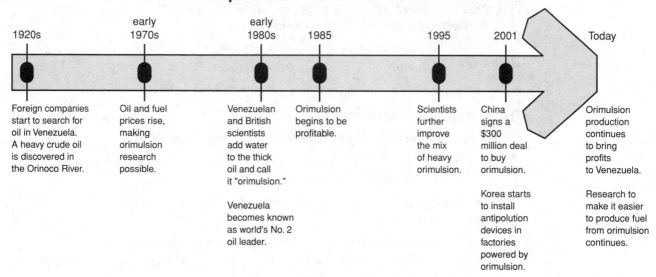

2 Complete the following sentences about orimulsion in Venezuela. Use present perfect tense verbs. Add other information from the timeline to your sentences. Compare your sentences in a group. The first one is done for you.

1. For over eighty years, *people have known that oil exists in Venezuela* .

2. Researchers _____ since the 1970s.

3. In recent years, scientists _____ the mix of oil and water.

4. For many years, orimulsion _____ profitable.

5. Korea _____ already _____ installing antipollution devices in its factories that run on orimulsion.

6. So far, Venezuela _____ a lot of profits from orimulsion.

7. Venezuela _____ one of the world's top ten oil producers.

DO IT YOURSELF
For more practice:

Present perfect tense, 228
Past tense verbs, 222
Irregular verb chart, 223

Comma Splices

As you learned in Chapter 1, a period, a question mark, or an exclamation point can be used to mark the end of a sentence. Commas should be used within a sentence, not at the end of the sentence. Using a comma to connect sentences without a conjunction (*and, but, so,* and so on or *when, because,* and so on) is called a comma splice error.

Study the punctuation in these sentences.

> **Incorrect:** Coal-fired power plants may contribute to global warming, they release carbon dioxide.

> **Correct:** Coal-fired power plants may contribute to global warming. They release carbon dioxide.

> **Correct:** Coal-fired power plants may contribute to global warming because they release carbon dioxide.

The incorrect sentence has a comma where a period should be. In the first correct sentence, there is a period between the two sentences. The second correct sentence shows another way to correct a comma splice: Add the conjunction *because* in place of the comma to join the two sentences.

Read the following paragraphs. Find and correct the comma splice errors. The first one is done for you.

1. Find the five remaining comma splice errors.

A Problem with Solar Power

Perhaps the greatest economic obstacle to solar power is the problem referred to in the industry as *intermittency*, ~~intermittency~~ means that the sun doesn't always shine, and solar plants are not reliable sources of electricity, the energy coming down from the sun is spread across the entire face of the Earth instead of being focused in one area, the sun's energy is only available in the daytime, it would have to be stored for use at night or on cloudy or rainy days. Solar collectors are available to collect and store sunlight, the problem is that the collectors are not very efficient, in fact, a typical solar plant operates at only 13 percent of its capacity.

2. Find the three comma splice errors.

Gasoline Taxes

One suggestion for reducing the use of oil in the United States is to increase gasoline taxes, in the United States, the need for gasoline accounts for about 40 percent of all the oil imported into the country. One reason behind this suggestion to raise gas taxes is the expectation that if gasoline prices are higher, people will buy less gasoline. In the United States, the average gasoline tax was about 80 cents per gallon in 2002, in Europe and Japan, the tax was about US$2 per gallon. Researchers say that Europeans and Japanese buy much less gasoline per person than Americans do, increasing gas taxes could reduce consumption.

DO IT YOURSELF
For more practice:
Comma splices, 261
Sentence-end
    punctuation, 259
Commas, 259

Writing the Final Draft

Use the checklist to edit your essay on a topic related to energy and natural resources. Then write your final draft.

Editing Checklist

❑ Are noun endings used correctly?

❑ Are present perfect tense verbs used appropriately?

❑ Are commas used appropriately?

❑ Are periods used at the ends of sentences?

Your instructor will grade your paper for its content, organization, and language using the evaluation sheet for this chapter on page 205. Read over the evaluation sheet. Then reread and edit your paper as necessary before you turn in the final draft.

On Your Own

More Writing Practice

Write an essay about one of the following topics.

REMEMBER Gather ideas before you begin to write. Include a thesis statement in the introduction. Begin each body paragraph with a major point sentence. Add details, facts, or examples to support each point. Add a conclusion paragraph to restate the main idea. After you finish, revise and edit your essay.

---

1. **The World's Most Serious Problem**

   Write an essay about the most serious problem that faces the world today. Describe the problem. Explain why it is so serious. Include facts, details, and examples. Suggest solutions to the problem. In your conclusion, make predictions or recommendations about the future.

2. **Automobile of the Future**

   Write an essay about two or three features of an ideal automobile of the future. The future car should be energy efficient and economical. Include facts, details, or examples to support your description. Explain the effects that your future car will have on the environment or the world's energy supplies.

3. **Energy-Saving Habits for Children**

   Write an essay about two or three energy-saving habits that parents can teach children. In the body paragraphs, describe the habits. Explain why they are important. Suggest how parents might teach the habits to their children. Use your experience and facts to support your ideas.

Chapter Goals   Take credit for achieving the learning goals in Chapter 6. Check (✔) all of the goals that you have achieved. If you are having problems with one of the areas, get extra practice by writing another essay on one of the topics above, or do the language exercises in the appropriate Do It Yourself section in the back of the book. Then talk to your instructor about your writing.

Chapter Goals Checklist

❏ Recognize and use noun endings.

❏ Use clustering to gather ideas for writing.

❏ Outline a problem-solution essay.

❏ Use transitions.

❏ Use present perfect tense verbs appropriately.

❏ Avoid comma splices.

CHAPTER 7

Your Chance to Shine

Chapter Goals

- Consider the *audience* and *purpose* for your writing.
- Outline a process essay.
- Use subordinating conjunctions appropriately.
- Use commands and modal verbs correctly.
- Keep pronouns consistent.

Approaching the Topic

Every one of us has skills and talents in a certain area or areas. In this chapter, you will read and write essays about how to *shine*, or show your talents, in academic tasks and other areas.

1. Look at the photos. Which of these skills interest you?

2. Which academic tasks do you do well?

3. What other special skills and talents do you have? Discuss your skills to see if your classmates might be interested in learning more about them.

READING FOR WRITING

Reading 1

Discuss these questions with your classmates before you read: What is *test anxiety?* Do you suffer from it? Which tests do you find the most challenging? Why? What do you think is the best way to be a successful test-taker?

The "Big Test"

1   Test taking is an important part of learning. That does not mean, however, that I approve of tests. To be honest, professors give tests to get a handle on[1] exactly how much we are learning and getting from the class. I think that they are good ways to let professors know if we are having a hard time without us actually having to tell them. The most important thing that I have learned about tests is that they do not measure my worth.[2] They are simply a measure of what I know about a certain thing at a certain point in my life. As someone who procrastinates[3] more than he should, testing is, and always has been, a fairly stressful experience for me. I have always tried to prepare myself for the "big test" and what was going to be on it, but it was not until I learned a few tricks that I became a better test-taker.

2   First of all, I learned that you have to approach the test with a relaxed, calm (yet focused) attitude. You also have to learn how to motivate yourself to do your best. If you do this, you will be mentally ready for the test.

3   Another thing I have learned is that you should not overload yourself with information that is not relevant[4] to the test. Listen to the professor, take good notes, read the text, study the handouts, and if necessary, get together with some friends and study together. This will save a lot of worry and stress.

4   Before I start the test, I try to look it over completely to get a good feel for what is being asked. From there, I start with a question that I know I can answer well. If I don't know the answer to a question, I move to the next one. I try not to get upset or stressed over the fact that I could not answer one question. The best advice for taking a test is to focus on the test questions and nothing else. Don't let your mind wander; just concentrate on the material. I know that I have a very short attention span.[5] Focusing is not easy for me, but when I do it, I score better on tests.

5   Finally, testing does not have to be fun to be rewarding. When you think back on the test and know that you did your best, there is something motivating in that. It makes you want to outdo yourself the next time.

Adam Smith, first-year journalism student, University of Kansas

¹*get a handle on:* get a clear idea about something, especially a problem or a difficult task; understand
²*worth:* value
³*procrastinates:* delays doing something that should be done
⁴*relevant:* directly relating to the subject or problem being discussed
⁵*attention span:* the period of time during which you watch, listen to, notice, or think about something

Discussion and Analysis

In a group, do the activities and discuss the questions. Then write answers to each question on a separate piece of paper. Write your answers in complete sentences.

1. This essay may be called a *process* essay because it explains a process, "a series of actions that someone does in order to achieve a particular result." What is the process being explained in this essay?

2. Reread the writer's thesis statement:

   > I have always tried to prepare myself for the "big test" and what was going to be on it, but it was not until I learned a few tricks that I became a better test-taker.

   Underline the words the writer uses to indicate that his essay will present the steps of a process.

3. According to the writer, what is the first part of the process? Underline the sentence that introduces this part.

4. Underline the sentence that introduces the second part.

5. Underline the sentence that introduces the third part.

6. In the conclusion paragraph, underline the sentence that includes the main idea of the thesis statement.

7. What is your opinion of the writer's ideas? Circle or highlight sentences that you agree or disagree strongly with. Explain your opinions.

Reading 2

Discuss these questions with your classmates before you read: Have you ever made a speech in public? How did you prepare? Explain the process that you went through. How and when do you think public speaking skills might be useful to you in the future?

Making a Speech

1   If you are afraid of making a speech in public, you are not alone. According to *The Book of Lists*, 3,000 Americans surveyed[1] listed public speaking as their *number one* fear. Public speaking came in ahead of sickness, financial troubles, and even *death!* However, the simple truth is that you are going to be asked to speak in many of your classes. From history to chemistry, from engineering to computer programming, speaking is a way of life for today's college students. The more you know about writing and delivering speeches,[2] the more confident you are going to feel in every class.

2   The first steps toward making a speech are choosing a topic and writing a thesis statement. Select a topic on which you are an expert or a topic in which you have a strong interest and enough preparation time to become an expert. If you choose topics that are new or unfamiliar to you, you will need to extend[3] your preparation time. Can you find sufficient[4] material and information for your speech? Is your topic appropriate to you and your audience? Can you adequately[5] discuss the topic within the given time? After you decide on a topic, write a thesis statement. The thesis statement is one sentence that tells your audience *exactly* what you hope to accomplish[6] in your speech. Here is an example of a thesis statement:

> You will understand the effects of domestic abuse, know how to look for warning signs, and know about resources for assistance.

3   Once you have selected your topic and developed your thesis statement, you are ready to begin gathering information to support your speech. As you begin to consider resources, you will want to investigate and explore a variety of sources, including the following: personal interviews with experts on your topic, books, the Internet, periodicals (magazines), and newspapers. You should have at least three or more sources supporting your thesis.

4   After you have researched your topic, organize and write your speech so that it has an introduction, body, and conclusion. Gamble and Gamble, in their book *Public Speaking in the Age of Diversity*, recommend that you share only information that you know to be true. This means that you should report the facts about your topic accurately. Second, do extensive[7] research so that you are fully prepared for questions. Third, make it easy for your audience to understand your message. The best way to make your speech clear is to make an outline for it, as you do for an essay.

5   The final step is to make notes for delivering your speech. Some speakers prefer to use note cards while others use several sheets of paper in outline form. Remember, write only key words in your notes. Do not write your speech out completely. You should not read it directly from the page. Rehearse your speech. Then you'll know your topic, and you'll be ready to talk to your audience. If you follow these steps, you'll be a successful public speaker.

[1]*surveyed:* asked a large number of people a set of questions in order to find out about their opinions or behavior
[2]*delivering speeches:* speaking or performing in public
[3]*extend:* lengthen
[4]*sufficient:* as much as you need for a particular purpose; enough
[5]*adequately:* having enough for a particular purpose
[6]*accomplish:* to succeed in doing something, especially after trying hard to do it; achieve
[7]*extensive:* containing a lot of information, details, work, etc.

Discussion and Analysis

In a group, do the activities and discuss the questions. Then write answers to each question on a separate piece of paper. Write your answers in complete sentences.

1. What process does this essay explain? Underline the writer's thesis statement.

2. What two steps make up the first part of the process? Underline the sentence that introduces the first part.

3. Underline the sentence that introduces the second part of the process.

4. Underline the sentence that introduces the third part.

5. In the conclusion, the writer includes the final steps of the process. Underline the sentences that introduce the final steps.

6. Underline the sentence in the conclusion paragraph that returns to the main idea of the thesis statement.

Journal Writing

Write a journal entry about your learning styles. Are you a "hands-on" learner who learns new skills by *doing* them? Are you an "observer" who learns by *watching* others? Do you learn by *reading?* Or do you combine these or other ways of learning new skills? Give examples of skills that you have learned. Explain how you learned them.

Language for Writing

Using Subordinating Conjunctions

In Chapter 3, you studied **main + dependent** clauses like this one:

┌─────DEPENDENT CLAUSE─────┐ ┌────────────MAIN CLAUSE────────────┐
If you follow these steps, you'll be a successful public speaker.

As you have learned, words that introduce dependent clauses (like *if*) are called *subordinating conjunctions*. When you write sentences with dependent clauses, make sure that you use the appropriate subordinating conjunction.

1 Study the list of subordinating conjunctions that follows. Most of the words relate to time, so they are useful in explaining a series of actions in a process. If some of the conjunctions are unfamiliar, ask your instructor.

after	as long as	if	when
although	because	since	whenever
as	before	until	while

2 Use subordinating conjunctions to complete the sentences in the following essay. Are there any sentences where more than one answer is possible? If so, write more than one conjunction in the blank. Discuss your answers with your whole class. The first one is done for you.

First Steps in Bouldering

Climbing boulders is one of the most satisfying outdoor sports. It may look difficult, but, in fact, bouldering is the easiest type of rock climbing. It's perfect for beginners

_____*because/since*_____ you don't climb
         1.

far off the ground. _____
                            2.

you concentrate and follow some simple guidelines, you should have a

successful experience. Here are some basics to get you started.

First of all, you need gear: climbing shoes, a bag with chalk, a piece of carpet or a mattress, a boulder (of course!), and tough skin.

_____ you don't have tough skin, don't worry. You will
       3.

soon develop it. As for shoes, the best choice is a pair of climbing shoes with special rubber roles. Sportiva and Boreal are two good brands that sell for between US$50 and US$100. _____ you can use 4. sneakers to start out, it's not a very good idea. You won't learn the skill of getting a foothold. Also, buy your shoes a size or two smaller than your normal size _____ your shoes should never feel loose. 5. The chalk, which you can find at sporting goods stores, is used for dusting your hands so that they stay dry. _____ you don't 6. use chalk, your hands will become sweaty and you can lose your handhold. Use a mattress "crash pad" to soften your fall.

_____ you do a lot of climbing, buy a crash pad. These 7. mattresses aren't cheap, but they're a lot softer to fall on than sharp rock.

_____ you have all your equipment, find an 8. experienced climbing partner to go with you. _____ 9. bouldering can be practiced alone, it's safer to have a partner with you. You'll not only pick up better climbing techniques, but you'll also be safer. Having someone to "spot" you (stand and support you if you fall) is useful. _____ you fall, your spotter can take hold of your 10. hips and guide your fall so that you land on both feet. In addition, an experienced climber or bouldering guide will also be able to choose a location for you _____ he or she will know which one has 11. boulders suited to your abilities.

_____ you start, you may look at the boulder and 12. wonder how you are going to pull yourself up. Actually, you're not. You are going to use your legs to push your body up to each of the handholds _____ your legs are much stronger than your 13. arms. Footwork is the key. Getting as much of your weight over your feet as possible will save your arm strength. _____ you 14.

have dusted your hands with chalk, look at the first foothold and then carefully place your foot on it. Look down at your feet _____
15.
you blindly put your foot to rock. Otherwise, you might get a surprise

_____ you try to stand on it. Feel around with your hands
16.
to find the next foothold up, and repeat the process. _____
17.
you get a feel for what works for you, you will climb confidently.

Of course, there are many more techniques to learn about climbing boulders, but these tips will get you started. The thrill of challenging yourself and the satisfaction you get from enjoying yourself outdoors may inspire you to climb more and more. Relax, and have fun bouldering!

Academic Words

1 Study the following academic word list and the example sentences. Check (✔) the academic words that you already know.

❑ **approach**   Always **approach** your research topic with an open mind.

❑ **investigate** Psychologists want to **investigate** why so many people fear public speaking.

❑ **motivate**   Observing her friends on the boulders **motivated** her to try a new technique.

❑ **objective**   Newspaper articles that contain the writer's opinions aren't **objective.**

❑ **relevant**   Look for information that is **relevant** to your research topic.

❑ **resource**   The Internet is a great **resource** for information.

❑ **sufficient**   Do you have **sufficient** time to complete the work?

❑ **survey**   The college plans to **survey** students to discover how they use computers.

2 Test your comprehension by matching one of the following definitions to an academic word from the list in Exercise 1. Write the word on the line.

1. _____ ask people questions to get their opinions

2. _____ enough

3. _____ relating to the subject

4. _____ source

5. _____ cause someone to be willing to do something

6. _____ to find out

7. _____ containing no opinion

8. _____ move closer to someone, something

3 If you have difficulty matching any word from Exercise 1 to its definition in Exercise 2, put it in the academic word list in your notebook. Write its definition and a sentence using the word.

WRITING

Assignment

Write an essay that explains the steps necessary to perform one skill or show one talent that you have. To write your essay, follow the steps of the writing process.

STEP 1

Getting Ideas

1 Make a list of activities that you do well. In a small group, discuss your skills and talents for these activities. Which of your skills or talents do your classmates want to learn more about? Which of your skills or talents do you have in common with others in your group?

2 Choose an activity that you do well and that your classmates are interested in. Write a sentence that introduces the activity and states that you will explain the steps or process to do the activity. This sentence will be the thesis statement for your essay.

Examples

Mountain biking is an exciting sport that's well worth the planning and preparation.

You can win at blackjack if you follow some basic strategies.

3 Make a list of steps that a person needs to follow to do the activity you have chosen.

Mountain biking is an exciting sport that's well worth the planning and preparation.

1. *First, you need to be physically fit, or start a training program to become fit.*
2. *Next, you need ~~~~~~~~~~~~~~~~~~~~~~~~~~~~~~*
3. *~~~~~~~~~~~~~~~~~~~~~~~~~~~~~~~~~~~~~~*
4. *~~~~~~~~~~~~~~~~~~~~~~~~~~~~~~~~~~~~~*
5. *~~~~~~~~~~~~~~~~~~~~~~~~~~~~~~~~~~~~~*

Audience and Purpose

When you write an essay that explains how to do something, you must think about your *audience,* or reader(s), and your *purpose,* or reason for writing. The *audience* for an academic essay is usually your instructor and sometimes your classmates. For this assignment, your *purpose* is to explain how to do something.

With your audience and purpose in mind, remember to explain the steps of the process in a simple way so that your *audience* will understand it. Also keep in mind that your *purpose* is to explain the steps of the process clearly and completely.

1 Read over your list of steps. Evaluate your list, using these questions. Make any necessary revisions.

- Are the steps written clearly so that your instructor and/or a classmate is able to understand them?

- Do you name and explain any materials or equipment that are needed?

- Do you include all the steps of the process?

- Do you explain the result of the process?

2 Share your thesis statement and list of steps with a classmate. Have your partner read over the steps and evaluate them, using the questions from Exercise 1. Ask your partner for feedback, and revise your steps again as necessary. Ask your instructor if you need extra help.

Organizing

Outlining a Process Essay

An essay that explains how to do something is called a process essay. The outline on page 144 suggests how to organize the steps in your process into paragraphs in an essay.

Home-Baked Bread

I. Introduction

In the first paragraph, introduce the process. Explain why it is important or useful. Is it difficult or easy? Briefly give any background to explain the process. Include the thesis statement that you wrote to introduce the activity and state that you will explain the process for doing it.

Example thesis statement: *You can enjoy a loaf of fresh homemade bread if you follow a few important guidelines.*

II. Body Paragraph 1

How does a person begin the process? What materials, information, tools, or equipment does he or she need? Begin this paragraph with a topic sentence that introduces the preparation needed to begin the process.

Example topic sentence: *Before you start, make sure that you have all the ingredients and tools that you need.*

Support: Include facts and details about this phase of the process.

III. Body Paragraph 2

What is the first part of the process? Are any warnings needed? Begin this paragraph with a topic sentence that introduces the first part of the process.

Example topic sentence: *The first step is to mix the flour and other dry ingredients with a prepared yeast mixture.*

Support: Include facts and details about this phase of the process.

IV. Body Paragraph 3

What is the next part of the process? Do you need to provide any warnings? Begin the paragraph with a topic sentence that introduces this part of the process.

Example topic sentence: *Next, knead the dough and allow it to rise.*

Support: Include facts and details about this phase of the process.

V. Conclusion

What are the final steps of the process? What is the end result? What will a person gain from performing these steps? Include sentences that restate the main idea of the essay and/or state the final steps or result(s) of doing the process.

Example concluding sentence: *With simple ingredients and in little time, you will have bread that is fresh and that tastes better than any store-bought loaf.*

Make an outline for your essay by using ideas from the list of steps that you made on page 142 (Step 1). Put those ideas into appropriate places in your outline.

Introduction Paragraph

As you learned in Chapter 4, there are several common types of introduction paragraphs: the funnel, the shared experience, and the turnabout. You can review these types of introductions on pages 71–72.

---

1 Read the following introduction paragraphs. What type or types of introduction does the writer use? Which of the introductions do you like the best? Why?

1.   Making beautiful ceramic pieces on a potter's wheel may seem to require a great deal of natural talent to anyone who's ever considered doing it. However, throwing pottery is a learned skill that nearly anyone can acquire. To become proficient in the art, beginning potters should start with good tools and materials, use careful techniques, and then practice.

2.   Meditation has been practiced for ages as a way to achieve inner peace. Even in the fast pace of modern times, meditating continues to be popular because it helps people reduce stress and become physically and mentally relaxed. Anyone can practice the art of meditation by learning these basic techniques.

3.   Taking a perfect photograph is more than just pointing the camera and clicking. Good photographers consider the composition, or arrangement, of elements in their photos. They also simplify scenes by moving closer to the subject or using different lenses. Finally, they use light and shadow to add interest to their shots. These are the key steps that good photographers take *before* shooting a great photograph.

4.   In my family, everyone eats meat. In fact, my mother rarely serves a meal without it. While I was growing up, I often wanted to become a vegetarian, but it was tough. My parents told me it was ridiculous not to eat meat, and everyone else in my family loved summer barbecues and holiday roasts. However, two years ago, I started living on my own. Since then I have become a vegetarian. Changing my eating habits was a challenging but worthwhile process.

2 Reread the introduction paragraphs of the following essays. What type or types of introductory paragraph does the writer use—the funnel, the shared experience, or the turnabout? Discuss your answers with a group of your classmates. Which type of introduction(s) do you prefer? Why?

1. "The 'Big Test,'" page 135
2. "Making a Speech," page 137
3. "First Steps in Bouldering," page 139

STEP 3

Writing the First Draft

Using your thesis statement (Step 1) and your outline with your list of steps and ideas (Steps 1 and 2), write the first draft of your essay about your activity, skill, or talent.

- Introduce the topic and present the thesis statement in the introduction paragraph.
- Be sure that the steps of your process are clear and complete.
- Conclude with sentences that relate to the thesis statement, or give the final steps or result of the process.

STEP 4

Revising

Exchange drafts with a partner. Read each other's essays and answer these questions.

- ❏ Does the essay follow the outline on page 144?
- ❏ Does the introduction paragraph introduce the topic and present the thesis statement?
- ❏ Does the writer tell the steps of the process clearly and completely?
- ❏ Are there any parts of the process that you do not understand?
- ❏ Does the conclusion relate to the main idea or tell the final steps or result of the process?

Discuss your partner's comments. Take notes on any revisions you need to make. Write a second draft of your essay.

STEP 5

Editing

PRE-TEST

Test your knowledge of the grammar presented in Chapter 7.

1. Complete the paragraphs by adding personal pronouns such as *I, you, he, she, it, we,* or *they* or by adding possessive pronouns such as *my, your, his, her, its, our,* or *their.* Words can be used more than once. The first one is done for you.

Ways to Save Money

A.   ___*You*___ can lower the price of a round-trip airfare by as
  1.

much as two-thirds by making certain _____ trip includes a
                                              2.

Saturday evening stayover and by purchasing the ticket in advance. To

make certain _____ have a cheap fare, even if _____ use a
              3.   4.

travel agent, contact all the airlines that fly where _____ want to
                                                        5.

go and ask what the lowest fare to _____ destination is.
                                     6.

B.   A used car can be a bargain, but the buyer must be careful. First,

the buyer should go to _____ local library to get a "blue book." This
                         1.

book gives the average retail price of cars. Then the buyer can compare a

seller's asking price with the car's "blue-book" price. Next, the buyer

should ask _____ mechanic to inspect the car's engine, _____
            2.   3.

transmission, _____ tires, and other parts. A consumer should
               4.

consider buying a car from someone _____ knows. A friend is more
                                     5.

likely to charge a lower price and point out any problems with the car.

2. Write five sentences about ways to save money.

   Examples

   You can save a lot of money in interest charges by paying off your entire credit card bill each month.

   Don't spend more money than you earn.

   _____

   _____

   _____

   _____

   _____

Have your instructor check your answers.

Grammar

Study the following grammar explanations and do the activities. They will help you recognize and correct grammar mistakes in your writing.

Modals and Commands

Modals and commands are frequently used to explain how to do something.

Modals

Use modal verbs to give advice or to express necessity, possibility, and future time.

Advice:	You **should exercise** at least three times a week.
Necessity:	You **must concentrate** when you play computer games.
	Every driver **needs to* learn** how to parallel park a car.
Possibility:	You **can purchase** the spices for this recipe at an Indian grocery store.
Future:	If you follow these steps, you **will make** friends more easily in college.

*Need to acts like a modal verb. It is often called a "semi-modal" verb.

Commands

Use commands to give orders, instructions, advice, or warnings. Notice that command sentences have no subject. The verb is in the base form.

Giving orders:	**Don't smoke** in my house.
	Be on time for the exam!
Instruction:	**Follow** the directions carefully.
	Wash fruit well before you eat it.
Advice:	**Don't take** too many clothes when you go on vacation.
	Wear sunscreen when you go to the beach.
Warning:	**Don't drink** while you drive, or you may have an accident.

---

1 Underline the commands and the modal + base verbs in the paragraphs on page 149. The first one has been done for you.

──────────────────── **Home-Baked Bread** ────────────────────

Like most people, you probably head for the store when you run out of bread. Grocery store shelves are full of so many varieties that you <u>might</u> never <u>think</u> about making your own bread. However, if you have ever tasted home-baked bread, you know how much better it tastes than store-bought bread. You can enjoy a loaf of your own homemade bread if you follow these steps.

Before you start, make sure that you have all the ingredients and tools that you need. The ingredients for making white bread are fairly simple: flour, yeast, milk, sugar, and salt. You should use unbleached white flour because it is more natural. You can use either granulated yeast, which is sold in jars, or fresh yeast, which is sold refrigerated in the dairy section of grocery stores. The tools vary, depending on whether you want to mix the bread by hand or machine. You can get by with just a large bowl, spoons, and a wooden cutting board. However, it's much easier if you have a heavy-duty mixer for mixing and kneading the dough.

The first step is to mix the flour and other dry ingredients with a prepared yeast mixture. In a large bowl, mix four cups of flour, one tablespoon of salt, and two teaspoons of sugar, if desired. With your hand, make a small hole or "well" in the middle of the flour. Meanwhile, mix two teaspoons of granulated yeast or one package of fresh yeast in a small bowl with one-quarter cup of warm water. The water temperature should be between 100 and 110 degrees Fahrenheit. The temperature is important because if the water is too hot, it can kill the yeast, and if it's too cold, the yeast won't work. Stir the yeast and water together and let it rest until the mixture begins to bubble. Then carefully add it to the flour mixture and stir. You can mix the dough with a wooden spoon, or you can do it with a heavy-duty mixer on a low setting. At this point, the dough should be sticky, but all the liquid should disappear into the flour. If the dough is too dry, slowly add more warm water.

2 Read the rules for being happy. Change each command verb sentence in the box into a modal verb sentence. Vary the modal verbs that you use. You may add words to the sentences, but do not change the basic meaning. Compare your sentences with a partner's. The first one is done for you.

Five Simple Rules for Being Happy

1. Free your heart from hatred.
   You must free your heart from hatred.

2. Free your mind from worries.
   _____

3. Live simply.
   _____

4. Give more.
   _____

5. Expect less.
   _____

---

3 On a separate piece of paper, write one command sentence and one modal verb sentence for each of the following items. Include the words provided in your sentences, or use synonymous phrases. Compare your sentences with a classmate's.

Example

take final exams
Get enough sleep before your final exams.
Students should study hard before they take final exams.

1. do homework
2. lose weight
3. wash your clothes
4. write a research paper
5. plan a trip
6. get to sleep easily
7. spend money wisely
8. avoid car accidents
9. save time

DO IT YOURSELF
For more practice:
Command
    verbs, 232
Modal auxiliary
    verbs, 232

Pronoun Consistency

Keep personal and possessive pronouns and related object pronouns consistent when you explain how to do something. In other words, speak to the same "person" throughout your writing.

First person:	**We** must improve **our** sleeping habits.
	My insomnia makes **me** feel irritable.
Second person:	If **you** want to exercise and have fun, learn to dance to **your** favorite music.
	You can download the music **you** like.
Third-person plural:	**People** should not talk on **their** cell phones while driving.
	They risk **their** own safety as well as the safety of others.
	If you see **friends** doing this, tell **them** to pull off the road.
Third-person singular*:	**Everyone** has a bad habit that **he** or **she** wants to eliminate.
	A **person** can improve **his** or **her** health by not smoking.
	It may be difficult for **him** or **her,** but the benefits will be great.

*(1) It's better to use third-person plural forms to avoid the awkward use of *he or she, his or her,* or *him or her* that occurs with some sentences in the third-person singular.
(2) Words that end in *-one* or *-body* (*anyone, anybody, everyone, everybody, no one, nobody, someone,* and *somebody*) are always third-person singular.

1 Read the following paragraph. Underline the second-person pronouns.

Once you have selected your topic and developed your thesis statement, you are ready to begin gathering information to support your speech. As you begin to consider resources, you will want to investigate and explore a variety of sources, including the following: personal interviews with experts on your topic, books, electronic card catalogs and computer databases, the Internet, periodicals (magazines), and newspapers. When you collect your research, you will find that information comes in a variety of forms. Do a variety of research to be able to objectively write your speech. You should have at least three or more sources supporting your thesis.

DO IT YOURSELF
For more practice:

Pronouns:
  Subject, object,
  and possessive
  pronouns, 243

2 Rewrite the Exercise 1 paragraph from page 151 on a separate piece of paper. Replace second-person pronouns like *you* and *your* with third-person plural nouns and pronouns. Make any other necessary changes. Compare your paragraph with one of your classmate's.

Once <u>students</u> have selected <u>their</u> <u>topics</u> and developed <u>their</u> thesis <u>statements</u>, . . .

Writing the Final Draft

Use the checklist to edit your essay on an activity, skill, or talent. Then write your final draft.

Your instructor will grade your paper for its content, organization, and language using the evaluation sheet for this chapter on page 206. Read over the evaluation sheet. Then reread and edit your paper as necessary before you turn in the final draft.

Editing Checklist

❑ Are subordinating conjunctions used appropriately?

❑ Are modal verbs used correctly?

❑ Are command sentences used correctly?

❑ Are personal pronouns, related nouns, and possessives used consistently?

On Your Own

**Personal
Spelling List**

1 Study the pair of words given with each sentence. Circle the correct spelling. Then write the correctly spelled word in the blank space above each pair. The first one is done for you.

1. It's _____*important*_____ to follow instructions.
   (important)/importent

2. You must _____ ingredients in a recipe accurately.
   measure/mesure

3. Colleges are _____ good places to make friends.
   usualy/usually

4. The writing _____ consists of several steps.
   process/proces

5. Learning _____ takes a long time.
   English / Inglish

6. First, you must _____ which type of car to buy.
   <u>dicide / decide</u>

7. A good _____ is hard to find.
   <u>friend / freind</u>

8. If you _____, you can make a label for your homemade CD.
   <u>preffer / prefer</u>

9. You will be a _____ student if you work hard.
   <u>successful / sucessful</u>

10. Busy students have _____ responsibilities.
    <u>a lot of / alot of</u>

11. If you exercise at a gym, you can use many kinds of _____.
    <u>equpment / equipment</u>

12. Gather all the _____ that you will need before you start to
    <u>materials / materails</u>
    paint a picture.

13. Pay _____ to the directions before you assemble the
    <u>attention / atention</u>
    bicycle.

14. You can ask a friend to help you study for a test, if _____.
    <u>necessary / necesary</u>

15. It's _____ difficult to remain calm in an emergency.
    <u>sometime / sometimes</u>

2 Use a dictionary to check your spelling in Exercise 1. Add the words that you misspelled to your personal spelling list.

3 Look over the writing that you have done in Chapters 6 and 7. Find the words that you misspelled, and add these words to your personal spelling list.

4 Work with your partner to test each other on your spelling words.

More Writing Practice

Write an essay about one of the following topics.

REMEMBER Brainstorm ideas and take notes before you begin to write. Organize your writing into introduction, body, and conclusion paragraphs. Add supporting details, facts, and warnings, if necessary. Be sure to make your explanation of the process clear and complete.

---

1. **Building a Good Relationship**
   Write an essay explaining the steps that a person can take to build a good relationship with a husband or wife, boyfriend or girlfriend, friend, co-worker, or family member. Explain why these steps will be helpful. Use your own experience or knowledge as support.

2. **In Case of an Accident**

   Write an essay explaining the steps to take in case of an accident, such as a medical emergency or a weather disaster. Write about a specific type of accident or disaster with which you have some experience or knowledge.

3. **An Academic Process**

   Write an essay explaining the steps that a student should take to accomplish an important task at school, such as registering for classes, getting financial aid, choosing a major, or solving problems with instructors. Write about a process that you have successfully completed yourself. Use facts and your own experience as support.

Chapter Goals

Take credit for achieving the learning goals in Chapter 7. Check (✔) all of the goals that you have achieved. If you are having problems with one of these goals, get extra practice by writing another essay on one of the topics above, or do the additional language exercises in the appropriate Do It Yourself section at the back of the book. Then talk to your instructor about your writing.

Chapter Goals Checklist

❑ Consider the audience and purpose for your writing.

❑ Outline a process essay.

❑ Use subordinating conjunctions appropriately.

❑ Use commands and modal verbs correctly.

❑ Keep pronouns consistent.

CHAPTER 8

Then and Now

Chapter Goals

- Use a Venn diagram to organize ideas.
- Write a thesis statement for a comparison/ contrast essay.
- Outline a comparison/ contrast essay.
- Use adjectives with *-ed* and *-ing* endings.
- Use comparative forms correctly.
- Use transitions for comparing and contrasting.

Approaching the Topic

In our modern world, it seems that change is occurring very rapidly. We have all lived long enough to notice changes in things, places, and ways of life. In Chapter 8, you will read and write essays about these kinds of changes.

Discuss the following questions in a group.

1. Look at the photographs. Do they remind you of places or objects you know that have changed? What changes do you see?

2. Have *you* undergone any major changes in your life in recent years? What has changed about your life? Are the changes positive or negative?

3. In what ways have practices in society changed during your lifetime, for example, in the family, marriage, or education?

Reading 1

Discuss these questions with a group of your classmates before you read: Have you ever moved from one place to another and revisited your former town or city after a long absence? What changes did you find? How did you feel about these changes?

Visiting My Home

1   I was very excited about going back to our small village in Bangladesh after five years away, but I was not prepared for the changes. Roads were paved where there had been dirt. People were riding buses where before they had used rickshaws.[1] And there were new shops and offices in the market area, selling items that before were available only in larger towns. I was very happy to see these changes. However, when I reached my family's old house, the changes there were even more surprising.

2   First of all, there were fewer family members living in our old house. Before, our household was very large—my family plus my uncles, aunts, cousins, and grandparents—all living in the same house. It was very crowded and noisy, but it was always fun being with the whole family. After five years, I found only my grandparents and one uncle and his family living there. My other uncle had moved to the city. I found our house half empty and very quiet.

3   Second, I discovered many changes outside our house. Before, there was a wooden fence around our house, and inside the fence, a big field where I used to play in the afternoons with the village children. There were lots of mango and banana trees and one lichee tree in our front yard. When the sun went down, the village children, my cousins, and I used to pick green mangoes and eat them in that field, lying on hay "beds" that we had made. We often played ball and hide-and-seek in that great field. Now, our field isn't a field anymore. It has become a large pond[2] with fish. My uncle sells the fish and makes money for the family. Also, there

are more palm trees planted on the edge of the pond. I am happy that my uncle has a good business, but I realized that I was not going to lie there and happily eat mangoes as before.

4   I was even more shocked when I went inside the house. I saw a nice living room with a sofa and color television in place of the wooden furniture and black and white television that we had had. Before, we didn't have a study room. However, after five years, I found a study room with a computer that one of my cousins uses for college. We didn't own a computer when we lived there. Also they have a phone connection, which we didn't have before. I thought it was strange that now my "old" house looked much like my new house!

5   Usually, change is a good thing. In fact, I was extremely happy to see the changes in the village itself—the better ways to travel and the new businesses. The changes in our family home were improvements, too, but I was nostalgic[3] for the way our family home was before I left.

Umme Salma, Bangladesh

---

[1]*rickshaws:* small vehicles used in Asia for carrying one or two passengers. A rickshaw is pulled by someone walking or riding a bicycle.

[2]*pond:* a small area of fresh water that is smaller than a lake

[3]*nostalgic:* the slightly sad feelings you have when you remember happy events from the past

Discussion and Analysis   In a group, do the activities and discuss the questions. Then write answers to each question on a separate piece of paper. Write your answers in complete sentences.

1. Underline the thesis statement of the essay.

2. In each body paragraph, the writer describes one main difference. Underline the sentences that introduce each difference.

3. In the body paragraphs, what are the main differences in the writer's family and home? Underline sentences that tell about these changes.

4. In the body paragraphs, underline words that express the writer's feelings about the way her family and her old home changed.

5. Does the conclusion paragraph include words or ideas that were in the thesis statement? If so, underline these words or ideas.

Reading 2

Traveling the Chunnel Train

1   The English Channel[1] Tunnel, called "the Chunnel," ranks[2] as one of the greatest engineering achievements of the twentieth century. The Chunnel is an undersea tunnel linking England and France. Before it opened in 1994, travelers went between England and the European continent[3] by sea or air. With the Chunnel, travelers have gained a way of traveling between England and continental Europe that is faster and simpler but somewhat costlier.

2   One major difference between crossing the Channel via[4] tunnel and via other means is travel time. The Chunnel's Eurostar Express passenger trains travel up to 186 miles per hour, and from London, they take only two and a half hours to reach Brussels and three hours to reach Paris. Before the Chunnel was completed, travelers going between London and Paris had two less efficient choices. Air travel between the cities takes roughly four hours, including check-in and baggage waits and airport-to-city travel. Travel over water is also time-consuming. To get from London to Paris, passengers have to go first to Dover, two to three hours south of London, by train or car. The trip across the Channel takes about 45 minutes on a hovercraft[5] and 75 minutes on a ferry. The train ride from Calais to Paris then takes about 75 minutes. People who used to take their cars across the Channel on hovercraft now have the choice of taking Le Shuttle—the car train through the Chunnel. The crossing time is the same; however, Chunnel drivers save a little time because the Chunnel's English and French customs checks are done simultaneously.

3   More important, Chunnel travel is relatively hassle free[6] compared to other means of travel. Travelers with tickets arrive at Waterloo train station in London ready to board their train. Check-in is as easy as zapping tickets through an automatic turnstile.[7] Passengers' baggage stays with them, so there is no need to check in suitcases or to wait for them on the other end. Also, no reservations are required for Le Shuttle car trains, and they run every 15 minutes during peak[8] times and at least once an hour at night. The Chunnel operates 24 hours a day, year-round. And Chunnel trains are not subject to weather delays, as are planes and boats. Chunnel trains run in all kinds of weather.

4   Unfortunately, the speed and ease of Chunnel travel means higher ticket prices. London-to-Paris round-trip Eurostar Express tickets cost more than ferry and hovercraft tickets. However, the boat passengers who must buy train tickets as well might find that the total price difference is not that great. Taking a car on Le Shuttle is considerably more expensive than ferrying a car over water, despite comparable travel times. Small, low-cost airline carriers have recently launched very inexpensive London-to-Paris flights, so for the budget-minded traveler, flying offers a tempting alternative to Chunnel travel.

5   Clearly, the choice of whether to travel by Chunnel train, by boat, or by airplane depends on the importance of convenience, time, and money to the individual traveler. The good news is that travelers now have a faster and more convenient way to move between England and the rest of Europe.

---

[1]*channel:* water that connects two seas
[2]*ranks:* has a particular position in a list of people or things
[3]*continent:* one of the main areas of land on the Earth
[4]*via:* by way of
[5]*hovercraft:* a high-speed boat that *hovers,* or "flies," atop the water
[6]*hassle free:* easy and simple; free of *hassles,* or problems
[7]*turnstile:* a gate that lets only one person through at a time
[8]*peak times:* busiest times

Discussion and Analysis

In a group, do the activities and discuss the questions. Then write answers to each question on a separate piece of paper. Write your answers in complete sentences.

1. What is the writer's main idea about the Chunnel? Underline the thesis statement.

2. What are the three major points that the writer presents? Underline the sentence in each body paragraph that introduces one of these points.

3. In each body paragraph (paragraphs 2–4), the writer makes comparisons. For each paragraph, write the two topics that are being compared in two columns. Then write the information about each topic in the proper column.

4. What kind of information does the writer include in the conclusion?

Journal Writing

Write a journal entry about how you deal with change. In general, do you accept change easily, or do you have trouble accepting change? Give some examples of large or small changes that have affected your life. How did you react to these changes?

Language for Writing

Word Families: Adjectives with *-ed* and *-ing* endings

Some words that end in *-ed* and *-ing* look like verbs, but, in fact, they are adjectives. They are useful for expressing feelings and opinions.

Adjectives ending in *-ed* have a *passive* meaning. The *-ed* word describes how the subject of the sentence is affected.

> Dmitri was **surprised** when he saw so many changes in his old neighborhood.
>
> (Dmitri was surprised *by* the changes.)

Adjectives ending in *-ing* have an active meaning. The *-ing* word describes the thing or person that produces the effect.

> His neighborhood had a **surprising** number of new buildings.
>
> (The *number* of new buildings produces the effect. It *surprises*.)

1 Fill in the chart with adjectives ending in *-ed* or *-ing*. (Remember to drop the final *e* of verbs ending in *e* and then add the appropriate ending.) The first one has been done for you.

Verb	I felt . . .	The change was . . .
1. amuse	amused	amusing
2. confuse	_____	_____
3. excite	_____	_____
4. frighten	_____	_____
5. interest	_____	_____
6. please	_____	_____
7. relax	_____	_____
8. tire	_____	_____

2 Complete each sentence by adding an adjective with an *-ed* or *-ing* ending. Choose an appropriate adjective from the list in Exercise 1. In some sentences, more than one word from the list may be appropriate. The first one has been done for you.

Being New Parents

Parenthood changes a couple's life in several ____interesting____
                                                        1.
ways. Before the baby comes, most new parents feel very

_____ about the coming baby. They read about child
        2.
raising and prepare the child's room. After the baby arrives, however,

new parents soon realize that being a parent can be stressful because an infant needs constant attention. Parents may become _____

3.

when they don't understand why their baby cries. It can also be

_____ when an infant gets sick. At this point, many new

4.

parents wish they could enjoy the _____ moments they

5.

had before parenthood. However, a positive change that occurs with new

parents is the simple joy of parenthood. It's very _____ for

6.

parents to watch their baby grow and respond to them. In the end, one

smile or laugh from the baby can make all the _____ work

7.

of raising the child seem worthwhile.

DO IT YOURSELF
For more practice:

Adjectives with
-*ed* and -*ing*
endings, 249

Academic Words

1 Study the list of academic words from Chapter 8 and the sentences in which they are used. Check (✔) the words that you already know.

❑ **categories**   Today there are several **categories** of nursing careers that students may choose from.

❑ **distinction**   Our culture makes a **distinction** between the way married women and the way single women should dress.

❑ **appreciate**   Do you **appreciate** improvements in technology in your home country?

❑ **items**   There were over a hundred **items** displayed in the Asian art exhibition.

❑ **period**   Many changes can occur over a **period** of ten years.

❑ **primary**   A shortage of classroom space was the **primary** reason that the university built a new building.

❑ **restriction**   Some cultures place **restrictions** on women's behavior.

❑ **seek**   Many people **seek** a perfect place to live, but few ever find it.

2 Test your comprehension of the academic words in Chapter 8 by matching one of the definitions that follow on page 162 to each boldfaced word in Exercise 1. Write the word on the line.

1. _____ difference
2. _____ try to get, find
3. _____ objects
4. _____ principal, main
5. _____ groups, types
6. _____ rules that limit what you can do
7. _____ be grateful for
8. _____ length of time

3 If you have difficulty matching any word from Exercise 1 to its definition in Exercise 2, put it in the academic word list in your notebook. Write its definition and a sentence using the word.

WRITING

Assignment

Write an essay about two or three changes that have occurred in a place, an object, or a way of life. To write your essay, follow the steps of the writing process.

STEP 1

Getting Ideas

1 Read the list of topics that relate to change. In a group, discuss how these things or events change people's lives or how these things or events have changed your own lives. Take notes on your discussion.

getting married	having a child	war
moving to a new city	my hometown	business
living on my own	being a college student	shopping
televisions	computers	fashion

2 In your group, add more topics to the list. To get more ideas, discuss these questions:

- Which is the most significant change in a thing, place, or way of life that you have noticed?

- Has your own life changed because of it? If so, how?

Take notes on your discussion. Share your ideas with the rest of the class.

3 Choose one or two topics that you may want to write about.

> ## Venn Diagram
>
> A *Venn diagram* is a type of graphic organizer that helps you visualize the similarities and differences between two subjects. For this assignment, the two subjects are your topic *in the past* and your topic *in the present*.

STEP 2

Organizing

1 Study the Venn diagram. Notes in the two circles describe major areas of change in television. Points that have not changed appear in the shaded area.

Discuss the following questions in a group.

1. What three major points about television in the past did the writer include in the past circle?

2. What three changes in these points does the writer show in the present circle?

3. According to the writer, what aspect of television hasn't changed?

Television Then and Now

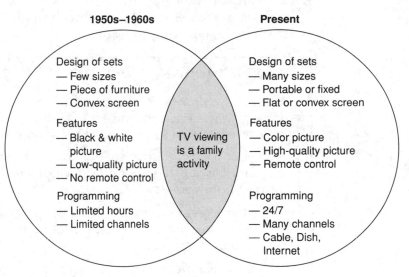

2 Make a Venn diagram using the diagram on page 164 to help you organize your ideas for your essay.

1. In the Past circle, write three or more points about your subject in the past.

2. In the Present circle, write notes about how the Past points have changed.

3. Make sure that the notes that you write in the Past and Present circles relate to the same points.

4. If any points are the same in both the past and the present, put these notes in the area where the two circles overlap.

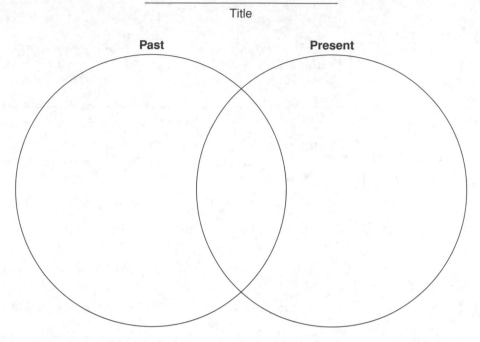

Title

Past   Present

3 Explain your notes to your partner. Choose two or three points to include in your essay. Draw a line through the ideas in your diagram that you do not want to include.

Thesis Statement for a Comparison/Contrast Essay

A *comparison/contrast* essay presents major similarities or differences between two topics. For this assignment, you are presenting the *contrasts*, or differences, in a subject in the past and the present.

1. With your partner, discuss the two or three main points in your Venn diagram. Answer these questions, which will help you write a thesis statement for your essay.

   ■ Are there great differences from the past to the present? Write a word or words to compare the degree, or number, of changes in the subject from past to present.

   Examples: *significant* changes   *several* changes   *important* changes

   ■ Are the changes positive or negative? In other words, do the changes make the place, object, or way of doing something better or worse than in the past?

2. Use your Venn diagram and the ideas from the previous exercise to write a thesis statement for your essay.

   Example Thesis Statements

   Television has changed vastly since the 1950s.

   Television has improved in three major ways.

   Today, there is a greater variety of television set designs, features, and programming than there was in the past.

Outlining a Comparison/Contrast Essay

Generally, in academic writing, there are two ways to organize a comparison/contrast essay. For this assignment, organize your essay in the following way:

- In the introduction, state your main idea about the comparison/contrast, that is, the differences in the subject from the past to the present.

- Use one body paragraph to present each difference. Begin each body paragraph with a topic sentence that presents one point that has changed. Include details and facts about the subject in the past and the present. Include two or three body paragraphs.

- Conclude your essay by restating the main ideas.

---

1 Work with a partner. Read the following outline of a comparison/ contrast essay titled "Television Then and Now." Discuss the questions that follow.

Television Then and Now

I. Introduction

Thesis statement: *Today, television has a greater variety of set designs, features, and programming than it did in the past.*

II. Change 1: Designs

Topic sentence: *First of all, television sets are now available in a range of sizes and designs.*

A. Design of television sets in the past

Supporting ideas (details, examples, facts) about design of TVs in the 1950s–1960s

B. Designs of television sets today

Supporting ideas (details, examples, facts) about design of TVs in the 1990s–2000s

III. Change 2: Features

Topic sentence: *Television also has many more features than it did in the past.*

A. Features of television in the past

Supporting ideas (details, examples, facts) about features of TVs in the 1950s–1960s

B. Features of television today

Supporting ideas (details, examples, facts) about features of TVs in the 1990s–2000s

IV. **Change 3: Programming**

Topic sentence: *Most important, television offers many more program choices than TV did in the past.*

A. TV programming in the past

Supporting ideas (details, examples, facts) about TV programming in the 1950s–1960s

B. TV programming options today

Supporting ideas (details, examples, facts) about TV programming in the 1990s–2000s

V. **Conclusion**

State an idea relating to the thesis statement.
State a result, a prediction, or a recommendation.

1. How many paragraphs does the outline show? How do you know this?
2. Read the thesis statement. What are the three points that the writer includes in this sentence? Does the outline present these three points in the same order as they were written in the thesis statement?
3. Look at the Venn diagram on page 163. In paragraph 2, what could the writer say about design of television sets in the past? In the present?

2 Make an outline for your essay using ideas from your Venn diagram and your thesis statement. As in the outline shown on page 165 and above, be sure to write complete sentences to express your thesis and your body paragraph topics.

3 Read your partner's outline. Make sure that it represents a four- or five-paragraph essay about two or three changes in a place, object, or way of life. Check your outline with your instructor.

Examples as Support

As you learned in Chapter 5, writers include examples of things, events, or people to show that opinions are true. Writers may include a series of general-to-specific statements to support opinions. In the following passage, study how the writer begins with a topic sentence that states his or her general opinion, then writes a more specific statement to lead into specific examples:

TOPIC SENTENCE (OPINION STATEMENT)
Having children permits parents to act like children again.
MORE SPECIFIC STATEMENT
Once parents have children, they can feel free to engage in games, sports, and other play activities that might not have seemed "normal" to them before they had children. SPECIFIC EXAMPLE A mother may sing funny songs or make silly clay creations. SPECIFIC EXAMPLE A father may climb on the playground equipment. SPECIFIC EXAMPLE For the parent of a young child, sledding after a winter snowstorm or playing hide-and-seek in the park are perfectly acceptable. Parents can join in the fun with their children, and no one will blame them for being childish.

1 Work with a partner. Read the paragraph. Mark the *topic sentence* (*opinion statement*) and the *more specific statements* that lead into *specific examples*. Compare your answers in a group.

Electronic mail is more convenient than regular mail. With electronic mail, a person can send messages very quickly across long distances. For example, a college student can attach his graduation photographs to an e-mail message, and his friends will receive them hours after the ceremony. Moreover, he can send an e-mail message to his parents asking them to send him money right away, and he doesn't have to spend money on a long-distance call to do it. Another convenient thing about e-mail is that there's no need to leave the comfort of home to send a message. The college student with an Internet connection doesn't need to go out and buy stamps, write a letter, and go to the post office to mail it. He can sit in his pajamas and communicate with others without setting foot outside. E-mail is a much easier way to keep in touch than regular mail.

2 With your partner, discuss the main idea of each topic sentence that follows. For each opinion statement, write a more specific statement that will lead into a specific example or examples. Write at least two sentences to support each opinion statement. Use the paragraph in Exercise 1 as an example.

1. Security is tighter at airports and other public buildings than it was before September 11, 2001.
2. Women now work in jobs that were dominated by men in previous generations.
3. For a newcomer, the unfamiliar surroundings of a city may be confusing.
4. Students in college work more independently than they did in high school.

3 Choose one of the topic sentences from Exercise 2. On your own, write an opinion paragraph that begins with the topic sentence. Support the opinion by writing more specific statements and specific examples. Include at least two examples to support the opinion in the topic sentence. Compare your paragraphs with classmates who chose the same topic.

STEP 3

Writing the First Draft

Using your discussion notes (Step 1) and the ideas in your Venn diagram (Step 2), write the first draft of your essay on changes in a place, object, or way of life. Follow your outline (page 166), making sure that your essay contains four or five paragraphs.

STEP 4

Revising

Exchange drafts with a partner. Read each other's essays and answer these questions.

❏ Does the introduction include a thesis statement that tells the main idea of the essay?

❏ Are there two or three body paragraphs? Does each body paragraph describe one area of change in the subject?

❏ Are examples used to support main ideas in the body paragraphs?

❏ Does the conclusion paragraph relate to the thesis statement?

Discuss your partner's comments. Take notes on any revisions you need to make. Write a second draft of your paper.

STEP 5

Editing

PRE-TEST

Test your knowledge of the grammar presented in Chapter 8.

Study the two photographs. On a separate piece of paper, write sentences to compare features of classrooms in the past and the present. Use at least six of the words in the list.

computers	ways to find information	difficult
paper and pencil	technology	boring
blackboards	convenient	

Have your instructor check your answers.

Grammar

Study the following grammar explanations and do the activities. They will help you recognize and correct grammar mistakes in your writing.

The Comparative

English has many patterns for making comparisons. You can use these patterns to show relationships of equality or inequality.

Comparatives of Equality

To show equality in a comparison, use *as* with the adjective, adverb, or noun.

Adjective: Telephones today are *as important as* they were in the past.

Adverb: Early computers did not run *as quietly as* today's computers do.

Noun: Videocassette tapes are almost **the same size *as*** eight-track audiotapes were.

Comparatives of Inequality

To show inequality in a comparison, use the comparative form of the adjective, adverb, noun, or verb with *than.*

Adjective:	Television screens are **larger** *than* they were 20 years ago.
Adverb:	Remote controls operate **more easily** *than* the knobs on old TVs.
Plural count nouns:	My hometown has **fewer shopping centers** *than* it did in the past.
Non-count nouns:	There is **more traffic** on this road now *than* there was a year ago.
Verb:	VCRs **cost less** today *than* they did 20 years ago.

Forming the Comparative

- Comparative adjectives are formed by adding *-er* to the word.

    dark → darker

- With two-syllable adjectives that end in *-y,* drop the *-y* and add *-ier.*

    pretty → prettier

- With adjectives and adverbs of two or more syllables, the words *more* and *less* are used instead of *-er.*

    more dependable machines
    fly less frequently

    Common exceptions to this rule are the words *quieter* and *simpler.*

- Following are some common adjectives and adverbs and their irregular comparative forms.

Adjectives	*Adverbs*
good → better	well → better
far → farther (further)	far → farther (further)
bad → worse	badly → worse

1 Work with a partner. Read the following specifications for two computers and the glossary of computer-related words. Discuss the differences and similarities between the two computers.

	Techco Dimension 440 US$799	Techco Dimension 440 Upgrade US$1,239
Processor[1]	Intel Pentium 4 at 1.6 GHz	Intel Pentium 4 at 2.66 GHz
Memory[2]	128 MB	256 MB
Hard drive[3]	60-GB Hard Drive	80-GB Hard Drive
Monitor	15-inch	17-inch
CD-ROM[4] drive	48× CD-ROM	16× DVD ROM Drive
Warranty	1-year limited warranty	3-year limited warranty
Software	Microsoft Works Suite	Microsoft Works Suite
Mouse	Microsoft IntelliMouse	Microsoft IntelliMouse Explorer
Floppy drive	3.5-inch floppy drive	3.5-inch floppy drive
Operating System	Windows XP Home Edition	Windows XP Home Edition

[1]*processor:* the brain of the computer. A computer performs tasks more quickly with a faster processor. Processor speed is measured in gigahertz (GHz).

[2]*RAM:* random access memory. RAM is where the computer temporarily stores data on its way to or from the processor.

[3]*hard drive:* performs long-term storage and is measured in gigabytes. A gigabyte (GB) equals 1,000 megabytes (MB).

[4]*CD-ROM (compact disc read-only memory):* device that reads software CDs and music CDs. A DVD-ROM (digital video disc read-only memory) device can read CDs and DVDs.

2 Complete the sentences using the computer specifications and glossary. Use a comparative form of the word or phrase under each blank. The first one is done for you.

1. The Techco 440 Upgrade is _____*more expensive*_____ than the Techco 440.
   <small>expensive</small>

2. The Techco 440 has a _____ hard drive than the
   <small>small</small>

   Techco 440 Upgrade.

3. The screen of the 15-inch monitor is not as _____ as
   <small>large</small>

   the screen of a 17-inch monitor.

4. A 1.6 GHz processor opens and runs programs _____
   <small>quick</small>

   than a 2.66 GHz processor.

5. The Techco 440 does not have _____ as the 440 Upgrade.
   <small>type of mouse</small>

6. The Techco 440 includes _____ as the 440 Upgrade.
   <small>software</small>

7. A DVD-ROM drive is _____ than a CD-ROM drive
   <small>useful</small>

   because it reads both DVDs and CDs.

8. Techco Computer Corporation provides _____ on the
   <small>years of warranty</small>

   440 model than it does on the 440 Upgrade.

9. Which of the two computers do you think is a _____
   <small>good</small>

   buy?

DO IT YOURSELF

For more practice:

Comparative
  forms, 251
Adjectives and
  adverbs, 251
Nouns, 253

3 Write five sentences of your own to compare the two computers. Use the comparative forms you have learned.

Examples

The Techco 440 is **cheaper than** the 440 Upgrade.

The Techco 440 has **the same components as** the 440 Upgrade.

Transitions for Comparing and Contrasting

Transitional expressions can also be used to show when items are similar or different.

Transitions to Show Similarities

Transition	Example
like similar to	Today's calculators are **similar to** the ones I used as a child.
in the same way* similarly likewise	Twenty years ago, telephones allowed people to communicate across long distances. **Likewise,** today's telephones connect us instantly with people far away.
and**	Electronic dictionaries give multiple definitions of words, **and** paper dictionaries do the same.

*Use a *period* or a *semicolon* before and a comma after these transitions, as in the example sentence.
**Use a *comma* before this transition.

Transitions to Show Differences

Transition	Example
whereas while	**Whereas** in the past food was most often cooked on gas or electric stoves, today food is often prepared in a microwave oven.
different from unlike	Ford automobiles today are **different from** the early Ford Model T's. **Unlike** the Fords of the 1920s, today's Fords have many features and comforts.
however on the other hand* in contrast	In my youth, my neighborhood was a quiet place. **However,** today it is noisy and crowded. A personal computer requires a desk or table to hold the monitor, processor, and keyboard; **on the other hand,** a Palm Pilot fits in your hand.
but** yet	I knew all my neighbors in my old neighborhood, **but** today I know only a few of my neighbors.

*Use a *period* or a *semicolon* before and a comma after these transitions, as in the example sentences.
**Use a *comma* before these transitions.

The Volkswagen Beetle then . . .	Today's Beetle . . .
■ Was first produced in Germany in 1937.	■ Is produced all over the world.
■ Cost about US$200.	■ Costs more than US$15,000.
■ Had its engine in the back.	■ Has its engine in the front.
■ Was unusual because of its "bug-like" shape.	■ Has the same "bug-like" shape.
■ Had a manual transmission.	■ Comes with either a manual or an automatic transmission.
■ Had a 25-horsepower engine.	■ Features a 115-horsepower engine.
■ Was built and sold in Mexico up until the year 2000.	■ Is built in the same Mexican factories that produced the original Beetle.
■ Could travel about 40 miles per gallon of gasoline.	■ Gets about 40 miles to the gallon of gasoline.

DO IT YOURSELF
For more practice:
Basic sentence
    patterns, 213
Punctuation, 259

Read the information about Volkswagen Beetles in the chart. Write at least eight sentences to compare Beetles in the past and present. Use appropriate transitions for comparison and contrast. Share your answers with your classmates.

Example

The original Beetle had its motor in the rear, **whereas** today's Beetle has the motor in the front.

Writing the Final Draft

Use the checklist to edit your work. Then rewrite your essay.

Editing Checklist

❏ Are comparative forms used correctly?

❏ Are transitions for comparing and contrasting used appropriately?

❏ Are adjectives with *-ed* and *-ing* endings used appropriately?

Your instructor will grade your paper for its content, organization, and language using the evaluation sheet for this chapter on page 207. Read over the evaluation sheet. Then reread and edit your paper as necessary before you turn in the final draft.

On Your Own

More Writing Practice

Write an essay about one of the following topics.

REMEMBER Brainstorm ideas and take notes before you begin to write. Organize your writing into introduction, body, and conclusion paragraphs. Add supporting examples, details, or facts. Your thesis statement can state that the two subjects are similar to or different from each other or that one is better than the other. Include the main idea in the conclusion paragraph.

1. **The Impact of _____**

   Write an essay about two or three changes that occur as a result of a major event in people's lives, such as graduating, moving to an unfamiliar city or country, or having a serious accident. In each body paragraph, write about one change that occurs in people's lives as a result of the event. Compare their lives before and after the event. Use facts, details, and examples to show how and why it affects people's lives. Use your own experiences to support your ideas.

2. **Changes in Beliefs**

   Write an essay that presents two or three points about a belief or idea that you had that has changed in your lifetime. For example, from the past to the present, you may have changed your religious beliefs or your beliefs about money, family, or education. In each body paragraph, explain how your belief or idea has changed. Use details, facts, and examples from your experience to explain the changes in your belief or idea.

3. **Personal Changes**

   Write an essay about two or three changes that you have seen in someone you know well. Specify the time period in which the changes have occurred. Use details, facts, and examples to show how the person has changed. Explain why he or she has changed.

Chapter Goals   Take credit for achieving the learning goals in Chapter 8. Check (✔) all the goals that you have achieved. If you are having problems with one of these goals, get extra practice by writing another essay on one of the topics on page 175, or do the additional language exercises in the appropriate Do It Yourself section in the back of the book. Then talk to your instructor about your writing.

Chapter Goals Checklist

❑ Use a Venn diagram to organize ideas.

❑ Write a thesis statement for a comparison/contrast essay.

❑ Outline a comparison/contrast essay.

❑ Use adjectives with *-ed* and *-ing* endings.

❑ Use comparative forms correctly.

❑ Use transitions for comparing and contrasting.

CHAPTER 9

Security versus Privacy

Chapter Goals

- Organize and write a summary of a reading.
- Make a concept map to show main ideas in a text.
- Organize and write a response to a reading.
- Paraphrase ideas in a text.
- Write reported speech sentences.
- Recognize and write passive and active sentences.

Approaching the Topic

In recent years, security has become a critical issue at many educational institutions—from elementary schools to colleges and universities. In Chapter 9, you will read and write about current practices for making schools and other public places safer.

1. Are schools in your community safe? If you have heard of any violence or crime that occurred there, describe these incidents.

2. In your view, what are the major causes of school violence or crime?

3. What other public places in your community face security problems? Describe the places and their problems.

READING FOR WRITING

Reading 1

Discuss these questions with classmates before reading: Which types of schools have security problems? What types of problems do they have? How can the problems be solved?

The Schools with Maximum Security

1   The days when school security meant a caretaker rattling his keys at the end of the day are long gone. Today closed circuit television (CCTV) cameras, high walls, smart cards,[1] and even a police presence are all part of the armory[2] of a modern school.

2   At one South London school recently, a mother who had come to pick up her daughter found two policemen with bullet-proof vests guarding the entrance. However, this frightening sight did have its funny side. Another mother, frustrated by the complicated security buzzer system, had climbed over the gates and set off the automatic alarm in the local police station.

3   Karen Haestier, of the Arson[3] Prevention Bureau, says three schools are hit by arsonists every day. The bill for 2000 is expected to reach £85 million, almost double the average over the past decade.

4   The entrances to every school in Newcastle are now monitored[4] by door-entry systems, and more than a quarter are protected by CCTV. Most of the city's schools are also surrounded by thick fencing made of galvanized steel. Before these schools were turned into fortresses,[5] one had 64 windows smashed in one night, according to Jim Rowtledge, the local education authority's security manager. "It was a massive problem," he says. "Now vandals[6] can't get in."

5   As part of this year's £22 million security package, which the government will give to local education authorities as of April, teachers will also be taught self-defense.

6   And last term a school in one of North London's toughest areas became the first in Britain to have its own policeman. Policeman Andy Briers, 35, is now in his second term at Northumberland Park School,

Tottenham. In the past students had been attacked and mugged[7] by students from other schools. "My presence makes them feel safer," says Briers.

7   He hopes his role at the 1,100-student school will become permanent. "Kids used to turn up from other schools looking for trouble. Now they don't. And robberies in the surrounding areas are down. If you dial 999 [the emergency line] here, it can be an hour before a police officer arrives. The kids tell me if they have been robbed or hassled and I hop on my bike and go straight out and deal with it. This is a return to community policing."

8   . . . "They don't fight outside here because they know I am here." He made 12 arrests in his first term at the school, for robbery, assault, and indecent exposure.[8] And he has managed to interest 20 Afro-Caribbean and Turkish youths in joining the police force.

9   In Bradford, one school is using electronic deterrents[9] at the children's request. Students at Yorkshire Martyrs Catholic College are protected from bullies[10] and intruders by a system of 30 security cameras that monitor halls, part of the grounds, and the toilets. The £50,000 system was set up last summer and includes electronic locking doors. The decision was "about valuing individuals and people. We want to cut down on bullying, and to make sure that anyone entering the school signs in," says the principal, Vincent McNicholas.

10   Yorkshire Martyrs is a school with 1,150 students aged 11 to 19. "We put cameras in areas such as the restrooms, where the children said they felt least safe. It was their idea, and the security is open, with no hidden cameras," McNicholas said.

11   It is not just inner-city schools that are responding to the threat of violence in modern Britain. In the quiet southwest London borough of Richmond, Grey Court School, a school of 1,000 students, has installed CCTV. "It was as a result of vandalism in the evenings and on weekends," says the principal, Geoff Conway. "One particularly bad year every window was broken on a systematic[11] basis." The problem, he says, has been 98 percent solved by the cameras, all placed on the outside of the school and facing outwards.

12   "These cameras are not meant to catch children having a cigarette. We would feel diminished if we had to spy on our own students." Grey Court also has an internal fire and break-in alarm system. "This is only sensible, given the number of schools burnt down."

13 Most independent schools now have CCTV, "but you need to achieve a balance," says Mike Sant, a school registrar. "No parent wants to see a school that looks like Fort Knox."[12]

14 Indeed no one does. But like it or not, schools have become high-security zones. The good news is that the children don't seem to mind. It makes them feel safer.

Cally Law, *The Times of London*

[1]*smart cards:* special plastic cards that are used to enter a secured place
[2]*armory:* a place where weapons are stored
[3]*arson:* the crime of deliberately making something burn
[4]*monitored:* carefully watched, listened to, or examined over a period of time to check for changes
[5]*fortresses:* large, strong buildings used for defending important places
[6]*vandals:* people who *vandalize,* that is, damage or destroy things deliberately
[7]*mugged:* attacked and robbed of money and valuables
[8]*indecent exposure:* the crime of showing your sex organs in a public place
[9]*deterrents:* things that *deter,* or make someone not want to do something
[10]*bullies:* people who threaten to hurt someone or frighten him or her, especially someone weaker or smaller
[11]*systematic:* as part of an organized plan or process
[12]*fort:* a strong building used by an army for defending an important place. The U.S. government stores money in Fort Knox, Kentucky.

Discussion and Analysis

In a group, do the activities and discuss the questions. Then write answers to each question on a separate piece of paper. Write your answers in complete sentences.

1. What is the most important news reported in this article from a newspaper? Underline the sentence or sentences that tells the main idea.

2. Complete this sentence: The newspaper article reports different types of _____ used in British schools.

3. Underline sentences that introduce each of these types.

4. Circle sentences that report the effects of each of these types or ways.

5. Are you surprised about the security methods used at these schools? Write a quick response to give your reaction.

Reading 2

Reading 2 is titled "Prying Eyes." *Pry* means "to try to find out details about someone's private life in an impolite way." Discuss the following questions in a group before you read: Do schools have the right to *pry* into students' activities with security cameras? Why? Should school officials search students' bags or their bodies? Why?

Prying Eyes

1   In the effort to make schools safe and drug-free, are authorities ignoring students' rights?

2   Thirty-two years ago, in a famous opinion defending the rights of students to protest the Vietnam War, United States Supreme Court[1] Justice Abe Fortas wrote that young people do not leave "their constitutional rights[2] at the schoolhouse gate."

3   That's still true.

4   But these days, depending on where you go to school, before you can enjoy those rights you may well have to make your way through a metal detector at the gate, encounter drug-sniffing German shepherds in the hallways, let school officials search your locker, smile for the security cameras, and be ready to urinate into a cup on demand to be tested for drugs. As to free speech, say what you want, but if you mention acts of violence you may be in trouble.

5   In most schools, of course, the picture is not that bad. But according to civil liberties groups[3] the rights of students are under attack as never before. Across the country, many school districts have adopted harsh "zero-tolerance" policies[4] in which even thinking about violating the rules can be reason for punishment. And in the process, civil liberties groups say, basic constitutional rights sometimes get ignored.

6   School officials are in a tough position. They are directed not only to educate their students but also to ensure their safety and maintain an atmosphere where learning can take place. Incidents like the 1999 Columbine[5] shootings have reminded them all too well that the failure to act against that rare student who gives warning signs and then actually does commit an act of serious violence could be deadly.

7   When the rights of students collide with[6] the will of school officials, it's up to the courts to decide where to draw the line.[7] Their decisions in these cases could help determine where the line is drawn in your school.

Eric Nagourney, *The New York Times*

---

[1]*United States Supreme Court:* the court of law with the most authority in the U.S.
[2]*constitutional rights:* rights that are officially allowed by the set of rules of a government or organization
[3]*civil liberties groups:* groups that defend the things you have a legal right to do
[4]*zero-tolerance policies:* policies that do not permit any violation of rules
[5]*Columbine:* Colorado high school where two students shot and killed twelve classmates and a teacher before committing suicide in April 1999
[6]*collide with:* to strongly oppose someone
[7]*draw the line:* to refuse to do something because you do not approve of it

Discussion and Analysis

In a group, do the activities and discuss the questions. Then write answers to each question on a separate piece of paper. Write your answers in complete sentences.

1. The title of the reading is "Prying Eyes." What does the title mean?
2. Underline the sentence that states the main idea or problem being discussed.
3. According to the reading, do students have rights in school? Underline the sentence that answers this question.
4. What are some types of security measures that schools use? Underline the sentence(s) that name some of these measures.
5. The reading states that "school officials are in a tough position." Why is this so?
6. According to the text, what role do courts play in this situation?
7. What is your reaction to the ideas in this text? Write a quick response to express your opinion.

Language for Writing

Word Families: Security-Related Verbs and Nouns

1 Verbs and nouns that you can use to write about security appear in the following charts. Use a dictionary to find the meaning of each word given. Then fill in the charts. The first one in each chart is done for you.

The verb is *to* . . .	The person or thing that does this action is called a . . .
1. deter	*deterrent*
2. detect	
3.	intruder
4. monitor	
5.	vandal
The verb is *to* . . .	**The act or condition of this action is called . . .**
6. *punish*	punishment
7. violate	
8.	defense
9.	improvement
10. tolerate	

2 Complete the words in the sentences with the correct form of the word from the charts in Exercise 1. Leave the space blank if you don't need to add anything. The first two are done for you.

At Fremont High School in Oakland, California, school officials have

taken several effective steps to improve_____ security. First, everyone
                                         1.

who enters the school must pass through a metal detect_*or*___. In
                                                       2.

addition, security officers monitor_____ the hallways, rooms, and
                                    3.

parking areas. Also, security cameras are used inside and outside the

school in order to catch an intrude_____ or vandal_____ on film. Finally,
                                    4.   5.

the school has a "zero-tolera_____" policy, which means officials
                             6.

punish_____ all students who violat_____ school security rules. Officials
       7.   8.

defen_____ the policy. The school principal says they are a strong
      9.

deter_____ against crime.
      10.

---

3 Write ten sentences. Use one word from each pair in the chart in Exercise 1. Write about security equipment, practices, or issues at your school or a public place in your city.

Example

improve

The airport needs to improve its security.

Words Used Together

As you have learned, many verbs and nouns are commonly used together. Notice the following verb + noun pairs from the reading:

The officials **installed cameras** in the high school.

The security guard **breaks up fights** at the school.

1 Work with a partner. Circle words in the lists that are commonly used with the boldfaced words given. Read the sentence aloud to help you decide which words go together. Compare answers with your partner's.

1. The college _____ **policies** regarding campus security.
   (developed)   put   did   (created)

2. **The tension** has _____ between students and security guards.
   grown   increased   risen   expanded

3. Strong security _____ **may reduce** crime in schools.
   policies   regulations   measures   works

4. Security guards _____ **students' bags** at some schools.
   check   search   see   inspect

5. Many criminal _____ **occur** in U.S. high schools each year.
   events   episodes   incidents   times

2 Write five sentences about security at a public place in your community. In each sentence, use one of the verb + noun pairs in Exercise 1 above. Add or change words to make the sentence true for you.

> **Example**
>
> The security guards **searched my bags** at the art museum.

Academic Words

1 Study the list of academic words and the example sentences. Check (✔) the academic words that you already know.

❑ **decade**   In the past **decade,** there has been an increase in terrorism.

❑ **authorities**   **Authorities** have tightened security at airports across the globe.

❑ **comprehensive**   The college conducted a **comprehensive** study of security issues.

❑ **diminish**   If police investigate passengers more carefully, they may **diminish** the number of airplane hijackings.

❑ **incidents**   There have been many **incidents** of bullying at high schools.

❑ **maintain**   Security guards try to **maintain** peace and quiet in schools.

❑ **commit**   Students who **commit** violent acts are often expelled from school.

❑ **encounter**   If you **encounter** a difficult situation, try to stay calm.

❑ **constitution**   A **constitution** is a set of laws and principles that describes the power and the purpose of a particular government.

2 Test your comprehension of the academic words in Chapter 9 by matching one of the definitions that follow to each boldfaced word in Exercise 1. Write the word on the line.

1. _____ experience or meet

2. _____ set of laws for a government

3. _____ make something stay the same

4. _____ people in charge

5. _____ ten years

6. _____ do or achieve something

7. _____ decrease

8. _____ events or occurrences

9. _____ including everything that is important

3 If you have difficulty matching any word from Exercise 1 to its definition in Exercise 2, put it in the academic word list in your notebook. Write its definition and a sentence using the word.

Journal

Write a one-page journal entry about airport security. What do you think are the major security problems that airports face? What are the best ways to solve these problems? Give examples of your own experiences of undergoing security checks at airports.

WRITING

Assignment

Write a one-paragraph summary of and a one-paragraph response to a reading about security in public places. To write your summary and response, follow the steps of the writing process.

STEP 1

Getting Ideas

1 With a group of your classmates, brainstorm places where security is an issue, such as high schools, colleges, airports, streets, parks, banks, and government buildings. Make a list of places that interest you.

2 Read the list of tips regarding finding sources. With your instructor, discuss which resources are available in your school library or computer facilities.

> ### Tips for Finding Readings on Security
>
> 1. **The Internet** Search for Web sites using a search engine like google.com. Type in "security" and a type of place, for example, "security and airport."
> 2. **Library periodicals** Search for sources using a database of magazines and newspapers. Type in key words just like you do when you search the Internet. Ask a librarian or your teacher to help you use the database.
> 3. **Library books** Search by topic (airport security) in your library's online card catalog. Ask a librarian or your teacher for help.

3 Decide on which resources to use, and schedule a time/place to search for readings.

4 Look for articles and book chapters one to two pages long and not too difficult to understand. Bring at least three sources to class. Show them to your instructor. Then choose one as your summary source.

STEP 2

Organizing | Summary Writing

As you learned in Chapter 5, a *summary* is a brief report of something that was written or spoken. A source summary should do the following:

- Identify the source by name and author (if available)
- Accurately report the main idea and major points in the source
- Include a few supporting details, if important
- Be shorter than the original
- Identify the author of the ideas
- Include *paraphrasing,* that is, rewording of ideas in the summary writer's own words
- Be *objective* (not include the summary writer's opinion)

Summarizing is an important skill for writing essays, exams, and research papers.

The Process of Summary Writing

Before you begin your own summary, practice the process of summary writing outlined here.

> The first step in summary writing: Write a one-sentence summary statement. This sentence should include the title of the article, the author's name, and the main idea of the text.

1 Choose the best one-sentence summary statement for "Prying Eyes." Discuss your answer with the rest of your class.

1. The essay "Prying Eyes" by Eric Nagourney states that the U.S. Supreme Court protects students' rights at school.

2. The essay "Prying Eyes" by Eric Nagourney states that student rights may be under attack because of security measures used at schools.

3. The essay "Prying Eyes" by Eric Nagourney says that school officials sometimes search students and their lockers for drugs.

> The second step in summary writing: Make a concept map, or graphic organizer that shows the main ideas of the article. You can write a summary just by looking at a concept map.

2 Study the concept map of "Prying Eyes" that follows.

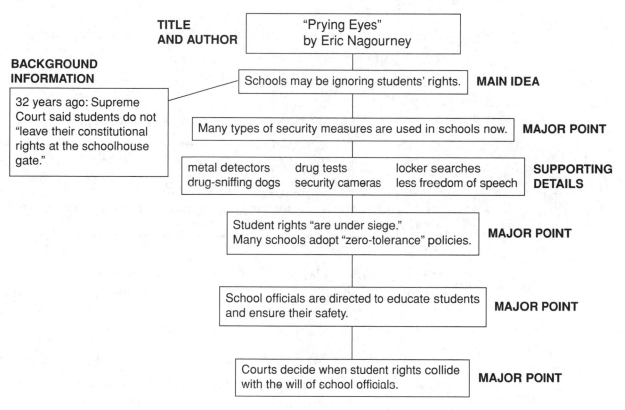

TITLE AND AUTHOR — "Prying Eyes" by Eric Nagourney

BACKGROUND INFORMATION — 32 years ago: Supreme Court said students do not "leave their constitutional rights at the schoolhouse gate."

Schools may be ignoring students' rights. — **MAIN IDEA**

Many types of security measures are used in schools now. — **MAJOR POINT**

metal detectors   drug tests   locker searches
drug-sniffing dogs   security cameras   less freedom of speech — **SUPPORTING DETAILS**

Student rights "are under siege."
Many schools adopt "zero-tolerance" policies. — **MAJOR POINT**

School officials are directed to educate students and ensure their safety. — **MAJOR POINT**

Courts decide when student rights collide with the will of school officials. — **MAJOR POINT**

3 Reread Reading 1, "The Schools with Maximum Security." Work with a partner to mark the main idea in the reading. Make a concept map of the reading. Share your map with groups of your classmates, and comment on the other maps.

The next step in summary writing: **Paraphrase,** or express what someone has written or said in a way that is shorter and easier to understand.

Study this example of a paraphrase.

Original text: *When the rights of students collide with the will of school officials, it's up to the courts to decide where to draw the line.*

Paraphrased version: *Courts must decide cases where student rights conflict with school policies.*

Guidelines for Paraphrasing:

- **Simplify vocabulary.**

  Use synonyms whenever possible.

  Don't change technological or scientific words, names of geographical places, parts of government, fields of study, or other types of specific or technical words.

- **Change the grammar or sentence structure to make sentences easier to understand.**

  Change word forms such as a noun form to an adjective form.

  Make verbs simpler, for example, *is done* to *do*.

  Change transition words and sentence connectors such as *on the other hand* to *but*.

- **Use appropriate punctuation and source identification.**

  Do not overuse quotation marks. Enclose the exact words of a source in quotes only if the words are special or memorable.

  Instead, put the author's ideas into your own words.

  Add phrases that identify the source, such as *the author said,* each time you present a new idea from the text.

4 Read the following original sentences taken from "The Schools with Maximum Security" and the paraphrases. Underline or highlight the parts of the original and paraphrased sentences that contain the same or similar ideas. Share your answers in a group.

1. **Original sentence:** At one South London school recently, a mother who had come to pick up her daughter found two policemen with bullet-proof vests guarding the entrance.

   Paraphrase: Policemen with bullet-proof clothes stood outside a school in London where a mother came to get her child.

2. **Original sentence:** The problem, he says, has been 98 percent solved by the cameras, all placed on the outside of the school and facing outwards.

Paraphrase: Outside cameras almost completely fixed the problem, he says.

5 On a separate piece of paper, paraphrase the following sentences from "Prying Eyes." Use the paraphrasing guidelines on page 188. Share your answers in your group.

1. . . . according to civil liberties groups, the rights of students are under attack as never before. (paragraph 5)
2. School officials are in a tough position. They are directed not only to educate their students but also to ensure their safety. . . (paragraph 6)

6 Read the two sample summaries of Reading 2, "Prying Eyes." Choose which summary you think best represents the main ideas of the reading, following the concept map on page 187. Discuss your answer with a group of your classmates.

Summary 1

The article "Prying Eyes" by Eric Nagourney states that student rights may be under attack because of security measures used at schools. The article in *The New York Times* describes many security methods currently being used—metal detectors, drug-sniffing dogs, locker searches, security cameras, and drug tests. However, according to the writer, a U.S. Supreme Court decision during the Vietnam War era gave students constitutional rights even at school. Civil liberties groups fear that the strict security policies now in force may violate students' rights, Nagourney says. Many schools have "zero-tolerance" policies that call for strict punishment of security violations. The problem is that school officials face a challenge because they must not only educate students but also keep schools safe, he writes. The article suggests that in the future, courts must decide when student rights conflict with school rules.

Summary 2

The newspaper article "Prying Eyes" by Eric Nagourney tells us about the types of security devices that are being used in schools today. Nowadays, students must enter schools through metal detectors, have their lockers searched, and undergo drug tests, among other things. These policies take away student rights. Students have rights under the U.S. Constitution, even while they are in school. Even though schools need to keep their buildings safe, they should not make the schools feel like prisons. Courts will need to help students keep their rights, or schools will continue to create more rules and policies that will trample on people's rights. Nobody wants violence in schools, but we also do not want students to be treated like criminals.

STEP 3

Writing the First Draft

Apply the process of summary writing to the source about security that you chose.

1. Analyze the source.
2. Write a one-sentence summary statement.
3. Create a concept map.
4. Summarize and paraphrase the major points and necessary details. Follow the guidelines for paraphrasing.
5. Summarize and paraphrase the conclusion of the text. Do not include your opinion of the text.

STEP 4

Revising

Exchange drafts and concept maps with a partner. Read each other's summaries and answer these questions.

❏ Does the summary follow the writer's concept map?

❏ Does the one-sentence summary statement include the title, author, and main idea?

❏ In the summary, does the writer include major points (and supporting details, if appropriate) from the original source?

❏ Is there a logical concluding sentence?

❏ Does the writer avoid including his or her own opinion about the subject?

Discuss your partner's comments. Take notes on any revisions you need to make. Write a second draft of your paper.

Sharing Your Writing

Writing a Response

A *response* is a statement of opinion about something that you have read. A response is similar to a summary in that you briefly restate a main idea or ideas from a reading, using paraphrasing. However, a response differs from a summary because you also present your opinions of or reactions to the main ideas in the reading. In a response, you may state your opinion of the overall main idea of a text or of one or more major points in the text.

1 Work with a partner. Read the sample one-paragraph response on page 191. Underline the following parts of the paragraph: (1) the sentence(s) that report idea(s) from the original text, and (2) the sentences that present the response writer's opinions. Discuss this question: Does the response writer give an opinion about the overall main idea of the original reading or about one major point?

Good Behavior at Schools

   One point that Eric Nagourney makes in "Prying Eyes" is that school officials must educate students as well as keep them safe. According to Nagourney, this puts schools in a difficult situation. In my opinion, schools must focus on their main purpose: education. Schools should not be in the difficult situation of having to "police" children. Teaching students how to behave should not be the school's responsibility. Therefore, the problem of keeping schools safe should not be the problem of educators. Parents should be held responsible for guiding their children and teaching them right and wrong. If students behave badly, they should not be allowed to attend school until they correct their behavior. Schools shouldn't have to pay so much attention to security. Let well-disciplined children attend school and get a good education. Prohibit trouble-making children from attending school. They get in the way of the serious students' learning. In short, school officials should not have to be police officers.

---

2 Next, write a one-paragraph response that states your opinions about the main idea or about one major point in the original reading that you summarized. To write your response, follow these steps.

1. Begin by writing a one-sentence summary statement that includes the title, author, and the overall main idea of the reading or one major point in the text.
2. Write sentences that give your opinion about this idea.
3. Write a conclusion sentence that restates your opinion.

3 Share your response with your partner. Discuss your opinions.

STEP 5

Editing

PRE-TEST

Test your knowledge of the grammar presented in Chapter 9.

1. Read the short speech that follows, given by a high school principal to students attending an assembly on electronic devices. Then write a short paragraph to report the main points that the speaker made.

Report: Student Assembly on Electronic Devices

Dr. Burt, the school principal:

Students should not bring cell phones or portable CD players to school. The school district has three main reasons for this rule. First, talking on the phone or listening to CD players can be dangerous. The school halls are noisy and crowded between classes. If you are paying attention to a phone or music, you might not hear important safety announcements. In addition, we want to avoid any thefts or arguments about these devices. Most important, cell phones and CD players distract you from learning. You are here to study, not to talk on the phone or to listen to music. Follow the rules, or you will be suspended from school.

In a speech to students, Dr. Burt, the school principal, said that _____

_____

_____

_____

_____

_____

_____

_____

_____

_____

2. Complete the sentences with the correct form of the verb under the blank.

Security at an Airport Gate

At an airport gate recently, an airline attendant

_____*selected*_____ two passengers for random searches. The two
1. select

passengers _____ in line to board their airplane. The
2. be

attendant _____ them to step aside. The passengers'
3. ask

carry-on bags _____ by a security guard. The passengers
4. search

_____ to take off their shoes. The guard
5. tell

_____ a security device to check their shoes for explosive
6. use

devices. The guard also _____ the passengers bodies
7. scan

with the security device. Afterward, the two passengers

_____ to enter the plane.
8. allow

Have your instructor check your answers.

Grammar

Study the following grammar explanations and do the activities. They will help you recognize and correct grammar mistakes in your writing.

Reported Speech

Study the following sentence:

The article "Prying Eyes" by Eric Nagourney says that students have rights.

Reported speech is used to report the speech or writing of others. Like the example, a reported speech sentence should include the **source of the idea,** a **reporting verb,** and **an important idea or ideas** from the text.

Follow these rules when you write reported speech.

1. **Vary the words you use to name the source,** for example, *the reading* or *the writer* or *the article.* The first time that you identify the writer, give his or her full name and title (if given). The most common style is to refer to the writer by his or her last name or a pronoun the second time you refer to him or her.

2. **Vary the reporting verbs** you use, for example, *the reading **says*** or *the writer **reports**.*

Study the boldfaced reporting verbs below.

The writer **reported** . . .	The author **showed** that . . .	The essay **said** that . . .
In the article, the writer **suggests** . . .	The author **thinks** that . . .	The article **tells us** that . . .
The writer **describes**	. . . the author **concludes**.	. . . the reading **points out**.

You may also use the phrase *according to* before the name of the source or writer in place of a reporting verb.

According to the article, students may undergo drug tests.

3. **Keep the tense of reporting verbs consistent.** In other words, write all the reporting verbs in the *present tense* or all in the *past tense.* Either tense is acceptable, but do not mix the verb tenses up.

4. **Change the verb tense of the statement being reported to match the verb tense of the reporting verb.**

Original sentence: "**I am** tired."—Mr. Bolleddu

Reported speech sentence: Mr. Bolleddu **said** that he **was** tired.

5. **You may add** *that* after the reported verb: *Mr. Bolleddu said **that**. . . .*

6. **Change pronouns** as necessary. Notice in the example that *I* in the original sentence is changed to *he* in the reported speech sentence.

7. **Do not overuse quotation marks.**

---

1 Compare the following original sentences taken from "The Schools with Maximum Security," pages 179–181, and the reported speech sentences. Underline the changes in the reported speech sentences. Discuss your answers with your classmates.

1. **Original sentence:** "My presence makes them feel safer," says Andy. (paragraph 6)

   Reported speech sentence: Policeman Andy Briers said that his presence made them feel safer.

2. **Original sentence:** "We would feel diminished if we had to spy on our own students." —Principal Geoff Conway (paragraph 12)

   Reported speech sentence: Principal Geoff Conway said that teachers would feel diminished if they had to spy on their own students.

2 Rewrite the original sentences from the reading into reported speech sentences. Follow the rules on page 194 and above. Compare your answers with a group of your classmates.

1. **Original sentence:** "They don't fight outside here because they know I am here." —Policeman Andy Briers

   Reported speech sentence: _____

   _____

   _____

2. **Original sentence:** "The kids tell me if they have been robbed or hassled. . ." —Policeman Andy Briers

   Reported speech sentence: _____

   _____

   _____

3. **Original Sentence:** "We. . .make sure that anyone entering the school signs in." —Principal Vincent McNicholas

   Reported speech sentence: _____

   _____

   _____

DO IT YOURSELF
For more practice:
Reported speech
   sentences, 256

Passive and Active Sentences

Study these two sentences. The first one is *active* and the second one is *passive*. In what ways are the sentences different?

School officials installed metal detectors in the school last week.

Metal detectors were installed in the school last week.

Uses of Passive Sentences

Most English sentences are active sentences. Use *passive* sentences for the following reasons:

- The person or thing who did the action is unknown.

  ┌——SUBJECT——┐ ┌——VERB——┐
  My car window was broken in the parking lot last week.

- The person or thing who did the action is unimportant.

  ┌——SUBJECT——┐┌——VERB——┐
  The window was repaired later.

Forms

- The passive verb is a combination of *be* + the past participle form of a verb. Most past participles are the *-ed* forms of verbs. Irregular past participles are listed on pages 223–225.

- Study the boldfaced verbs in the active and passive sentences below.

Verb Tense	Active Sentence	Passive Sentence
Simple present tense	I **write** my essays on a computer.	My essays **are written** on a computer.
Simple past tense	I **wrote** my summary in two hours.	My summary **was written** in two hours.
Future tense	I **will revise** it tomorrow.	It **will be revised** tomorrow.
Other modal verbs	The students **can find** articles on the Internet.	Articles **can be found** on the Internet.
Present perfect tense	My classmates **have finished** all the work.	All the work **has been finished.** All the work **has been finished** by my classmates.*

*Sometimes you may want to include the *actor* (the person or thing that did the action) in a passive sentence. Do this by adding *by* + the actor at the end of the sentence.

1 Identify the following sentences as active (**A**) or passive (**P**). Compare your answers with a partner's.

_____ 1. Airports have improved security measures since September 11, 2001.

_____ 2. Soldiers and police officers are seen at many airports.

_____ 3. Airline officials use hand-held devices to search for bombs.

_____ 4. Specially trained dogs are used to smell for bombs and drugs.

_____ 5. Only passengers are allowed at the gated areas of airports.

_____ 6. On some flights airline officials hand-search the bags of selected passengers.

_____ 7. Airline employees must go through the same security checks as passengers.

2 Complete the sentences in the following article. Circle the appropriate active or passive form of the verb. Discuss your answers with a group of your classmates.

"Trusted Traveler" ID Card

Feb. 7, 2002—Frequent travelers think that all U.S. airports

_____ a "trusted traveler card" system, according to a

1. should use / should be used

survey by Travelocity.com Inc. In the survey, 76% of frequent travelers

said that they _____ the use of a voluntary "trusted

2. support / are supported

traveler" identification card. Encrypted, or coded, information, including

a photograph, fingerprints, flight history and/or facial/retinal (eye)

characteristics _____ on the card. The card _____

3. includes / is included   4. allows / is allowed

passengers to move more quickly through security. About four out of

five frequent travelers said that if such a card _____

5. becomes / is become

available, they _____ it. In a similar Travelocity.com survey

6. will use / will be used

released in October 2001, 71% of frequent travelers said they hope a

national travel ID card _____ available by the U.S.

7. will make / will be made

government. Travelers said the cards _____

8. should not require / should not be required

by the government but _____ only to those people

9. should give / should be given

who want to use them.

DO IT YOURSELF
For more practice:
Passive voice
sentences, 230

Writing the Final Draft

Use the checklist to edit your summary and response paragraphs on the topic of security. Then write your final drafts.

> ### Editing Checklist
> ❑ Are the correct forms of security-related words used?
> ❑ Are reported speech sentences written correctly?
> ❑ Are active and passive sentences used appropriately?

Your instructor will grade your paper for its content, organization, and language using the evaluation sheet for this chapter on page 208. Read over the evaluation sheet. Then reread and edit your paper as necessary before you turn in the final draft.

On Your Own

More Writing Practice   Write an essay about one of the following topics.

REMEMBER Brainstorm ideas for an essay or take notes for a summary before you begin to write. Follow the steps for essay or summary writing.

---

1. **Security Problems and Solutions**

   Write a four- or five-paragraph essay about two or three security problems that exist at one type of public place. Then suggest solutions to the problems. In the thesis statement, introduce the place and its problems. Begin each body paragraph with a topic sentence about one problem. Give facts, examples, and details about each problem in the body paragraphs. In the conclusion, suggest solutions.

2. **Political Conflict**

   Write a summary of an article or chapter that reports about a political conflict. The text may describe a disagreement between two political groups, a war, an attack, or other politically related incident. Use your library or the Internet as a resource. Find an article about one to three pages in length. Follow the steps and guidelines that you have practiced to write your summary.

3. **Minorities on Campus**

   Write a summary of an article or chapter about any issue relating to minority students on high school, college, or university campuses. Use your library or the Internet as a resource. Find an article about one to three pages in length. Follow the steps and guidelines that you have practiced to write your summary.

Chapter Goals   Take credit for achieving the learning goals in Chapter 9. Check (✔) the goals that you have achieved. If you are having problems with one of these goals, get extra practice by writing another summary or essay on one of the topics above, or do the additional language exercises in the appropriate Do It Yourself section in the back of the book. Then talk to your instructor about your writing.

Chapter Goals Checklist

❑ Organize and write a summary of a reading.

❑ Make a concept map to show main ideas in a text.

❑ Organize and write a response to a reading.

❑ Paraphrase ideas in a text.

❑ Write reported speech sentences.

❑ Recognize and write passive and active sentences.

Writing Evaluation Sheets

To the Student

As a quick way to check your own writing *before* you turn it in to your instructor, we have included one-page writing evaluation sheets. Each chapter's evaluation sheet includes a list of good writing features that you have already studied.

After you write, reread your paper. Pay attention to the features that relate to content, organization, and language use. Then, revise and edit your writing as necessary. The evaluation sheets will help you to quickly check the individual aspects of your writing that you have already studied.

Of course, every teacher evaluates writing in his or her own way. Ask your instructor to explain the way that he or she will grade your writing. Your teacher may use the evaluation sheets provided in this textbook, or he or she may use another system for grading.

To the Teacher

The nine one-page writing evaluation sheets included in this textbook can assist teachers and students in evaluating the features of writing that students have studied in each chapter.

Instructors may choose to use or adapt the evaluation sheets to grade and respond to student writing. Teachers can rate each feature of students' writing—in content, organization, and language use—by checking "well done," "satisfactory," or "needs work." Then, the teacher can estimate students' scores for each category based on the checkmarks. The scoring system places equal weight on content, development, and organization (50%) and language use and mechanics (50%), using a standard 100 point scale. The evaluation sheets make it easy to respond to student writing in one-on-one conferences.

The sheets can also be used in peer- or self-editing tasks directed by the teacher. An instructor may wish to summarize the writing features of the chapter and then guide students in evaluating their own or their classmates' writing in pairs, small groups, or on their own.

Chapter 1   Paragraph Evaluation Sheet

Good Writing Features

Content and Ideas	Well Done	Satisfactory	Needs Work
Writing on assigned topic	_____	_____	_____
Supporting ideas	_____	_____	_____
Interesting content	_____	_____	_____
	Score _____ /25		
Organization	Well Done	Satisfactory	Needs Work
Paragraph with one idea	_____	_____	_____
Topic sentence	_____	_____	_____
Controlling idea	_____	_____	_____
Major point organization	_____	_____	_____
	Score _____ /25		
Language Use	Well Done	Satisfactory	Needs Work
Vocabulary	_____	_____	_____
Academic words	_____	_____	_____
Complete sentences	_____	_____	_____
Verb tense and form	_____	_____	_____
	Score _____ /30		
Mechanics and Format	Well Done	Satisfactory	Needs Work
Sentence end punctuation	_____	_____	_____
Spelling	_____	_____	_____
Complete sentences	_____	_____	_____
Paragraph format	_____	_____	_____
	Score _____ /20		
Overall Comments	**Total Score _____ /100**		

Chapter 2   Paragraph Evaluation Sheet

Good Writing Features

Content and Ideas	Well Done	Satisfactory	Needs Work
Writing on assigned topic	_____	_____	_____
Supporting ideas	_____	_____	_____
Specific details	_____	_____	_____
Interesting content	_____	_____	_____
	Score _____ /25		
Organization	Well Done	Satisfactory	Needs Work
Paragraph with one idea	_____	_____	_____
Topic sentence	_____	_____	_____
Controlling idea	_____	_____	_____
Major point organization	_____	_____	_____
	Score _____ /25		
Language Use	Well Done	Satisfactory	Needs Work
Vocabulary	_____	_____	_____
Academic words	_____	_____	_____
Complete sentences	_____	_____	_____
Sentence patterns	_____	_____	_____
Verb tense and form	_____	_____	_____
	Score _____ /30		
Mechanics and Format	Well Done	Satisfactory	Needs Work
Sentence end punctuation	_____	_____	_____
Spelling	_____	_____	_____
Complete sentences	_____	_____	_____
Paragraph format	_____	_____	_____
	Score _____ /20		
Overall Comments	**Total Score _____ /100**		

Chapter 3   Essay Evaluation Sheet

Good Writing Features

Content and Ideas	Well Done	Satisfactory	Needs Work
Writing on assigned topic	_____	_____	_____
Supporting ideas	_____	_____	_____
Specific details	_____	_____	_____
Interesting content	_____	_____	_____
		Score _____ /25	

Organization	Well Done	Satisfactory	Needs Work
Essay organization	_____	_____	_____
Thesis statement	_____	_____	_____
Body paragraphs	_____	_____	_____
Topic sentences	_____	_____	_____
		Score _____ /25	

Language Use	Well Done	Satisfactory	Needs Work
Vocabulary	_____	_____	_____
Academic words	_____	_____	_____
Word endings	_____	_____	_____
Complete sentences	_____	_____	_____
Sentence patterns	_____	_____	_____
Compound/ complex sentences	_____	_____	_____
Verb tense and form	_____	_____	_____
		Score _____ /30	

Mechanics and Format	Well Done	Satisfactory	Needs Work
Sentence-end punctuation	_____	_____	_____
Spelling	_____	_____	_____
Complete sentences	_____	_____	_____
Essay format	_____	_____	_____
		Score _____ /20	

Overall Comments	Total Score _____ /100

Good Writing Features

Content and Ideas	Well Done	Satisfactory	Needs Work
Writing on assigned topic	____	____	____
Supporting ideas	____	____	____
Specific details	____	____	____
Interesting content	____	____	____
	Score ____ /25		
Organization	Well Done	Satisfactory	Needs Work
Essay organization	____	____	____
Thesis statement	____	____	____
Introduction paragraph	____	____	____
Body paragraphs	____	____	____
Topic sentences	____	____	____
	Score ____ /25		
Language Use	Well Done	Satisfactory	Needs Work
Vocabulary	____	____	____
Academic words	____	____	____
Word endings	____	____	____
Complete sentences	____	____	____
Sentence patterns	____	____	____
Compound/ complex sentences	____	____	____
Verb tense and form	____	____	____
Subject-verb agreement	____	____	____
Gerunds and infinitives	____	____	____
	Score ____ /30		
Mechanics and Format	Well Done	Satisfactory	Needs Work
Sentence end punctuation	____	____	____
Spelling	____	____	____
Complete sentences	____	____	____
Essay format	____	____	____
	Score ____ /20		
Overall Comments	**Total Score ____ /100**		

Good Writing Features

Content and Ideas	Well Done	Satisfactory	Needs Work
Writing on assigned topic	_____	_____	_____
Supporting ideas	_____	_____	_____
Specific details	_____	_____	_____
Examples	_____	_____	_____
Interesting content	_____	_____	_____
	Score _____ /25		
Organization	Well Done	Satisfactory	Needs Work
Essay organization	_____	_____	_____
Thesis statement	_____	_____	_____
Introduction paragraph	_____	_____	_____
Body paragraphs	_____	_____	_____
Topic sentences	_____	_____	_____
	Score _____ /25		
Language Use	Well Done	Satisfactory	Needs Work
Vocabulary	_____	_____	_____
Word endings	_____	_____	_____
Complete sentences	_____	_____	_____
Sentence patterns	_____	_____	_____
Compound/ complex sentences	_____	_____	_____
Verb tense and form	_____	_____	_____
Subject-verb agreement	_____	_____	_____
Gerunds and infinitives	_____	_____	_____
Articles	_____	_____	_____
	Score _____ /30		
Mechanics and Format	Well Done	Satisfactory	Needs Work
Sentence end punctuation	_____	_____	_____
Spelling	_____	_____	_____
Complete sentences	_____	_____	_____
Essay format	_____	_____	_____
	Score _____ /20		
Overall Comments	**Total Score _____ / 100**		

Good Writing Features

Content and Ideas	Well Done	Satisfactory	Needs Work
Writing on assigned topic	____	____	____
Supporting ideas	____	____	____
Specific details	____	____	____
Examples	____	____	____
Interesting content	____	____	____
		Score ____ /25	
Organization	Well Done	Satisfactory	Needs Work
Essay organization	____	____	____
Thesis statement	____	____	____
Introduction paragraph	____	____	____
Body paragraphs	____	____	____
Topic sentences	____	____	____
		Score ____ /25	
Language Use	Well Done	Satisfactory	Needs Work
Vocabulary	____	____	____
Word endings	____	____	____
Transitions	____	____	____
Complete sentences	____	____	____
Sentence patterns	____	____	____
Compound/ complex sentences	____	____	____
Verb tense and form	____	____	____
Subject-verb agreement	____	____	____
Gerunds and infinitives	____	____	____
Articles	____	____	____
		Score ____ /30	
Mechanics and Format	Well Done	Satisfactory	Needs Work
Sentence end punctuation	____	____	____
Comma splices	____	____	____
Spelling	____	____	____
Complete sentences	____	____	____
Essay format	____	____	____
		Score ____ /20	
Overall Comments	Total Score ____ /100		

Good Writing Features

Content and Ideas	Well Done	Satisfactory	Needs Work
Writing on assigned topic	_____	_____	_____
Supporting ideas	_____	_____	_____
Specific details	_____	_____	_____
Examples	_____	_____	_____
Interesting content	_____	_____	_____
Audience and purpose	_____	_____	_____
		Score _____ /25	

Organization	Well Done	Satisfactory	Needs Work
Essay organization	_____	_____	_____
Thesis statement	_____	_____	_____
Introduction paragraph	_____	_____	_____
Body paragraphs	_____	_____	_____
Topic sentences	_____	_____	_____
		Score _____ /25	

Language Use	Well Done	Satisfactory	Needs Work
Vocabulary	_____	_____	_____
Word endings	_____	_____	_____
Transitions	_____	_____	_____
Complete sentences	_____	_____	_____
Sentence patterns	_____	_____	_____
Compound/ complex sentences	_____	_____	_____
Verb tense and form	_____	_____	_____
Commands and modals	_____	_____	_____
Subject-verb agreement	_____	_____	_____
Gerunds and infinitives	_____	_____	_____
Articles	_____	_____	_____
Pronouns	_____	_____	_____
		Score _____ /30	

Mechanics and Format	Well Done	Satisfactory	Needs Work
Sentence end punctuation	_____	_____	_____
Comma splices	_____	_____	_____
Spelling	_____	_____	_____
Complete sentences	_____	_____	_____
Essay format	_____	_____	_____
		Score _____ /20	

Overall Comments	Total Score _____ /100

Chapter 8 Essay Evaluation Sheet

Good Writing Features

Content and Ideas	Well Done	Satisfactory	Needs Work
Writing on assigned topic	___	___	___
Supporting ideas	___	___	___
Specific details	___	___	___
Examples	___	___	___
Interesting content	___	___	___
Audience and purpose	___	___	___
		Score ___ /25	

Organization	Well Done	Satisfactory	Needs Work
Essay organization	___	___	___
Thesis statement	___	___	___
Introduction paragraph	___	___	___
Body paragraphs	___	___	___
Topic sentences	___	___	___
		Score ___ /25	

Language Use	Well Done	Satisfactory	Needs Work
Vocabulary	___	___	___
Word endings	___	___	___
Transitions	___	___	___
Complete sentences	___	___	___
Sentence patterns	___	___	___
Compound/ complex sentences	___	___	___
Verb tense and form	___	___	___
Commands and modals	___	___	___
Subject-verb agreement	___	___	___
Gerunds and infinitives	___	___	___
Articles	___	___	___
Pronouns	___	___	___
Comparative forms	___	___	___
		Score ___ /30	

Mechanics and Format	Well Done	Satisfactory	Needs Work
Sentence end punctuation	___	___	___
Comma splices	___	___	___
Spelling	___	___	___
Complete sentences	___	___	___
Essay format	___	___	___
		Score ___ /20	

Overall Comments	Total Score ___ /100

Chapter 9   Summary/Response Evaluation Sheet

Good Writing Features

Content and Ideas	Well Done	Satisfactory	Needs Work
Writing on assigned topic	____	____	____
Paraphrasing	____	____	____
Interesting content	____	____	____
Score ____ /25			

Organization	Well Done	Satisfactory	Needs Work
Summary topic sentence	____	____	____
Supporting ideas	____	____	____
Response topic sentence	____	____	____
Supporting ideas	____	____	____
Score ____ /25			

Language Use	Well Done	Satisfactory	Needs Work
Vocabulary	____	____	____
Word endings	____	____	____
Transitions	____	____	____
Complete sentences	____	____	____
Sentence patterns	____	____	____
Compound/ complex sentences	____	____	____
Passive/active sentences	____	____	____
Verb tense and form	____	____	____
Commands and modals	____	____	____
Subject-verb agreement	____	____	____
Reported speech	____	____	____
Gerunds and infinitives	____	____	____
Articles	____	____	____
Pronouns	____	____	____
Comparative forms	____	____	____
Score ____ /30			

Mechanics and Format	Well Done	Satisfactory	Needs Work
Sentence end punctuation	____	____	____
Comma splices	____	____	____
Spelling	____	____	____
Complete sentences	____	____	____
Essay format	____	____	____
Score ____ /20			

Overall Comments	Total Score ____ /100

Do It Yourself

"Do it yourself" means to work independently, without someone else's help. If you need extra practice with a language topic, you can do the additional exercises in this section on your own. Then check your answers on pages 266-278.

I. Sentences

A. Complete Sentences

> A complete sentence must have at least one subject and one complete verb and express a complete thought.
>
>   SUBJECT   VERB
>   <u>Motivated people</u> <u>know</u> that losing is a part of winning.
>
>   SUBJECT   SUBJECT   VERB   VERB
>   <u>Paul</u> and <u>his friends</u> <u>study</u> full-time and <u>work</u> part-time.

1 Read the following "sentences" taken from student writing. Mark the complete sentences **C** and the incomplete sentences **I**. Add, delete, or change a word or words to correct the incomplete sentences. The first one is done for you.

                      are

___*I*___ 1. If you ^ late to your class too much, you will miss important parts of the lecture.

_____ 2. On February 27 is a beautiful celebration in my country.

_____ 3. My best friend is Maria. We have two classes together and live in the dormitory, so we always together.

_____ 4. When I have free time, I take care of myself. I take a shower and wash my hair. Blow my hair out. Do my nails.

_____ 5. Money will bring me happiness. Because if I have plenty of money, I will buy a lot of things.

_____ 6. When I came to the United States, I knew only one or two words in English.

_____ 7. Khalil's apartment is very noisy, so wants to find another place.

_____ 8. Dr. Gao a very good mathematics teacher. Because he explains everything well. And answers the students' questions.

_____ 9. At first, I couldn't speak English, didn't understand what other people were saying.

_____ 10. If you have money is easy to make a living and support your family.

_____ 11. My brother he is living in Los Angeles.

_____ 12. She working very hard in her classes this year.

2 Complete the following sentences. Be sure each sentence has a subject and a complete verb and expresses a complete thought.

1. Studying hard *will help me pass my exam* _____.

2. Every person _____.

3. _____ is a good way to succeed.

4. A serious student _____.

5. At the beginning of each school year, _____.

6. _____ when I want to relax.

7. _____ are my best qualities.

8. My favorite class _____.

9. _____ wakes me up early every day.

10. After class, I _____.

3 Complete the following student paragraph by adding a subject or a verb to make each sentence complete.

A Good Use of Time

If you _____ the Internet, don't feel guilty because _____ is really a good way to use your time. The Internet _____ an incredible amount of information. _____ can be answered on the Internet. _____ can get help on a research paper or math homework. If you _____ what to major in, _____ has many career exploration sites. Indeed, _____ is like having an older, wiser friend right in your home. It's also a great source of entertainment. _____ you feeling bored? You _____ today's joke, a Web site just for bored people, or a partner for a game of solitaire. If _____ are interested in music, you can _____ to your favorite songs on the Internet. You _____ photographs of your favorite movie stars and even _____ film clips. And, while you _____ fun, you also _____ an added bonus. _____ will be improving your typing. In today's technological world, you _____ computers and the Internet. If you _____ time on the Internet, you _____ wasting time.

4 Edit the following sentences to make them complete sentences. Begin each sentence with a capital letter and end it with a period. Add or change a word or words to correct incomplete sentences. See page 264 for examples of capital letters. The first one is done for you.

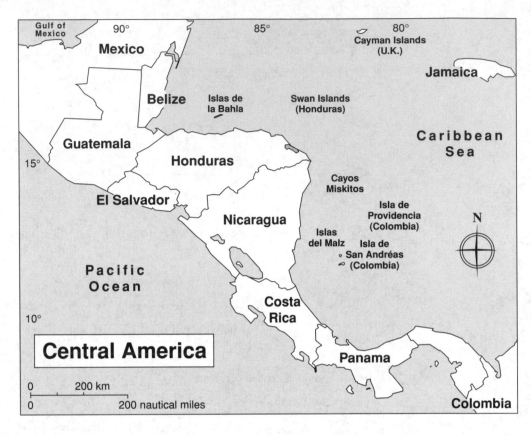

T   *is*

1. the geography of Central America very interesting.

2. first, connects North America and South America

3. it located between Mexico to the north and Colombia to the south

4. also, Central America several countries

5. guatemala, Honduras, and Nicaragua the largest

6. guatemala like a bridge between Mexico and the rest of Central America

7. next to Guatemala, Belize also a border with Mexico

8. as continue south, lies southeast of Guatemala and south of Honduras

9. further south the countries of Nicaragua and Costa Rica

10. finally, Panama Central America and Colombia in South America

11. of course, has the famous Panama Canal

12. Ships through the canal to save time on long sea journeys

13. is not easy to remember the exact location of the countries of Central America

14. perhaps one day visit Central America to see the countries firsthand

B. Four Basic Sentence Patterns

Review the four basic sentence patterns:

■ **Pattern 1: Subject + Action Verb + (Object + Adverb)**

These sentences *must* have a subject and verb. They *may* have an object or adverb.

    SUBJECT   VERB   OBJECT   ADVERB
My cousin Elizabeth received an award at the graduation ceremony.

■ **Pattern 2: Subject + Linking Verb + Complement**

                COMPLEMENT
Linear mathematics is an interesting subject.

■ **Pattern 3: *There is* and *there are* sentences** (*There is* + singular noun or *There are* + plural noun)

      PLURAL NOUN
There are several reasons that I want to get a college degree.

■ **Pattern 4: *It is* sentences** (*It is* + adjective or *It is* + noun or noun phrase)

  NOUN   ADJECTIVE
It is a rainy night. **It is** difficult to drive in the rain.

1 Complete the following sentences by adding words that make sense. Then, write the correct number to identify the pattern of your sentence.

_____ 1. On a typical weekday, I _____.

_____ 2. When I meet my friends, we _____.

_____ 3. Working part-time _____.

_____ 4. _____ very easy to _____.

_____ 5. _____ is bad for me.

_____ 6. Some of my classmates _____.

_____ 7. _____ in my neighborhood.

_____ 8. _____ the most exciting day of my life.

_____ 9. The city _____.

_____ 10. _____ too much work to do.

2 Write five sentences about a busy area of your school, like the cafeteria, library, a building entrance, or a computer lab. Write sentences about things and activities that happen in that place. Use Patterns 1, 2, and 3.

Examples

Many students are typing in the computer lab. (*Pattern 1*)

The library is a quiet place to read. (*Pattern 2*)

There is a long line in front of the cashier's office. (*Pattern 3*)

3 Use Pattern 4 (*it is* sentences) to write about the following topics. Be sure to write complete sentences.

1. Today's weather _____

2. The present day and date _____

3. The temperature last night _____

4. The time that you woke up this morning

_____

5. The level of difficulty to write in English

_____

C. Sentence Combining

You can combine simple sentences into compound sentences and complex sentences.

Simple Sentences	**Compound Sentence**	**Complex Sentence**
Alexis had a toothache. He left class early.	Alexis had a toothache, so he left class early.	Because Alexis had a toothache, he left class early.

1. **Compound Sentences**

   Use this pattern to form compound sentences:

   SIMPLE SENTENCE +   COORDINATING +   SIMPLE SENTENCE
                   CONJUNCTION

   I tried to call you,   **but**   you weren't home.

   Coordinating conjunctions: *and, but, so, for, yet,* and *or.*

2. **Sentences with Dependent Clauses**

   Form sentences with dependent clauses in the following ways:

   INDEPENDENT CLAUSE +   SUBORDINATING +   DEPENDENT CLAUSE
                   CONJUNCTION

   <u>Rinna is going to the learning lab</u> because <u>she needs more help wih her writing</u>.

   OR DEPENDENT CLAUSE + SUBORDINATING CONJUNCTION +   INDEPENDENT CLAUSE
   Because <u>Rinna needs more help with her writing, she is going to the learning lab.</u>

   An *independent clause* is the same as a simple sentence or complete sentence. A *dependent clause* is a group of words with a subject and verb that begins with a subordinating conjunction.

   a. Subordinating Conjunctions

   Study the list of subordinating conjunctions and their meanings.

Subordinating Conjunction	Meaning
while **whereas**	Contrast
although **even though** **though** **despite the fact that**	Concession (giving in)

Subordinating Conjunction	Meaning
because since	Reason or cause
after as soon as before when while until whenever as as long as	Time relationship or order
if even if unless	Condition
so that in order that	Purpose

1 Choose a logical subordinating conjunction to complete the following sentences.

1. Weilun has to use crutches _____ he sprained his ankle. He fell down _____ he was playing basketball.

2. _____ Najeeb doesn't like the food in the cafeteria, he bought his lunch there today. He had to eat there _____ it was raining, and he didn't want to walk to a restaurant.

3. _____ I finish my shopping early, I can go to the movies with you. Then, we can try that new Colombian restaurant _____ we get out of the movie.

4. The weather is beautiful outside. Unfortunately, I can't enjoy it _____ I finish all this homework. _____ I look at my stack of books, I get very depressed.

5. Raoul is saving all his money _____ he can have an exciting vacation in Haiti. _____ he gets off the plane, he plans to go to the beach.

2 Correct the errors in the following sentences from student writing. The errors relate to subordinating conjunctions.

1. My brother quit his job in the grocery store. Because being a cashier made him nervous.

2. Even though I had an operation, but I came to school to finish my English class.

3. Maria missed many days of work, her children were sick.

4. If people lie and let me catch them. Next time I won't believe them.

5. Because my family didn't want to waste money on rent, so we bought our own house.

6. Time passes and children grow old enough, they should should move out of their parents' home and live independently.

7. I need to have high self esteem before I become independent, I need to get a good-paying job.

8. I would like to change my indecisiveness because sometimes it's hard for me. When I have to make an important decision about my studies, career, etc.

9. I take a long time to think about something, I sometimes never do anything.

10. Although it won't be easy, but I can do it and overcome my indecisiveness.

3 Read the following sentences taken from a student paragraph. Use coordinating conjunctions or subordinating conjunctions to combine the pairs of sentences into one sentence.

1. Some of my teachers say that I'm quiet. My teachers are wrong.

   _____

2. Sometimes I am really nervous at first. I try not to show it in front of people.

   _____

3. I usually don't ask questions in class. I understand everything that the teachers said.

   _____

4. In class, I don't like to talk that much. I think it's rude to talk when the teacher talks.

   _____

5. I don't understand something. I never ask questions.

   _____

6. Some of my classmates ask questions. They don't listen to what the teachers say.

   _____

7. You pay attention and concentrate. You can understand everything.

   _____

8. However, sometimes you listen and you still don't understand. You have to ask questions.

   _____

II. Common Verb Tenses

A. Present Tense Verbs

1. Simple Present Tense

Simple present tense verbs tell about regular activities, habits, beliefs or opinions, facts, or ownership.	
Be **Forms**	**+ Negatives**
I **am** a nice person.	**I am not/I'm not** a nice person.
He/She **is** my friend.	**He is not/He's not/He isn't** my friend.
It **is** important.	**It is not/It's not/It isn't** important.
You/They/We **are** happy.	**We are not/We're not/We aren't** happy.
Clark and Laura **are** sad.	**They are not/They're not/They aren't** sad.
Other Verb Forms	**+ Negatives**
I/You/They/We **live** in Miami.	I/You/They/We **don't live** there.
Patti and Michael **live** in Houston.	Patti and Michael **don't live** there.
He/She **lives** in Chicago.	He/She **doesn't live** there.
Leo/Mary **lives** in a big house.	Leo/Mary **doesn't live** there.
The dog **lives** in a dog house.	The dog **doesn't live** there.

1 Complete the following sentences. Use a simple present tense verb that is appropriate for the sentence. The first one is done for you.

1. Parents ———— *are* ———— their children's first teachers.

2. A successful parent _____ his or her child values and behavior.

3. Honesty and kindness _____ also important values for a child.

4. Being honest _____ that you _____ lies.

5. A good parent _____ his or her children the best ways to act with others.

6. A child _____ how to behave unless the parents _____ him good behavior.

7. Children also _____ morals from their parents.

8. If parents _____ their children to have good morals, the children will not know what is right or wrong.

9. Learning to judge right from wrong _____ children to make good decisions in their lives.

10. The best parents _____ a lot of patience because it _____ time to teach a child good behavior.

2 Write sentences about the academic habits of a student that you know. Use the following words in your sentences.

Example

time to study *Lian never has enough time to study.* _____

1. every morning _____

2. to school _____

3. before class _____

4. during class _____

5. bilingual dictionary _____

6. with other classmates _____

7. after class is over _____

8. the teacher's office _____

9. homework _____

10. in the library _____

2. Present Progressive Tense

> Simple present tells about an action that continues over a long time. Present progressive tells about an action that is in progress now or an action that is temporary.
>
> | **Simple Present** | **Present Progressive** |
> |---|---|
> | Bob always **works** hard. | Right now he **is working** at a grocery store. |
> | Lin **doesn't talk** very much. | Lin **is talking** to her teacher now. |

1 Complete the sentences on page 219. Use the simple present or the present progressive tense forms of the verbs in parentheses.

1. Nadia _____is preparing_____ (*prepare*) for her final examinations this week. She
   _____ (*have*) a laptop computer to help her study.

2. Sentisouk _____ (*help*) his mother with housework every day.
   Right now he _____ (*wash*) the clothes.

3. Kerlen usually _____ (*come*) to every class. However, this week
   she _____ (*stay*) with her sick mother in Haiti.

4. Mike rarely _____ (*keep*) his room neat. His mother got angry, so
   he _____ (*clean*) his room at the moment.

5. Celia and Jenny often _____ (*play*) ping pong after class. Today,
   however, they _____ (*not, play*) because the gymnasium is closed.

2 Use the following words to write positive or negative statements about events
that are happening at the present time. Change the form of the verb to the
present progressive tense.

Example

currently economy go down _Currently the economy is going down._____

1. price of gasoline rise _____

2. unemployment decline _____

3. the war in _____ continue now _____

4. the Earth orbit the sun at the moment _____

5. satellites circle the Earth right now _____

6. cost of living rise in _____ _____
   (name of country)

7. crime rise in _____ _____
   (name of city)

8. population grow around the world _____

9. natural resources dwindle _____

10. technology change at the present time _____

3. Non-Progressive Verbs

Some verbs are not usually used in the *-ing*, or progressive, form.

My mother **knows** how to cook very well.
Our family **has** one car.

Here is a list of some common non-progressive verbs:

Feelings and emotions: *like, love, hate, prefer, want, need*
Mental states: *think, believe, understand, seem, forget, remember, know, mean*
Senses: *hear, see, smell, feel, sound*
Possession: *belong, own, have*

1 Read the following paragraph. Complete each sentence with a non-progressive verb that makes sense. Change the form, or ending, of the verb to match the subject.

People _____ different types of worries about material goods, depending on their economic level. For example, many middle-class Americans _____ a great number of material things: houses, furniture, computers, televisions, etc. They constantly _____ to acquire *more* things. The phrase "keeping up with the Joneses" _____ that Americans _____ to have as many material goods as their neighbors. Often, they _____ dissatisfied if they _____ the latest models of products. On the other hand, people with less money to spare may never _____ about buying the latest model of a car. They _____ about how they can fulfill their basic needs. Acquiring food, water, and other basics _____ what they worry about the most. After they satisfy their basic needs, they may _____ other material goods. Therefore, people of different economic levels _____ their own types of worries.

4. Subject-Verb Agreement

> In sentences containing present tense verbs, the subject and the verb must agree in number. Add *-s* to simple present tense verbs if the subject is *he, she, it,* or a singular noun. With present progressive verbs, use *is* + the *-ing* verb when the subject is *he, she, it,* or a singular noun.
>
> **Singular Subjects and Verbs**
>
> A successful <u>student</u> <u>works</u> hard. <u>Samuel</u> <u>is working</u> on his homework right now.
>
> **Plural Subjects and Verbs**
>
> The <u>books</u> in my backpack <u>are</u> so heavy that I can't carry them. The <u>seams</u> of the bag <u>are starting</u> to rip open, so I need to buy a new backpack.

1 Read the following sentences taken from student writing. They contain subject-verb agreement errors. Underline the errors and write the correct form above them.

1. Some of my friends has bachelor's degrees from universities.

2. Taking notes in class help me to succeed academically.

3. My classmate Javier always sit in the front row in class. He want to hear what the teacher is saying.

4. It feel very comfortable when you study in your room.

5. This semester our class are reading the book *Dracula*.

6. If a student don't listen in class, he don't get good grades.

7. Computer skills is very important for us.

8. Now I goes to school and work. That is very good for me because I gets new opportunities.

9. Right now my brother and I am living in an apartment.

10. When students is listening in class, they should take notes.

2 Read the following paragraphs. Find the eight subject-verb agreement errors in each paragraph. Underline the errors and write the correct form above them.

A.   **A Great Tourist Destination**

One of the best cities to visit on the east coast of the United States are Washington. It have some of the most interesting landmarks and tourist spots in the country. There is many monuments to visit, such as the Lincoln Memorial, the Jefferson Memorial, and the Washington Monument (the tallest building in Washington). Washington also have interesting museums like the Smithsonian Institute. For more excitement, the area called Georgetown in northwest Washington are famous for its shopping, restaurants, and nightclubs. Nearby, there is Virginia Beach. It have nice beaches with features like horseback riding, sailboat rentals, and seafood restaurants. People goes there in great numbers in the summer. Washington, D.C., is not as large or as famous as New York City, but it have an appeal all its own.

B.   **A Strange Dream**

Sometimes my friend Maria has strange dreams, and she tell me about them. She wants to know the meaning of her dreams. In one dream, Maria and a friend is walking through a city at night. In the next scene, they are sitting in a club. A band is playing jazz music, and all the people is smoking. A strange man come up to her table and asks her to dance. Maria feel excited, so she accepts his offer. Then, while they are dancing, the man change into a lion. Suddenly, the lion is opening his mouth, and Maria is running away. She keep turning her head, and the lion follows her. Then, just at the moment when the lion is about to catch up to her, she wake up. What do you think the dream means?

3 Read each of the following sentences. Then, write another sentence on a similar subject, using the words provided. Make the verb agree in number with the subject.

1. I always eat breakfast every morning.

   My classmate <u>*Hana never eats breakfast*</u>.

2. Many students at my college smoke cigarettes.

   Smoking cigarettes _____.

3. Computers get less expensive every year.

   A hand-held computer _____.

4. At my university, international students pay three times the tuition that residents pay.

   My tuition _____.

5. Oksana and Sergey are buying a new house.

   An apartment _____.

6. The students in Chinese 101 are learning to write Chinese characters.

   The Chinese language _____.

7. Flat-screen televisions with 24-inch screens cost about $7,500.

   A flat-screen TV _____.

8. People from all over the world celebrate the Carnival in Brazil.

   The Mardi Gras festival _____.

9. Children play in the parks and in the streets in my neighborhood.

   Playing in the street _____.

10. Some fast-food restaurants serve their customers in less than one minute.

    My favorite restaurant _____.

B. Past Tense Verbs

English has several past tense verbs.

- **Simple past tense** is the most common verb tense for telling about past actions. Regular verbs form the simple past tense with -*ed* added to the base form of the verb. See the chart of irregular past tense verbs on pages 223–225.

Regular Past Forms		
I	**worked**	very hard yesterday.
You	**worked**	on your homework last night.
John	**worked**	every day last week.
Michele and I	**worked**	at the high school last semester.
They	**worked**	all day to clean up the basement.

- **Past progressive tense*** is used for telling about actions that are in progress in the past. This verb may be used to present an action that was in the middle of happening when it was interrupted by another action, expressed in the simple past tense.

> PAST PROGRESSIVE SIMPLE PAST
> While I **was walking** down the street, I **met** my friend.

*Past progressive = was/were + -ing form

- **Past perfect tense*** is used for telling about actions that occurred *before* other past actions. This verb may be used in a sentence with two actions; one action is expressed with a simple past tense verb, and another action that occurred before is expressed with the past perfect tense.

> PAST PERFECT SIMPLE PAST
> I **had** never **been** to California until I **went** there last summer.

*Past perfect = had + past participle form

Irregular Verb Chart

Base Form	Past Form	Past Participle Form	Base Form	Past Form	Past Participle Form
arise	arose	arisen	buy	bought	bought
awake	awoke	awoken	cast	cast	cast
be	was/were	been	catch	caught	caught
bear	bore	born	choose	chose	chosen
beat	beat	beaten	cling	clung	clung
become	became	become	come	came	come
begin	began	begun	cost	cost	cost
bend	bent	bent	creep	crept	crept
bet	bet	bet	cut	cut	cut
bind	bound	bound	deal	dealt	dealt
bid	bid, bade	bid, bidden	dig	dug	dug
bite	bit	bitten	do	did	done
bleed	bled	bled	draw	drew	drawn
blow	blew	blown	dream	dreamed, dreamt	dreamed, dreamt
break	broke	broken			
breed	bred	bred	drink	drank	drunk
bring	brought	brought	drive	drove	driven
broadcast	broadcast	broadcast	dwell	dwelt, dwelled	dwelt, dwelled
build	built	built	eat	ate	eaten
burn	burned, burnt	burnt	fall	fell	fallen
burst	burst	burst	feed	fed	fed

Base Form	Past Form	Past Participle Form	Base Form	Past Form	Past Participle Form
feel	felt	felt	lie	lay	lain
fight	fought	fought	light	lit, lighted	lit, lighted
find	found	found	lose	lost	lost
fit	fit	fit	make	made	made
flee	fled	fled	mean	meant	meant
fling	flung	flung	meet	met	met
fly	flew	flown	mislead	misled	misled
forbid	forbade	forbidden	mistake	mistook	mistaken
forecast	forecast	forecast	misunderrstand	misunderstood	misunderstood
foresee	foresaw	foreseen	mow	mowed	mowed, mown
foretell	foretold	foretold	overcome	overcame	overcome
forget	forgot	forgotten	overdo	overdid	overdone
forgive	forgave	forgiven	override	overrode	overridden
freeze	froze	frozen	overrun	overran	overrun
get	got	got, gotten	overtake	overtook	overtaken
give	gave	given	overthrow	overthrew	overthrown
go	went	gone	pay	paid	paid
grind	ground	ground	prove	proved	proven, proved
grow	grew	grown	put	put	put
hang	hung[1]	hung[1]	quit	quit	quit
have	had	had	read	read	read
hear	heard	heard	rid	rid	rid
hide	hid	hidden	ride	rode	ridden
hit	hit	hit	ring	rang	rung
hold	held	held	rise	rose	risen
hurt	hurt	hurt	run	ran	run
keep	kept	kept	say	said	said
kneel	knelt	knelt	see	saw	seen
know	knew	known	seek	sought	sought
lay	laid	laid	sell	sold	sold
lead	led	led	send	sent	sent
lean	leaned, leant	leaned, leant	set	set	set
leap	leaped, leapt	leaped, leapt	sew	sewed	sewn, sewed
learn	learned, learnt	learned, learnt	shake	shook	shaken
leave	left	left	shed	shed	shed
lend	lent	lent	shine	shone	shone, shined
let	let	let	shoot	shot	shot

Base Form	Past Form	Past Participle Form	Base Form	Past Form	Past Participle Form
show	showed	shown	swell	swelled	swollen, swelled
shrink	shrank	shrunk	swim	swam	swum
shut	shut	shut	swing	swung	swung
sing	sang	sung	take	took	taken
sink	sank	sunk	teach	taught	taught
sit	sat	sat	tear	tore	torn
sleep	slept	slept	tell	told	told
slide	slid	slid	think	thought	thought
slit	slit	slit	throw	threw	thrown
smell	smelled, smelt	smelled, smelt	thrust	thrust	thrust
speak	spoke	spoken	undergo	underwent	undergone
speed	sped	sped	understand	understood	understood
spend	spent	spent	undertake	undertook	undertaken
spill	spilled, spilt	spilled, spilt	undo	undid	undone
spin	spun	spun	uphold	upheld	upheld
spit	spit	spit	upset	upset	upset
split	split	split	wake	woke	woken
spread	spread	spread	wear	wore	worn
spring	sprang	sprung	wed	wed	wed
stand	stood	stood	weep	wept	wept
steal	stole	stolen	win	won	won
stick	stuck	stuck	wind	wound	wound
sting	stung	stung	withdraw	withdrew	withdrawn
stink	stank	stunk	withstand	withstood	withstood
strike	struck	struck	wring	wrung	wrung
strive	strove, strived	striven, strived	write	wrote	written
swear	swore	sworn			
sweep	swept	swept			

[1]**hung,** meaning "to hang a picture on the wall." *Hang* as in ". . . when the prisoner **hanged** himself in the jail" is a regular verb.

1 Study the present and past forms of the following irregular verbs. For each group, what sound and spelling change(s) occur from present to past? Find a classmate or friend to help you study. Say a sentence to your study partner, using the past tense verb. Include time word(s) like *yesterday, last night,* or *when I was a child* to show the time.

Example

I **cut** my finger yesterday when I was cooking.

Group A		Group B		Group C		Group D	
bet	bet	bring	brought	bleed	bled	drink	drank
cut	cut	buy	bought	feed	fed	ring	rang
let	let	fight	fought	feel	felt	sing	sang
put	put	seek	sought	flee	fled	sink	sank
quit	quit	think	thought	keep	kept	sit	sat
read	read	teach	taught	leave	left	spring	sprang
set	set			meet	met	stink	stank
shut	shut			sleep	slept		
split	split			speed	sped		
upset	upset			sweep	swept		
wed	wed			weep	wept		

2 Read the following student paragraph. Correct errors in simple past tense verbs. The first one is done for you. There are 10 more errors.

Getting Lost

went
Last week, I ~~go~~ to Summit Grove Camp in York, Pennsylvania. The camping trip for my church begin on Friday night. All my friends went to the camp on Friday, but I had to work on Friday night, so I went to the camp by myself on Saturday morning. I drived alone about an hour on Interstate 95. In the early morning, there weren't many cars on the highway. I feeled sleepy, so I thought I would get some coffee so I might feel better. I turned at the exit that said "service area." I follow the signs, but I get lost. I went on a road that take me into a forest. There are a lot of trees. I didn't see anybody there. I was very frightened. I turned back, but I got lost again. Luckily, I saw one car coming towards me from the opposite direction. It was a small road, so I wave him down and ask directions to get back to I-95. Once I got back on the highway, I drove straight to the camp. I don't feel sleepy anymore because I was frightened. Finally, I got to the camp. I met my friends, and I had a good time.

C. Using Present and Past Tense Verbs Together

> Pay attention to verb tenses when you write about both present and past actions.
>
> When I first **came** to the United States, I **didn't speak** English. Now I **speak** very well. I also **understand** what people **say** to me.

1 Complete the following sentences by using the simple present or simple past tense form of the verb in parentheses.

Lee, the Computer Genius

My friend Lee _____ (*not, touch*) a computer before he

_____ (come) to America. He _____ (*buy*) his first

computer in 1998. In a five-year period, he _____ (*break*) two hard

drives, two CD-Rom drives, and one modem, but he _____ (*gain*) a

lot of experience about caring for a computer. Now, he _____ (*know*)

so much about computers that he _____ (*teach*) his friends how to

maintain and repair them.

Lee often _____ (*give*) me advice about how to take care of my

computer. He always _____ (*remind*) me that a computer is a

machine. It _____ (*need*) good ventilation. As the computer

_____ (*work*), it _____ (*produce*) more heat. Lee

_____ (*say*) that when my computer _____ (*run*)

slowly, or _____ (*give*) me a "system error" message, it may be

overheated.

Last night my computer _____ (*freeze*) up on me two times. I

_____ (*get*) very annoyed because I _____ (*keep*)

having to restart it. Then I _____ (*remember*) what Lee

_____ (*tell*) me. I _____ (*shut*) down the computer

and _____ (*give*) it a break. This morning my computer

_____ (*run*) fine.

Another tip that I _____ (*learn*) from Lee about the overheating

problem _____ (*be*) to open up the cover of the central processing

unit (CPU). Lee _____ (*say*) that I can use a fan to cool off the CPU

while its cover _____ (*be*) off. I _____ (*try*) this one

time, but I _____ (*think*) the computer _____ (*look*)

very ugly this way. Also, I _____ (*be*) afraid that a lot of dust would

fall into my computer from the fan.

Every time I _____ (*talk*) to Lee about computers, I

_____ (*discover*) something new. Thanks to my friend, my computer

_____ (*run*) very well.

D. Present Perfect Tense

Present perfect tense verbs are used to refer to two time periods.

- They may refer to something in the past that started in the past and continues in the present.

  Our family **has lived** in the United States <u>since 1998</u>. (*We still live here.*)

- Or, they may also refer to one or more indefinite, or not exact, periods of time in the past.

  I **have read** that book <u>before</u>. (*"Before" does not tell the exact time in the past.*)

This verb has two parts: *have* or *has* + the past participle form of the verb.

Lara's Life in the United States

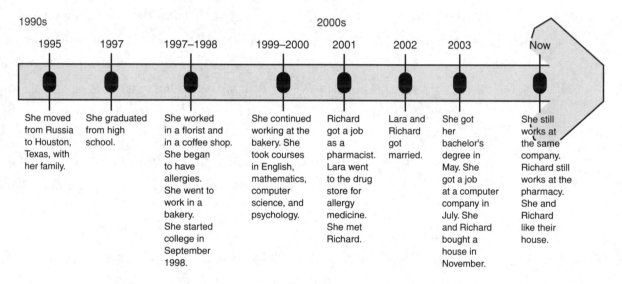

1990s   2000s

| 1995 | 1997 | 1997–1998 | 1999–2000 | 2001 | 2002 | 2003 | Now |

She moved from Russia to Houston, Texas, with her family.

She graduated from high school.

She worked in a florist and in a coffee shop. She began to have allergies. She went to work in a bakery. She started college in September 1998.

She continued working at the bakery. She took courses in English, mathematics, computer science, and psychology.

Richard got a job as a pharmacist. Lara went to the drug store for allergy medicine. She met Richard.

Lara and Richard got married.

She got her bachelor's degree in May. She got a job at a computer company in July. She and Richard bought a house in November.

She still works at the same company. Richard still works at the pharmacy. She and Richard like their house.

1 Use the timeline of Lara's life to complete the following sentences. Add verbs that make sense. Use appropriate verb tenses.

1. In 1995, Lara and her family _____ Russia and _____ to the United States.

2. She _____ many jobs since she _____ to the United States.

3. She _____ in a florist, a coffee shop, and a bakery. At present, she _____ at a computer company. She _____ there since 2002.

4. Lara _____ two diplomas in the United States. First, she _____ her high school diploma in 1997. Then, in 2003, she _____ from the university and _____ a bachelor's degree diploma.

5. Also, Lara _____ very lucky in love. She _____

her future husband, Richard, in 2001. They _____ a year later.

6. Richard _____ to work as a pharmacist in 2001. He

_____ in the same pharmacy since then. He

_____ Lara since 2001.

7. The only problem that Lara _____ since she _____

to the United States is her allergies. She _____ allergy problems since

1997. Of course, she _____ her husband because of her allergies.

8. Now, Lara and Richard _____ their own home. They

_____ there since 2003.

2 Write sentences about your own life. Use the phrases below in your sentences. In each sentence, use the present perfect tense or another appropriate tense of the verb given.

Example

be a student *I Have been a student since I was six years old.* _____

1. study English _____

2. live in the place where you live now _____

3. see many movies _____

4. wear glasses _____

5. have health problems _____

6. work in a restaurant _____

7. take a computer science course _____

8. travel on a ship _____

9. visit Paris _____

10. choose my college major _____

3 Write a college application statement on a separate piece of paper. Include the information asked for in the following instructions. Pay attention to the verb tenses that you use.

Application Statement

Great Technology Institute

Write a statement indicating why you are applying for your preferred program. Explain why you want to attend this school. Describe your current educational activities. Explain what education and/or experience you have had in this field in the past and other past experiences that may benefit your studies. Finally, explain what you hope to achieve through your education and state your long-range career plans.

E. Passive Voice Sentences

> Passive voice sentences have two important features.
>
> ■ The **subject** of the sentence is not the person who or thing that *does* the action, but the person who or thing that *receives* **the action.** You can add a *by* phrase after the verb to identify the *doer* of the action.
>
> SUBJECT (RECEIVER
> OF ACTION)   VERB   DOER OF ACTION
>   Vehicles <u>are searched</u> by police at several key points.
>
> ■ The **verb** is formed by adding a *be* verb + the *past participle* form of the main verb.
>
> **Comparing Active Voice Sentences with Passive Voice Sentences**
>
> ■ In **active voice** sentences, the **subject** of the sentence **does the action.**
>
> SUBJECT (DOER
> OF ACTION)   VERB
>   Police   <u>search</u> vehicles at several key points.
>
> Active voice sentences are more common than passive voice sentences.

1 Choose the appropriate verb forms to complete the following paragraph. Pay attention to the subjects of the sentences to determine if the sentences are active voice or passive voice sentences.

Many new security measures _____ in the United
                          1. have established/have been established
States since the September 11, 2001, attacks. Police _____
                                          2. have been intensified/have intensified
their searches of people and their belongings as they

_____ government buildings and other places. For
       3. are entered/enter
example, security guards at popular monuments like the Statue of Liberty

_____ visitors more carefully. Visitors' bags
  4. are being searched/are searching
_____ by electronic devices. Also, tours of the White
  5. are scanned/are scanning
House _____ as a result of security fears. Even the
      6. have canceled/have been canceled
streets in front of government buildings like the Independence Hall National Park in

Philadelphia _____ to drivers. Across the country, police
            7. have been closed/have closed
_____ checkpoints outside of airports. For instance,
  8. are setting up/are being set up
police _____ vehicles at several key points on highways
      9. are inspected/inspect
leading to Bush International Airport in Houston, Texas. The

police _____ drivers and
      10. are stopped/stop

_____ them to open their car trunks. Even visitors to
      11. ask/are asked

Disneyland and Disney World _____ at the entrance
                             12. are stopped/stop

gates. Police _____ their bags and
         13. open/are opened

_____ through them. All these security measures
    14. are looked/look

_____ to prevent bombings and other acts of violence.
    15. are being taken/are taking

However, they _____ life less convenient for many
           16. make/are made

Americans.

2 Write sentences about security actions that you have experienced or security devices that you have seen. Think about the times that you went to an airport, a building, a school, or other public place where you or your belongings were searched, or other security measures were used. For each of the following items, write two sentences. Label one an **active voice sentence** and one a **passive voice sentence.**

                    ACTIVE VOICE SENTENCE

1. inside an airport *We showed our tickets to the guard inside the airport.* _____

    PASSIVE VOICE SENTENCE
    Our baggage was scanned at the ticket counter. _____

2. before getting on a flight _____

   _____

3. in a museum or a monument _____

   _____

4. in a school _____

   _____

5. outside a school _____

   _____

6. at the entrance of _____ (a building) _____

   _____

7. in a library or computer lab _____

   _____

8. at a music concert _____

   _____

9. on clothing in a store _____

   _____

III. Other Verbs

A. Command Verbs

- Command verbs are commonly used to give orders, instructions, advice, and warnings.

    Be quiet!   **Do** your work.

- Command verb sentences have no stated subject. The verb is in the base form.

    Don't be lazy.   **Be** careful! (*"You" is the understood subject.*)

B. Modal Auxiliary Verbs

Modal auxiliary verbs, shown in boldfaced type, express the following meanings.

Necessity:	Alexis **must** finish his research paper by April 28.
Advice:	Hyo **should** quit his job at the Korean restaurant.
Ability:	Samuel **can** play ping pong very well. When he was in high school, he **could** beat his father.
Possibility:	Phuong **may** continue to be a Buddhist monk for another year. Then, he **might** work in his father's grocery store. He **could** take over the family's business in five years.
Future Time:	Francisco **will** leave for Colombia on May 5.

Notice that modals have several characteristics:

- They are used along with another verb to show different meanings like necessity or possibility.

- The other verb does not vary with subject or tense. For example, you write "She can come," not "She can comes," and "He could not come last week," not "He could not came last week."

Semi-Modal Verbs

Other verbs that act like modal auxiliary verbs are called "semi-modals." The boldfaced semi-modal verbs express these meanings:

Necessity:	Khalil **had to** go to court to pay his traffic ticket.
	I **have got to** get a new car.
Obligation:	Kim **was supposed to** hand in her homework on Monday.
	Children **ought to** obey their parents.
Ability:	I **was** finally **able to** get my car started last night.
Future:	It **is going to** rain tomorrow.
Past Habit:	When Umme was a child, she **used to** eat mangoes.

Semi-modals have these characteristics:

- Some semi-modals change form depending on the subject or the tense (*have to, have got to, be supposed to, be able to, be going to*).

Examples
> We **have to** go.
> She **has got to** go.
> Yesterday I **was supposed to** go.

> She **isn't able to** meet you today.
> They **are going to** go.

1 Complete the following sentences by adding an appropriate command, modal auxiliary, or semi-modal verb.

Your Nutritional Needs

1. Before you reach for a piece of pizza, you _____ think of more than the energy it _____ give you.

2. For good health, the number of calories in the food that you eat _____ match the caloric needs of your body.

3. Most nutrition experts believe that about 50 to 60 percent of a person's calories _____ come from carbohydrates.

4. At a meal, you usually eat more carbohydrates than your body _____ immediately use.

5. If you have a craving for sweets, _____ naturally sweet foods, such as fruits and fruit juices.

6. Animal fats and the fats in dairy products _____ affect the cholesterol level in your blood.

7. When you are choosing the food you eat, always _____ the amount and kind of fat that it contains.

8. You _____ choose three to five servings of vegetables and two to four servings of fruit every day.

9. Grain foods like bread, rice, and spaghetti are high in carbohydrates, so you _____ eat six to eleven servings of grains per day.

10. When you want a nutritious snack, _____ a doughnut. Instead, _____ a piece of fruit.

2 Complete the following sentences. Include a command, modal auxiliary, or semi-modal verb in each sentence.

1. If you are going on a vacation, _____.

2. When you walk in the city at night, _____.

3. _____ at the shopping mall.

4. _____ before you hand in your paper.

5. _____ if you don't want to go to a Chinese restaurant.

6. Before you leave for the airport, _____.

7. _____ if the water is very deep.

8. _____ if you want to go to the movies.

9. Whenever you have free time, _____.

10. Before you lock the door, _____.

3 Write one paragraph of advice based on each of the following student interviews. Use commands, modals, and semi-modal verbs in your writing.

A. Javier, a native of Peru and a U.S. citizen, lives with his family in Los Angeles. He is considering two different paths after he finishes his ESL classes. Either he will study computer engineering at University of California-Berkeley like his father, or he can join the U.S. Air Force Reserves. He has already filled out his enlistment papers. He feels less confident about succeeding in his studies at Berkeley. He thought that if he served in the military, he would improve his English. If he joins the Air Force, he will go to Texas in September to start his basic training. If not, he will start at Berkeley the following January. What should he do? What might be better for his future?

B. Svetlana is a first-year ESL student. She is studying only English. She was a nurse in the Ukraine. She is very shy about speaking in English. She works at a daycare center for the children of Russians and Ukrainians. Svetlana loves her job, but it doesn't pay very well. She lives in a Russian-speaking neighborhood of Chicago with her husband and daughter. Her favorite pastime is reading novels in Russian. She thought about studying to be a nurse, but she is 35. What can she do to improve her life in the United States?

IV. Gerunds and Infinitives

A. Gerunds

> Gerunds have a variety of common uses, including the following:
>
> - Subject of sentence
>   **Being** an only child has its advantages.
> - Object in a sentence
>   Tom kept **working** until midnight.
> - Object of a preposition
>   Can you learn English just by **reading** books?
> - Subject complement
>   My greatest fear was **getting** lost.

Don't confuse gerunds with continuous verbs.

> GERUND
> **Learning** another language seems difficult at times.
>
> VERB
> Nour **is taking** a Spanish class.

B. Infinitives

Infinitives are commonly used in the following ways:

- Object in a sentence

  The protesters began **to march** toward City Hall.

- In *It is* sentences

  It was not easy **to move** through the crowds of people.

- Subject complement

  The reason for the march was **to protest** the war.

Infinitives don't take endings like *-ed* or *-s.*

Patti plans to go on a cruise. NOT Patti plans to go~~es~~ on a cruise.

She started to pack last night. NOT She started to pack~~ed~~ last night.

1 Read the following sentences. Then, write two sentences to state the same idea. In your first sentence, use a gerund as the subject. Write your second sentence as an *It is* sentence with an infinitive. The first one is done for you.

1. Sendji takes five classes every semester. This is tough.

   Taking five classes every semester is tough for Sendji.

   It is tough for Sendji to take five classes in a semester.

2. The students are learning to use Microsoft Excel. This is beneficial.

   _____

   _____

3. Lynne studied Spanish in Costa Rica. That was amazing.

   _____

   _____

4. Gilberto won a scholarship. That was rewarding

   _____

   _____

5. Our English class performed in the International Festival talent show. That was enjoyable.

   _____

   _____

2 Next, think about your academic experiences. What you are studying, doing, learning, reading, and writing about this semester? What classes are you taking? Do any of these adjectives describe your academic activities: *difficult, easy, pleasant, interesting, fascinating, boring,* or *challenging*? Write three sentences using gerunds as subjects and three *It is* sentences with infinitives to describe your studies. Include adjectives like the ones above in your sentences.

C. Gerunds, Infinitives, and Simple Verb Forms as Direct Objects

Gerunds and infinitives, and in a few cases simple verbs, are used as **direct objects** in sentences. A direct object **receives** the action performed by the subject. To find the direct object, say the subject and verb followed by whom or what.

VERB DIRECT OBJECT
Tanya enjoys **performing** in school plays.

What does Tanya enjoy? *performing*   Direct object = gerund

VERB DIRECT OBJECT
The restaurant plans **to open** in November.

What does the restaurant plan? *to open*   Direct object = infinitive

VERB DIRECT OBJECT
My classmate Anbin let me **borrow** $2 for the bus.

What did Anbin let me do? *borrow $2*   Direct object = simple verb

In English some verbs take only gerunds as direct objects while other verbs take only infinitives and still others can take either. A few verbs may be followed by the simple verb form. The following are examples of these types of verbs.

Verbs That Take Only Gerunds as Direct Objects

admit	dislike	used to	quit
appreciate	enjoy	give up	recall
avoid	get/be through	keep	recommend
be fond of	finish	keep (on)	regret
can't help	get/be	mind	risk
consider	accustomed to	miss	stop (quit)
delay	get/be through	postpone	suggest
deny	get/be tired of	practice	tolerate
detest	get/be	put off	

Examples

People should always <u>avoid</u> **drinking** before driving.
I <u>don't recall</u> **meeting** you before.

Verbs That Take Only Infinitives as Direct Objects

agree	expect	intend	neglect	promise
attempt	hesitate	learn	plan	propose
decide	hope	need	pretend	want

Examples

I <u>hope</u> **to finish** my ESL classes soon.
He <u>promised</u> **to help** me with my math homework.

Verbs That Take Gerunds or Infinitives as Direct Objects

begin	forget	like	prefer	start
continue	hate	love	remember	try

Examples

Reni <u>loves</u> **to go** shopping.

Reni <u>loves</u> **going** out to the movies, too.

Note: With the verbs *forget* and *remember*, the use of gerunds or infinitives as direct object changes the meaning of the sentence.

1. I remember to lock the door. (*He always does it.*)
2. I sometimes forget to lock the door. (*He regularly forgets.*)
3. Yesterday I forgot to lock it. (*He never did it.*)
4. I don't remember locking the door. (*He did it, but he didn't remember later.*)
5. I remember locking the door. (*He did it, and he remembers now.*)
6. I forgot locking it. (*He did it, but he didn't remember later.*)

Sense Verbs That Take an Object Plus a Gerund or a Simple Verbas Direct Objects

feel	notice	see	watch
hear	observe	smell	

Examples

Maria <u>heard</u> her baby **crying.**

Maria <u>heard</u> her baby **cry.**

Other Verbs That Take a Simple Verb as Direct Objects

have	help	let	make

Examples

<u>Have</u> him **call** me on Monday.

Our instructor <u>let</u> the class **go** early.

Notes: In the sentence above, *have* means "to tell someone to."

Help may also be followed by an infinitive.

He <u>helped</u> me **do** the work.

He <u>helped</u> me **to do** the work.

1 Complete each of the following sentences with a gerund, infinitive, or simple verb form and any other words you wish to add. Choose words that make sense in the sentence.

1. Our new neighbors appear ————————— pleasant people.

2. We all appreciate your ————————— our party.

3. Can you be prepared ————————— in half an hour?

4. More and more people stop ————————— every year.

5. Michele stopped ————————— in the parking lot because she had not had a cigarette for several hours.

6. Have you begun ————————— your vacation?

7. Peter continued ————————— long after his friends had gone to bed.

8. What time do you prefer ————————— dinner?

9. Do you like ————————— letters?

10. Do you want me ————————— to the movies with you?

11. Elizabeth asked us ————————— the cookies that she baked.

12. A friend let Walter ————————— his car.

13. George helped his friend ————————— his car.

14. Mr. Kelly made his children ————————— the garage.

15. We saw a dog ————————— in the river.

16. I noticed a dog ————————— in your driveway.

17. Do you like —————————?

18. It is expected ————————— tomorrow.

19. We are tired of ————————— English grammar.

20. Are you accustomed to ————————— in your new apartment?

2 Complete the sentences in the following essay by adding the gerund, infinitive, or simple verb form of the verb in parentheses.

Alberto was studying English 091 (High-Beginning Writing). He was serious about his studies, but he had to work full-time. Sometimes Alberto didn't have enough time to do his homework. Once he tried a timesaving way ————————— (*do*) his homework but learned a lesson instead.

In the third week of class, his teacher asked him ————————— (*write*) a paragraph about his country and turn it in one week later. Unfortunately, Alberto postponed ————————— (*do*) his work until the night before it was due. He tried ————————— (*think*) of something to write, but he had no ideas. He considered ————————— (*ask*) his teacher if he could hand in the paper late, but he didn't do it because he wanted ————————— (*make*) a good impression. He also wanted _____ (*get*) a good grade on the assignment, so he found a Web site with information about his country. He wrote one sentence of his own. Then, he began _____ (*copy*) sentences from the Web site to add to his paper. The next day he turned it in with a smile. He expected _____ (*get*) a good grade.

Two days later, he was surprised when his teacher handed back the paragraph. It was unmarked except for a short message: "Come to my office after class." Later, his teacher asked: "Would you like _____ (*explain*) where this came from?" Alberto denied _____ (*copy*) the paragraph. The teacher looked unhappy. "If you expect me _____ (*believe*) that, you must think that I'm stupid," she said. Then, Alberto's teacher asked him _____ (*open*) his folder. "*This* is your writing," she pointed. Alberto felt embarrassed and started _____ (*sweat*).

In the end, the teacher made Alberto _____ (*write*) the paragraph over, so he didn't save time after all. He didn't make this mistake again.

3 Write a one-page journal entry about your plans for the coming weekend. Use verbs such as *decide, hope, intend, plan, want,* and *wish* in your writing.

V. Nouns and Pronouns

A. Count and Non-Count Nouns

In English, there are two main types of nouns: *count* nouns and *non-count* nouns.

- *Count* nouns are nouns that you can pluralize, usually by adding *-s*. You can "count" these nouns on your fingers (*one book, two books, three books,* or *one person, two people,* etc.).

- *Non-count* nouns are always singular and do not take *-s* endings. Non-count nouns include groups of items (*homework, furniture,* etc.), fluids (*milk, oil,* etc.), abstract ideas (*love, happiness,* etc.), and other nouns.

Common Non-Count Nouns by Types

- **Things that come in small pieces**

  dirt, flour, pepper, rice, salt, sand, sugar

- **Wholes made up of parts**

  baggage, cash, clothing, equipment, food, fruit, furniture, homework, jewelry, mail, money

- **Academic subjects**

  biology, computer science, engineering, economics, English, mathematics

- **Abstract ideas**

    advice, anger, beauty, fun, happiness, hatred, information, knowledge, love, luck, trouble, work

- **Fluids**

    blood, coffee, gasoline, juice, milk, oil, tea, water

- **Gases**

    air, hydrogen, oxygen

- **Solids and minerals**

    concrete, cotton, glass, gold, ice, silver, wood

- **Sports and recreational activities**

    baseball, basketball, chess, hockey, jogging, soccer, volleyball

- **Natural phenomena**

    fog, gravity, rain, snow, thunder

- **Diseases and medical conditions**

    AIDS, cancer, flu

B. Article Usage

Rules for using articles (*a/an/the*) with count and non-count nouns are stated on pages 105-106. Study common problems that occur with the use of articles.

Problem 1: Not including articles with singular count nouns

I needed **a** car, so I went to **a** car dealership.

NOT   I needed car, so I went to car dealership.

Problem 2: Using the article *a* with plural nouns

She gave me a book to read. OR She gave me some books to read.

NOT   She gave me a books to read.

Problem 3: Using *the* incorrectly with a general noun

Computers are useful in our lives.

NOT   The computers are useful in our lives.

Problem 4: Not including *the* when the noun is specific

The Africans in the novel *Amistad* were charged with murder.

NOT Africans in the novel *Amistad* were charged with murder.

Articles with Proper Nouns (Specific Names of Places and People)

Proper nouns are the names of specific people, places, and things. Study the rules for using articles with proper nouns.

In general, don't use an article . . .

- **With the name of a city, state, country, or continent**

Tokyo	Paris	Kiev	Seoul
California	Texas	Mexico	Russia
Africa	Asia		

- **With singular islands, lakes, and mountains**

Bermuda	Lake Titicaca	Mount Fuji

- **With the names of languages**

French	Russian

Use *the* . . .

- **With names of countries containing a plural noun like "States"**

  the United Arab Emirates   the United States

- **With names of countries containing "of"**

  the People's Republic of China

- **With these other countries**

  the Sudan
  the Ukraine
  the former Soviet Union

- **With geographical locations: canals, deserts, forests, islands, oceans, rivers, seas**

the Panama Canal	the Amazon River
the Gobi Desert	the Pacific Ocean

1 Complete the following sentences by adding *a, an, the,* or Ø (no article) when appropriate. Refer to the rules on pages 105-106.

The *Amistad*

In 1997, _____ film was made about _____ true story of _____ group of _____ Africans who were kidnapped in _____ Africa.

_____ Africans were captured and transported across _____ Atlantic Ocean to _____ Cuba on _____ ship named _____ *Tecoro*. On _____ journey to _____ Cuba, about one-third of _____ Africans died. They had shortages of _____ food and _____ water, so _____ sailors put about 50 Africans in _____ net weighted down with _____ heavy balls and threw _____ Africans into _____ sea.

When _____ remaining Africans arrived in _____ Havana, they were sold as _____ slaves to two Spanish landowners. On _____ trip from _____ Havana to _____ owners' sugar fields, _____ slaves got free and killed _____ sailors. They forced _____ two owners to sail _____ ship, called _____ *Amistad*, back to _____ Africa. However, _____ owners tricked _____ Africans. At night, they sailed back toward _____ Cuba.

Eventually, _____ *Amistad* ran aground near New York. _____ U.S. ship captured _____ Africans and put them in _____ prison in _____ Connecticut. When _____ court case started, _____ few Americans who opposed _____ slavery spoke in favor of _____ Africans. _____ lawyer defended _____ Africans. _____ Africans won their first court battle; however, _____ case was appealed to _____ U.S. Supreme Court.

In _____ end, _____ Africans won, and they were allowed to return home to _____ Africa.

C. Pronouns: Subject, Object, and Possessive Pronouns

- The subject pronouns *I, you, he, she, it, we,* and *they* can take the place of nouns.

  Success in life depends in part on a person's **self-image.** If **it** is positive, a person is more likely to succeed.

  Challenging situations help to make a person stronger. **They** help a person identify his strengths and weaknesses.

- Use the object pronouns—*me, you, him, her, it, them,* and *us*—as objects in a sentence.

  | S | V | OBJECT | | S | V | OBJECT |

  You must adjust to the **changes** in your life. You can learn from **them.**

- Use possessive pronouns—*my, your, his, her, its, their,* and *our*—to show ownership or possession.

  POSSESSIVE
  PRONOUN

  Young adults should establish relationships with people outside of **their** families.

  Study the following common problems that occur with pronoun use:

  Problem 1:   Using subject or object pronouns incorrectly

  My best friend and **I** are going to the movies.

  NOT   My best friend and **me** are going to the movies.

  We told **him** to meet **us** here at 1 o'clock.

  NOT   We told **he** to meet **we** here at 1 o'clock.

> **Problem 2:** **Mixing up pronouns with the same or similar sounds**
> **His** friend is coming to pick him up.
> NOT **He's** friend is coming to pick him up.
> **You're** not ready yet. Hurry up!
> NOT **Your** not ready yet. Hurry up!
> The old wood floor has lost **its** shine.
> NOT The old wood floor has lost **it's** shine.
>
> **Problem 3:** **Using subject pronouns where possessive pronouns are needed**
> Tomas and Ray left **their** books in the library.
> NOT Tomas and Ray left **they** books in the library.

1 Complete the following sentences by adding subject, object, or possessive pronouns.

1. If ___*you*___ look up the term *adult* in the dictionary, _____ will find the definition "fully developed and mature."

2. Certainly, most people reach maturity, the state of being full grown, by _____ late teens or early twenties.

3. If a person has been healthy and has had adequate nutrition and exercise, _____ is likely to reach _____ physical peak during young adulthood.

4. One major concern of young adults is finding an occupation at which _____ are effective, productive, and satisfied.

5. Although work can be rewarding, _____ also can be a source of stress.

6. Young adults may live at home or away from _____ families. When young adults live away from home, _____ may experience a sense of loss. Getting together with _____ family members for special occasions can help _____ adjust to life away from home.

7. You are more likely to form lasting friendships during young adulthood because as a young adult _____ have a better sense of who _____ are.

8. In addition, most people marry during young adulthood. People usually select _____ marriage partners on the basis of shared age, education, and social background.

2 Correct the errors in subject, object, and possessive pronouns in the following sentences taken from student writing.

1. A young boy doesn't know how to behave. ~~He's~~ *His* parents have to teach him because he is young.

2. Some people copy songs from the radio onto a cassette tape, but them are not good quality.

3. Nowadays, everyone wishes they had more money to make their lifestyle better.

4. Some people are scared of robbers who will get into they house.

5. You have special qualities, so your different from everyone else.

6. When I meet children, I feel like their mother and their teacher. I like to play with they and make they lives more interesting and fun.

7. The key to happiness is to learn how to live with what your have.

8. My friends and me can travel around the world if I am rich.

9. Nowadays, if a person wants to buy something, he just turns on him computer. He just clicks or types some words and he can buy something quickly.

10. Technology changes so quickly that its like trying to jump into a fast-moving vehicle. Technology improves so much every day that it is difficult to keep up with it's speed.

3 Read the following sentences. Change all the boldfaced nouns and pronouns from singular to plural. Make any necessary changes in verbs, articles, and other words. The first one is done for you.

1. A **person** may want to change **his** or **her** behavior, character, or physical appearance.
   People may want to change their behavior, character, or physical appearance.

2. A **computer** has a **program** to protect **its** files from viruses.

   _____

3. The **child** played in front of **her** house. **Her** dogs were running with **her** and **her** father sat on the lawn and watched his **child** play.

   _____

4. My **friend** finally reached the highway. When **he** was sure that **he** was not lost, **his** mood became better.

   _____

5. The **noise** bothered me. **It** was shrill and loud. **Its** sound gave me a headache.

   _____

4 Next, change the plural nouns and pronouns in the following sentences to singular nouns and pronouns. Make any other necessary changes when you rewrite the sentences.

1. When I got angry, I yelled at my **brothers.** I threw the television remote control at **them.** Then, **they** got hurt. After that, I apologized to **them.**

   _____

2. I love my new **cars. They**'re beautiful red Hondas. **They** have clean, soft seats, and I don't let my friends eat food inside of **them.**

   _____

3. **Pretzels** are salted pieces of bread. **They** are twisted like knots. Most people don't know where **they** came from, but some say that monks first made **them** in Italy.

_____

4. If **people** have trouble going to sleep, **they** should imagine a beautiful, peaceful place. **They** can think about the place, and this will help **them** to fall asleep.

_____

5. **Flight attendants** get excellent benefits. Enjoying new scenery is part of **their** daily work routine. **They** also get bargain prices on airline tickets when **they** take **their** own vacations.

_____

VI. Parts of Speech

A. Common Noun Endings

Learning common noun endings, or *suffixes*, will expand your vocabulary and help you write more correctly. Study the following noun suffixes and their meanings:

Suffix	Meaning	Examples
-er, -ar, -or	One who	lawyer liar
-er, -ar, -or	Something that	freezer skyscraper
-ist	One who	artist motorist
-an, -ian	One who is skilled at; Of, relating to, or resembling	mathematician Russian
-ery, -ory, -ary	A place where something happens or is done	laboratory library
-ion	The act of doing something or the state of being something	circulation translation
-ence, -ance	The act of doing something or the state of being something	confidence preference
-ment	The act of doing something or the state of being something	argument improvement
-ics	Science, art, study, or knowledge of, or skill in; qualities or operations of	mathematics mechanics

Suffix	Meaning	Examples
-hood	Condition, state, quality	falsehood neighborhood
-ism	Action, process, practice; characteristic behavior or quality; state, condition, quality; doctrine, theory, system of principles	heroism capitalism
-ness	The state of being something	kindness weakness
-ship	The state of being something	leadership scholarship
-ity	The state of being something	durability similarity

1 Use the chart on page 245 and above to help you define the following words. Write your guess of the word's meaning on the line next to the word. Check your definitions in a dictionary, if necessary.

1. illustrator _____

2. overeater _____

3. strainer _____

4. novelist _____

5. pharmacist _____

6. guardian _____

7. vegetarian _____

8. Cuban _____

9. armory _____

10. bakery _____

11. circulation _____

12. hesitance _____

13. encouragement _____

14. phonetics _____

15. parenthood _____

16. terrorism _____

17. seriousness _____

18. hardship _____

19. simplicity _____

2 Complete the following paragraph by adding the appropriate suffixes.

Hist_____ of Genet_____

The hist_____ of genet_____ began with a monk named Gregor Mendel working in the garden of a small monast_____ in Europe. He joined the priest_____ at the age of 25. In 1851, Mendel was sent to the Univers_____ of Vienna to study science and mathemat_____. After he graduated, he taught high school and took care of the monast_____ garden. Here he conducted experim_____s on pea plants to see if he could find a pattern in the way certain characterist_____s were handed down from one generat_____ of pea plants to the next.

Although Mendel did not realize it at the time, his experim_____s would come to be considered the beginning of the science of genet_____. For this reason, Mendel is called the Fath_____ of Genet_____. Genet_____ is the study of hered_____, or the passing on of traits from an organ_____ to its offspring.

3 Write 10 original sentences, using one noun with a suffix that you studied in the chart and exercise above in each sentence. You may need to add -*s* to the nouns. Write sentences that help you to remember the meaning of each word.

Example

I have suffered many **hardships** in my life, but I have overcome my difficulties.

B. Common Adjective Endings

In English many adjectives have the following suffixes.		
Suffix	**Meaning**	**Examples**
-*less*	without	careless useless
-*ful*	Full of, covered with	beautiful grateful
-*y*	Full of, covered with	dirty easy
-*ous*	Full of, covered with	famous nervous
-*ese*	Of, relating to, or resembling	Chinese Viennese
-*ar*	Of, relating to, or resembling	polar insular
-*al*	Related to, tied to, connected to	accidental historical
-*ish*	Like, similar, related to	childish Jewish

Suffix	Meaning	Examples
-ic	Like, similar, related to	athletic gigantic
-ile, -ine	Like, similar, related to	marine juvenile
-ent, -ant	Like, similar, related to	ancient fragrant
-ive	Causing, having power, related to	active massive

1 Use the chart on page 247 and above to help you define the following words. Write your guess of the word's meaning on the line next to the word. Check your definitions in a dictionary, if necessary.

1. limitless _____
2. senseless _____
3. restful _____
4. youthful _____
5. breakable _____
6. taxable _____
7. stormy _____
8. needy _____
9. ambitious _____
10. victorious _____
11. Vietnamese _____
12. stellar _____
13. coastal _____
14. devilish _____
15. angelic _____
16. feminine _____
17. obedient _____
18. imaginative _____
19. secretive _____

2 Complete the paragraph on page 249 by adding the appropriate suffixes.

Breeding the Perfect Cat

Did you know that cars are more popul_____ than dogs as pets in the Unit_____ States? Many people adopt home_____ cats from anim_____ shelt_____s, and oth_____s prefer to buy purebred cats from cat breed_____s. Two of the most popul_____ kinds of purebred cats are Siam_____ cats and Pers_____ cats. Both of these breeds are very old. Siam_____ cats have long, thin bodies. They are short-hair_____, with dark markings on the face, feet, and tail. Pers_____ cats are long-hair_____, with short, stock_____ bodies.

In the 1930s, these two breeds were combined in a series of genet_____s experi_____s conducted by scient_____s at Harvard Medic_____ School. The scient_____s were trying to find out how certain traits in cats are inherited. The result of their work was a new, artifici_____ breed of cat called the Himalay_____. The first Himalay_____ cat was born in 1935. The kitten had long hair like a Pers_____ and the markings of a Siam_____.

After the birth of the first Himalay_____ kitten, profession_____ cat breed_____s took over. In the 1960s, Himalay_____s were recognized by groups such as the Cat Fanc_____s Associat_____.

3 Write 10 original sentences, using one adjective with a suffix that you studied in the chart and exercise above in each sentence. Write sentences that help you to remember the meaning of each word.

> **Example**
> An **ambitious** person is someone who has set high goals for his or her future.

Adjectives with -*ed* and -*ing* Endings

As you have learned, some adjectives have -*ing* and -*ed* endings. These adjectives are called *verbal adjectives* because they may look like verbs but function like adjectives.

Use the -*ed* adjective to express how you feel:
I felt **bored** at the party, so I left early.

Use the -*ing* adjective to describe a subject:
I didn't have an **interesting** time at the party because I didn't know anyone.

Here are some common adjectives ending in -*ed* and -*ing*.

amused	excited	pleased	surprised
amusing	exciting	pleasing	surprising
bored	frightened	relaxed	thrilled
boring	frightening	relaxing	thrilling
confused	interested	shocked	tired
confusing	interesting	shocking	tiring

1 Complete the adjectives in the following paragraph by adding an *-ed* or *-ing* ending.

Last summer my friends and I took a trip to the Grand Bahama Island. The night before we left, we were so excit_____ that we couldn't sleep. I was a little frighten_____ by the plane ride over the ocean, but by the time we arrived I was completely relax_____. The first surpris_____ thing that we saw was that everything was green: the palm trees, the grass, and the plants. Our hotel was beautiful, and the view from our room was very invit_____. We couldn't wait to change into our swimsuits and take a refresh_____ dip in the ocean. After we swam for an hour, we were tir_____, so we rested on the beach. It was interest_____ just to watch all the people riding on "banana boats" and playing volleyball. We spent four excit_____ days on the island, and next summer, we plan to go again.

2 Write five original sentences about a trip that you took. Use an *-ed* or *-ing* ending from the chart above in each sentence.

VII. Comparative Forms

A. Adjectives and Adverbs

Here are some of the patterns for making comparisons with adjectives and adverbs.

Comparative Forms of Adjectives	
Nora's room is 8 feet by 10 feet. Gina's room is 10 feet by 12 feet. 1. Nora's room is **smaller than** Gina's (room is). 2. Gina's room is **larger than** Nora's (room is).	Add *-er* to an adjective with one syllable. Use *than* after the comparative form.
Two women want to be John's girlfriend. Martha is pretty, but Lynn is extremely pretty. 3. Lynn is **prettier than** Martha (is).	If a two-syllable adjective ends with *-y, -ow, -er, -some,* or *-ite,* add *-er* or use *more* + adjective to make the comparative form.
The tickets to the play cost $100. The tickets to the concert cost $150. 4. The tickets to the concert are **more expensive than** the tickets to the play (are)	Use *more . . . than* with most adjectives with two or more syllables.

5. Antonio's pizza is **better than** Luigi's pizza.	The comparative forms of *good, bad, far,* and *little* are irregular.
6. My headache feels **worse** now **than** it did this morning.	good—better
7. The bus stop is far from our house, but the train station is even **farther**.	bad—worse far—farther little—less
8. Tonight I have **less** homework **than** I did on Monday night.	

Comparative Forms of Adverbs

I can drive an automatic car very well. I can also drive a standard car very well, but it's harder. 1. I can drive an automatic car **more easily than** a standard car.	Use *more* + adverb + *than* to compare verbs.
Farid is a construction worker. He doesn't know how to drive a car very well. Najeeb is a taxicab driver. He drives very carefully. 2. Farid works **harder than** Najeeb (does). 3. Najeeb drives **better than** Farid (does).	Irregular adverbs include *hard, fast, well, bad,* and *far.* hard–harder fast—faster well—better bad—worse far—farther
I bought a DVD player for $150. I paid $75 for a VCR. 4. My DVD player cost **more than** my VCR. 5. I paid **less** for my VCR **than** I paid for my DVD player.	Use *more . . . than* and *less . . . than* to compare verbs.
Spoken versus Written English *Written:* My friend Richard likes gardening more than **I do.** *Spoken:* My friend Richard likes gardening more than **me.**	

Comparative Forms with as . . . as	
Tuyen is 5′ 2″ tall. Phuong is 5′ 2″ tall. Louarda is 5′ 4″ tall. 1. Tuyen is **as tall as** Phuong (is). 2. Tuyen and Phuong **are not as tall as** Louarda.	Use verb + *as . . . as* with adjectives to show equality or similarity Use *not as . . . as* with adjectives to show a difference.
Frantz and Alexis both finished writing their essays at the same . time Lian is still finishing her essay. 3. Frantz wrote his essay **as quickly as** Alexis (did). 4. Lian did **not** write her essay **as quickly as** the other two students (did).	Use a verb + *as . . . as* with adverbs to write about equality or similarity. *Not as . . . as* with adverbs shows a difference.

1 Write a sentence to compare each pair of items. Use the comparative form of the adjective in parentheses. The first one is done for you.

1. village   town   (small)

   A village is smaller than a town.

2. a refrigerator   a toaster   (expensive)

   _____

3. watching television   running   (restful)

   _____

4. yogurt   ice cream   (healthy)

   _____

5. laptop computers   hand-held computers   (large)

   _____

6. sending an e-mail   sending a letter   (fast)

   _____

7. married men   single men   (responsible)

   _____

8. college   high school   (difficult)

   _____

2 Write sentences to compare yourself and your best friend.

1. old ___My best friend is older than I am._____

2. athletic _____

3. lazy _____

4. has a lot of friends _____

5. has a good sense of humor _____

6. work hard _____

7. eat fast _____

8. sleep well _____

B. Nouns

Here are some of the ways to make comparisons with nouns.	
1. Kelly has **more freedom than** Maria (does). 2. Maria has **more responsibilities than** Kelly (does).	Use *more* + noun + *than.*
3. California has **nicer beaches than** New Jersey (does).	Use *-er* with one-syllable and some two-syllables adjectives + noun + *than.*
4. Pat's Deli makes **better sandwiches than** Lee's (does). 5. I had a **worse time than** he did at the party.	Use *better / worse* + noun + *than.*
6. Nadia has **less money than** she did one month ago.	Use *less* + non-count noun + *than.*
7. Merida has **fewer museums than** Mexico City (does).	Use *fewer* + plural count noun + *than.*
Comparisons with *as . . . as* **and** *the same . . . as*	
1. You may take **as much time as** you need to finish the test.	Use *as* + *much* + noun + *as* with non-count nouns to show equality or similarity.
2. My father does **not** have **as much patience as** my mother (does).	Add *not* to show a difference.
3. Does your research paper have **as many pages** as mine (does)?	Use *as* + *many* + noun + *as* with count nouns.
4. This semester, Josh is taking **the same classes as** Pierre (is/is taking).	Use *the same* + noun + *as.*

1 Write sentences to compare this school with another school that you attended. Use comparative forms of the following nouns.

1. library *My old school has a smaller library than my present school* _____ .

2. food _____

3. students _____

4. buildings _____

5. classrooms _____

6. tuition _____

7. reputation _____

8. computers _____

2 Read the following student essay. Correct the errors in comparative forms.

My Two Boyfriends

I am very lucky to have two boyfriends. The first boy is named Leo. I have known him about seven years. The second boy is named Sammie. I met him about three years ago. Both boys are wonderful, but they are very different from each other, in particular, in their personalities, habits, and background.

First, the major difference between the two is personality. Sammie has a more mild temper than Leo, but he is not independent as Leo. Sammie always makes me happy when I feel sad. Also, he has a good sense of humor than Leo. Sammie likes to talk, and he makes people feel relaxed. Leo is mature than Sammie. He is quiet and independent, but he never makes me happy as Sammie does. When I am with Leo, the only thing I feel is bored!

Second, I have discovered many different habits between Leo and Sammie. Sammie plays pool better Leo. When Sammie plays pool, I always stand by his side and watch. He always beats everybody very quickly. On the other hand, Leo is a skilled tennis player than Sammie, but I don't like tennis. At least, in the same way, they both like sports.

Third, Leo and Sammie have extremely different backgrounds. Leo is more rich than Sammie because Leo owns several restaurants. In contrast, Sammie only works in a restaurant. Also, Leo speaks perfect English and some Chinese, unlike Sammie, who only speaks a little English but is good than Leo in Chinese. The thing that is similar about them is that they both come from China.

Each of these two men has his individual character, and they are very different. I like both of them, but in my opinion, I feel Sammie is the one that suits me better.

3 Read the following advertisements for two vacations. Write a paragraph comparing the two vacations. State which one is better. Compare these points about the two vacations: *length of time, cost, entertainment, food, rooms, enjoyment,* and *interest.*

All-Inclusive Four-Day Bahamas Vacation!

Freeport

Grand Bahama Island

$429 per person

May 15–August 15

Your Vacation Includes:
- *Spacious oceanfront room (2 queen beds) for three nights*
- *Breakfast, lunch, and dinner daily*
- *Unlimited drinks (including alcoholic beverages)*
- *Scuba lessons*
- *Beach games, water aerobics, dance classes*

Join us at Oceanview Beach Resort — 26 acres of fun with private, white-sand beach, oceanfront swimming pool, jacuzzi, tennis courts, gym, and sauna
www.oceanviewresort.com

Five-Day Cruise to Mexico!

Get away for a long weekend to see the very best of the Gulf of Mexico. In Cozumel, you'll explore Mayan ruins, shop in colorful markets, and snorkel around colorful reefs. In Playa del Carmen, you'll ride in a submarine and swim with dolphins.

- Your Cruise Includes:
- Shipboard cabin (4 nights)
- Ocean transportation
- Meals and some beverages
- Midnight buffets *plus* 24/hr room service
- Nightly Las Vegas-style shows and comedy acts
- Non-stop movies, swimming, gym, and games

May 15–August 15
$499/person, interior cabin
$599/person, oceanview cabin

Note: Package does not include tours or activities at Cozumel or Playa del Carmen or alcoholic beverages.
www.cruisecozumel.com

VIII. Reported Speech Sentences

> Reported speech is used to tell what someone said or wrote. When you write reported speech sentences, follow these rules:
>
> ■ **Add a reporting verb (with or without *that*) before the original speech or writing.**
>
> > Richard: "My plane will arrive at 10 A.M. on Friday."
> >
> > Reported speech: Richard **said (that)** his plane would arrive at 10 A.M. on Friday.

■ **Reporting verbs are usually past tense, and the verb tense in the original speech or writing shifts to become further in the past.**

	Original Speech	Reported Speech
Present tense verbs become past tense verbs.	Lisa: "I need to borrow some money."	Lisa told me (that) she needed to borrow some money.*
Present perfect verbs become past perfect verbs.	Shirley: "I **have** not **eaten** breakfast yet."	Shirley **said** (that) she **had** not **eaten** breakfast yet.
Past tense verbs become past perfect verbs.	Michelle: "I **lost** my keys."	Michelle said (that) she **had lost** her keys.
Most modal verbs also change.	Ben: "I **can** help you."	Ben **said** (that) he **could** help me.
	The weatherman: "It **may** rain on the weekend."	The weatherman **said** (that) it **might** rain on the weekend.
	Jay: "The test **will** be next Friday."	Jay said (that) the exam **would** be next Friday.

■ **Some verb tenses in original speech do not change in reported speech.**

	Original Speech	Reported Speech
Present tense verbs in original speech with present tense reporting verbs	Beth: "I **am** in love with Eric."	Beth **says** (that) she **is** in love with Eric.
Past perfect verbs in original speech with past tense reporting verbs	Newspaper article: The economy **had been** in good shape before 2001.	A newspaper article **said** (that) the economy **had been** in good shape before 2001.

■ **Pronouns change when the speaker and listener are not those of the original speech.**

Original Speech	Reported Speech
Paula: "**My** exam will be over at 2 P.M. on Friday. **I** can meet you in the cafeteria."	Paula said (that) **her** exam would be over at 2 P.M. on Friday. **She** said that **she** could meet **me** in the cafeteria.

*Tell must be followed by a pronoun or noun phrase: Lisa **told me** that she needed to borrow some money.

Verbs to Introduce Reported Speech

> *Say* and *tell* are commonly used to introduce speech. Here are some other common reporting verbs:
>
> | | | | |
> |---|---|---|---|
> | add | declare | point out | state |
> | ask | explain | remark | think |
> | claim | indicate | reply | warn |
> | comment | mention | report | write |

1 Read each of the following quotations. Write a sentence to report the original speech. Make appropriate changes in verbs and pronouns. Use a variety of reporting verbs. The first one is done for you.

1. A professor at Beijing Normal University: "Beijing was considered the best city in China in which to study, but that's changing. Now students want to stay in the south or be on the coast because they have more opportunities and can make more money."

   A professor at Beijing Normal University said that Beijing had been

   considered the best city in China in which to study, but that was changing.

   He explained that students now wanted to stay in the south or be on the

   coast because they had more opportunities and could make more money.

2. Lester Pearson, a former prime minister of Canada: "The best defense of peace is not power, but the removal of the causes of war."

   _____

   _____

   _____

3. A Japanese garden architect: "When I am arranging one stone after another, I am always entangling the stone with my dream and pursuing an ideal world of beauty."

   _____

   _____

   _____

4. One [male] writer: "I still like Bangkok because it is a city of secrets."

   _____

   _____

   _____

5. A journalist who visited Rio de Janeiro, writing about the city's slums, or *favelas:* "The houses, built illegally on hillsides or swampland, generally consist of wood planks, mud, tin cans, corrugated iron, and anything that comes to hand."

_____

_____

_____

6. One journalist: "Throughout Siberia, boats ply rivers only in the summer; winter turns artery into bone. On the frozen surface, transportation is far easier."

_____

_____

_____

7. Old proverb: "Moscow is the heart of Russia, and St. Petersburg is its head, but Kiev is its mother."

_____

_____

_____

8. One Eritrean, speaking after Eritrea won its independence from Ethiopia: "There is almost a demonic determination to get things done. It's one of those things I think comes out of suffering."

_____

_____

_____

9. Jawaharial Nehru, first prime minister of India, speaking hours before India's independence: "At the stroke of the midnight hour, while the world sleeps, Indians will awake to life and freedom."

_____

_____

_____

10. A United Nations special delegate to Sierra Leone: "Africa never runs out of surprises. The lesson here in Sierra Leone is that things can always change for the better, and it is never too late to save a situation."

_____

_____

_____

IX. Punctuation

A. Sentence-End Punctuation

> The **period (.)** marks the end of a complete sentence. A **question mark (?)** ends a sentence that is a question, and an **exclamation point (!)** ends a sentence that tells a command or shows a strong feeling.
>
> You are responsible for seeking out educational opportunities.
>
> How can education help you succeed?
>
> Wake up! It's after 10 o'clock.

1 Read the following paragraphs. Add the appropriate punctuation at the ends of the sentences. Capitalize the first letter of the word that begins each sentence.

How Can I Decide on a Major?

Question

My older brothers and sisters and most of my friends seemed to know what they wanted to do right out of high school that's not the case with me when I first came to college, I wanted to go into physical therapy and be an athletic trainer, but I don't know if there's a future in that I've also considered teaching, but many teachers I know work other jobs to make ends meet I want to work only one job so that I have time to do other activities that I like

It seems like every day one of my brothers has a new idea for a major for me sometimes I tell people I'm thinking about it just to get them off my back lately, I've been thinking that I'll just major in business or liberal arts because those can be applied to just about any field can you offer a few suggestions for how I can decide on a major that's right for me

—Hector Perez, Student, University of Idaho

2 Write a paragraph to answer the student's question in Exercise 1 above. When you write, pay special attention to sentence-end punctuation.

B. Commas

> Use commas to show a brief pause between ideas inside a sentence. Here is a summary of some of the rules for comma use.
>
> - Use commas after introductory phrases.
>   **In my case,** chronic lateness is one of my biggest problems.
>
> - Use commas after items in a list of three or more items.
>   Being a college student can be a **challenging, chaotic, and demanding situation.**

- Use commas before coordinating conjunctions (*and, but, so, yet, for*).
  You can register for fall classes now, **or** you can wait until the summer.

- Use a comma after a dependent clause at the beginning of a sentence.
  Even if the task is difficult, you can do it.

- Use a comma with dates and years, geographic locations, and numbers.
  The University of Kansas is located in **Manhattan, Kansas.**
  The World Trade Center was destroyed on **September 11, 2001.**
  The average cost in the United States for a year's full-time tuition in 1998 was about **$1,318** for two-year public colleges to over **$17,000** for four-year private universities.

- Use commas with transitions.
  Employers value many skills, **for example,** organization and leadership skills.
  However, many people do not continue to develop their skills.

- Use a comma with reporting verbs and quotations.
  The teacher **asked,** "Do you have any questions?"

1 Add commas and periods correctly to the following sentences.

1. When you're doing something that you like time seems to pass quickly

2. Shenxin knew that he needed to write his essay but he just could not think of a topic perhaps if he took a little rest he could work on the paper later on his way to his bedroom he suddenly stopped he told himself "You can do it"

3. Chirag did well in high school so he thought that college would be easy he didn't realize that he would have to work study and maintain a social life at the same time

4. You can learn a lot about your interests by taking college courses for example taking an anthropology class may teach you that you have a passion for learning about diverse cultures or you may take a photography course and learn that you have a real artistic talent

5. Doing research without having a clear purpose is like driving without knowing where you are going therefore before you go to the library always decide what you want to accomplish before you begin

6. If you receive a federal grant you need to budget your grant money for example a $1200 grant for one 14-week semester equals about $300 per month

7. It's important for students to have positive self-images successful students tell themselves "You are smart strong and hard-working so you will succeed."

C. Comma Splices

> The incorrect use of a comma at the end of a sentence—rather than a period—is called a comma splice.
>
> **Incorrect:** Najeeb is in a college away from home, he feels lonely sometimes.
>
> **Correct:** Najeeb is in a college away from home. He feels lonely sometimes.
>
> Najeeb is in a college away from home, so he feels lonely sometimes.

1 Read the following student essay, written in response to the true story of a group of Africans who were imprisoned for killing their kidnappers and were later freed. Find and correct the comma splice errors.

The Africans' Problems

The Africans from the *Amistad* faced two difficult problems. First, they needed to escape from slavery, and second, they needed to communicate.

The Africans faced a problem when they were kidnapped and taken as slaves. They were held in chains in the ship, they couldn't move or eat. Cinque, the leader, helped them to be free from the chains. Then, they killed the sailors, after that, they left the ship to get water, they were in a small boat. When they came back, they heard some sounds, there were men who shot at them with guns. Some of the Africans jumped into the sea. Cinque jumped, too, he heard his wife's voice, she called him back to their home. After that he came up out of the water and found a gun pointed at his head. He was enslaved again.

Afterwards, the Africans faced a lot of difficulties because of language. In the court, their lawyer tried to prove that the Africans were not slaves, they were free men before. However, there wasn't any proof that showed that. The Africans needed to talk about how they were kidnapped and who brought them there, but they couldn't speak English. This was another problem for them. With English, they could answer the judge's questions, they could defend themselves. They needed to find someone to communicate with them, they could use sign language or draw pictures. If they that could do that, they would solve the language problem.

In the end, the Africans solved their problem of slavery by solving their language problem, a former slave from Africa translated for them in the court, and they were finally set free.

2 Read over the following sentences from student writing. Correct any comma splice errors.

1. In Morocco, we lived with my entire family, our house was very large with many bedrooms and two stories, in the United States my house is small because I live here by myself.

2. All people need to dream every night, nobody can remain sound if he or she is deprived of dreams for a long time.

3. Sometimes dreams lead to creative solutions or ideas about waking problems. For example, before I decided to immigrate to America, I saw a dream where the military was fighting a losing battle, I abandoned the battlefield, my war was over. When I woke up, I was ready to leave Russia.

4. Vietnam is a poor country, and it is a very small country, Vietnam is only as big as the state of Texas. Vietnam has only one big city: Ho Chi Minh City, it has many small districts with many poor inhabitants.

5. In New Orleans, the weather always changes, the people must follow the weather and wear clothes accordingly.

6. I was very excited when I took a vacation to Puerto Rico last year. It had been two years since I last saw my parents, they were so happy to see me.

7. My wife wants to return to college, but she has to work full-time. We have to talk about how both of us can go to school and still pay for our expenses, it's lucky that we own a house, so we don't have to pay rent.

8. In the supermarket where I work, I practice speaking English, the customers ask for things in the store, and I show them where to find them. I'm learning a lot of English in my job.

X. Capitalization Rules

1. Capitalize the first word of every sentence.

   My city has many interesting places to visit.

2. Capitalize the names of people, including titles.

   Mr. Steve **J**ones is my favorite teacher.

3. Always capitalize the pronoun *I*.

   Patti and **I** are going to the movies.

4. Capitalize family words if they are used with a name, but do not capitalize family words used without a name.

   We called **U**ncle **F**arid on the telephone last night.
   My **u**ncle lives in Washington, D.C.

5. Capitalize the names of the days of the week, months of the year, and holidays, but do not capitalize the names of seasons.

    On **N**ew **Y**ear's **D**ay, we had a party.

    I came to the United States on **W**ednesday, **O**ctober 7, 1998.

    In New York, there are four seasons: spring, summer, fall, and winter.

6. Capitalize names of languages, nationalities, races, and religions.

    Vietnamese   **H**aitian   **M**uslim

7. Capitalize the names of countries, states, provinces, counties, cities, and towns.

    Mexico   **T**exas   **Q**uebec   **W**ebb   **C**ounty   **M**oscow

8. Capitalize the specific names of oceans, lakes, rivers, islands, mountains, deserts, beaches, etc.

    the **I**ndian **O**cean   **L**ake **T**iticaca   the **Y**angtze **R**iver   the **C**anary **I**slands the **A**tlas **M**ountains   the **S**ahara **D**esert   **S**outh **M**iami **B**each

9. Capitalize geographic words that refer to specific areas, but do not capitalize geographic words if they do not refer to specific geographic areas.

    the **F**ar **E**ast   **S**outheast **A**sia   the **N**ortheast   the **s**outhern part of my country   **n**orth of the college

10. Capitalize specific names of companies, but do not capitalize words that tell about general types of companies.

    Yevgeniy works for **U**nited **P**arcel **S**ervice.

    He wants to get a job with a **c**omputer **c**ompany.

11. Capitalize specific names of courses, but do not capitalize the names of subjects of study.

    I love **m**athematics. Next semester, I will take **C**alculus 161.

2 Edit the following paragraph for errors in capitalization. The first sentence is corrected for you.

The Importance of Education

I know now that ~~E~~ducation is very important, but I didn't always have this ~~I~~dea. I remember when I was younger, I didn't like School. I thought that I would never need School in my Life because I thought that school would never get me anywhere. I remember every time my Mother used to send me to School, I pretended I was sick. I told Her that I couldn't go to School. after I graduated from High School I realized that Education is one of the best things in my Life. I realize that I won't be able to get a good Job without Education. it's easy for anybody to find a better Job with school Knowledge. In Some places when you apply for a Job, the first thing they ask you is if you graduated from High School. when you are educated, you get more respect than somebody who doesn't have School Knowledge. nothing can make you succeed better than education.

XI. Handwriting Guide

Study the charts below to see how to write capital (large) and lowercase (small) letters correctly in English.

Cursive (Handwritten) Letters
(Used in writing essays, letters, etc.)

Aa	*Bb*	*Cc*	*Dd*	*Ee*	*Ff*	*Gg*
Hh	*Ii*	*Jj*	*Kk*	*Ll*	*Mm*	*Nn*
Oo	*Pp*	*Qq*	*Rr*	*Ss*	*Tt*	*Uu*
Vv	*Ww*	*Xx*	*Yy*	*Zz*		

Printed Letters
(Used in writing lists, signs, etc.)

Aa	Bb	Cc	Dd	Ee	Ff	Gg
Hh	Ii	Jj	Kk	Ll	Mm	Nn
Oo	Pp	Qq	Rr	Ss	Tt	Uu
Vv	Ww	Xx	Yy	Zz		

Look over two or three of your compositions. Compare your cursive capital and lowercase letters with the samples in the first chart. Show your handwriting to another person to make sure that all of your letters are clearly written. Also, make sure that you use capital and lowercase letters appropriately. Rewrite any letters that look very different from the samples or seem unclear to another reader.

XII. Common Editing Symbols

art.	article error	*art.* I live in <u>the</u> Chicago. (*Correct:* I live in Chicago.) *art.* I have __ large family.
pl.	plural	*pl.* His <u>parent</u> own a dry cleaning business.
s-v	subject-verb agreement	*s-v* My sister <u>work</u> at a Chinese restaurant.
sp.	spelling error	*sp.* My <u>douther's</u> name is Alina.
v.t.	wrong verb tense	*v.t.* When I was a child, my family <u>visit</u> Agra.
v.f.	wrong verb form	*v.f.* I <u>am come</u> from Vietnam.
w.f.	wrong word form	*w.f.* I am happy to live in a <u>freedom</u> country.
w.w.	wrong word	*w.w.* She <u>said</u> me to go home.
◯	word or punctuation mark missing	We took a train ◯ we got lost. I bought ◯ car last summer.
⋏	insert	◯ *v.f.* She ⋏ going for a walk.
≡	capitalize letter	<u>m</u>y classes end on <u>m</u>ay 15.
⌐⌐	wrong word order	I |always|am| late for class.
/	lowercase letter	My best /Friend is named Joan.
⌐	indent	Move the line to the right five spaces.

Correct the mistakes in the example sentences in the Common Editing Symbols chart above. The first sentence is done for you. Share your answers with your classmates.

Do It Yourself Answer Key

I. Sentences

A. Complete Sentences

1 1. If you **are** late to your class too much, you will miss important parts of the lecture.
2. On February 27 **there** is a beautiful celebration in my country.
3. My best friend is Maria. We have two classes together and live in the dormitory, so we **are** always together.
4. When I have free time, I take care of myself. I take a shower and wash my hair. **Then I b**low my hair out **and d**o my nails.
5. Money will bring me happiness **b**ecause if I have plenty of money, I will buy a lot of things.
6. **C**
7. Khalil's apartment is very noisy, so **he** wants to find another place.
8. Dr. Gao **is** a very good mathematics teacher **b**ecause he explains everything well **a**nd answers the students' questions.
9. At first, I couldn't speak English**. I** didn't understand what other people were saying.
10. If you have money**, it** is easy to make a living and support your family.
11. My brother ~~he~~ is living in Los Angeles.
12. She **is** working very hard in her classes this year.

2 Possible answers
1. Studying hard <u>will help me pass my exam</u>.
2. Every person <u>needs to enjoy life</u>.
3. <u>Getting an education</u> is a good way to succeed.
4. A serious student <u>concentrates in class and takes notes</u>.
5. At the beginning of each school year, <u>I organize all the things that I need for my</u> studies.
6. <u>I listen to music</u> when I want to relax.
7. <u>Honesty and determination</u> are my best qualities.
8. My favorite class <u>is computer science</u>.
9. <u>An alarm clock</u> wakes me up early every day.
10. After class, I <u>take the bus home</u>.

3 Possible answers

A Good Use of Time

If you <u>spend a lot of time on</u> the Internet, don't feel guilty because <u>it</u> is really a good way to use your time. The Internet <u>contains</u> an incredible amount of information. <u>Any question that you have</u> can be answered on the Internet. <u>Students</u> can get help on a research paper or math homework. If you <u>don't know</u> what to major in, <u>the Internet</u> has many career exploration sites. Indeed, <u>the Internet</u>/using the internet is like having an older, wiser friend right in your home. It's also a great source of entertainment. <u>Are</u> you feeling bored? You <u>can find</u> today's joke, a Web site just for bored people, or a partner for a game of solitaire. If <u>you</u> are interested in music, you can <u>listen</u> to your favorite songs on the Internet. You <u>can copy</u> photographs of your favorite movie stars and even <u>watch</u> film clips. And, while you <u>are having</u> fun, you also <u>get</u> an added bonus. <u>You</u> will be improving your typing. In today's technological world, you <u>need to know how to use</u> computers and the Internet. If you <u>spend</u> time on the Internet, you <u>are not</u> wasting time.

4 Possible answers
1. **The** geography of Central America **is** very interesting.
2. **First, Central America** connects North America and South America.
3. **It is** located between Mexico to the north and Colombia to the south.
4. **Also,** Central America **consists of** several countries.
5. **Guatemala, Honduras, and Nicaragua are** the largest.
6. **Guatemala is** like a bridge between Mexico and the rest of Central America.
7. **Next to** Guatemala, Belize also **shares** a border with Mexico.
8. **As you** continue south, **El Salvador** lies southeast of Guatemala and south of Honduras.
9. **Further south lie** the countries of Nicaragua and Costa Rica.
10. **Finally,** Panama **connects** Central America and Colombia in South America.
11. **Of course, Panama** has the famous Panama Canal.
12. Ships **travel** through the canal to save time on long sea journeys.
13. **It** is not easy to remember the exact location of the countries of Central America.
14. **Perhaps** one day **you can** visit Central America to see the countries firsthand.

B. Four Basic Sentence Patterns

1 Possible answers

_1_ 1. On a typical weekday, I <u>go to school from 8 A.M. to 1 P.M. and work from 3 P.M. to 11 P.M.</u>.

_1_ 2. When I meet my friends, we <u>have a good time together</u>.

_2_ 3. Working part-time <u>is better than working full-time</u>.

_4_ 4. <u>It is</u> very easy to <u>spend a lot of money on clothes</u>.

_2_ 5. <u>Drinking alcohol</u> is bad for me.

_1_ 6. Some of my classmates <u>live in apartments</u>.

_3_ 7. <u>There are many cars parked on the streets</u> in my neighborhood.

_2_ 8. <u>My high school graduation was</u> the most exciting day of my life.

_2_ 9. The city <u>is quiet at night</u>.

_1_ 10. <u>College students have</u> too much work to do.

2 Possible answers

1. The students are smoking in front of the Mint Building. (*Pattern 1*)
2. There is a parking garage for students on 17th Street. (*Pattern 3*)
3. The food in the cafeteria is expensive. (*Pattern 2*)
4. There are many quiet areas in the library. (*Pattern 3*)
5. There are benches and trees near the entrance to the Bonnell Building. (*Pattern 3*)

3 Possible answers

1. It's cold and windy today.
2. What is today's date? It is September 2.
3. It was warm last night.
4. It was 6 A.M. when I woke up this morning.
5. It's not easy to write in English.

C. Sentence Combining

1 Possible answers

1. Wellun has to use crutches <u>because</u> he sprained his ankle. He fell down <u>while</u> he was playing basketball.
2. <u>Even though</u> Najeeb doesn't like the food in the cafeteria, he bought his lunch there today. He had to eat there <u>because</u> it was raining, and he didn't want to walk to a restaurant.

3. <u>If</u> I finish my shopping early, I can go to the movies with you. Then, we can try that new Colombian restaurant <u>after</u> we get out of the movie.
4. The weather is beautiful outside. Unfortunately, I can't enjoy it <u>until</u> I finish all this homework. <u>When</u> I look at my stack of books, I get very depressed.
5. Raoul is saving all his money <u>so that</u> he can have an exciting vacation in Haiti. <u>As soon as</u> he gets off the plane, he plans to go to the beach.

2 1. My brother quit his job in the grocery store **b**ecause being a cashier made him nervous.
2. Even though I had an operation, ~~but~~ I came to school to finish my English class.
3. Maria missed many days of work **because** her children were sick.
4. If people lie and let me catch them**, n**ext time I won't believe them.
5. Because my family didn't want to waste money on rent, ~~so~~ we bought our own house.
6. **As t**ime passes and children grow old enough, they should move out of their parents' home and live independently.
7. I need to have high self esteem before I become independent, **so** I need to get a good-paying job.
8. I would like to change my indecisiveness because sometimes it's hard for me **w**hen I have to make an important decision about my studies, career, etc.
9. **Even though** I take a long time to think about something, I sometimes never do anything.
10. Although it won't be easy, ~~but~~ I can do it and overcome my indecisiveness.

3 1. Some of my teachers say that I'm quiet**, but m**y teachers are wrong.
2. **Although s**ometimes I am really nervous at first**,** I try not to show it in front of people.
3. I usually don't ask questions in class **if** I understand everything that the teachers said.
4. In class, I don't like to talk that much **because** I think it's rude to talk when the teacher talks.
5. **Unless** I don't understand something, I never ask questions.
6. Some of my classmates ask questions **because t**hey don't listen to what the teachers say.
7. **When y**ou pay attention and concentrate**, y**ou can understand everything.
8. However, **if** sometimes you listen and you still don't understand**, y**ou have to ask questions.

II. Common Verb Tenses

A. Present Tense Verbs

1. Simple Present Tense

1 1. Parents <u>are</u> their children's first teachers.
2. A successful parent <u>teaches</u> his or her child values and behavior.
3. Honesty and kindness <u>are</u> also important values for a child.
4. Being honest <u>means</u> that you <u>don't tell</u> lies.
5. A good parent <u>shows</u> his or her children the best ways to act with others.
6. A child <u>doesn't know</u> how to behave unless the parents <u>teach</u> him good behavior.
7. Children also <u>learn</u> morals from their parents.
8. If parents <u>don't teach</u> their children to have good morals, the children will not know what is right or wrong.
9. Learning to judge right from wrong <u>helps</u> children to make good decisions in their lives.
10. The best parents <u>have</u> a lot of patience because it <u>takes</u> time to teach a child good behavior.

2 Possible answers
1. Xinli wakes up early every morning.
2. Alex rides his bicycle to school.
3. Before class, Nour talks to his classmates.
4. During class, Lian sometimes falls asleep.
5. Mahdi always looks up words in his bilingual dictionary.
6. Samuel sometimes goes with other classmates to the library.
7. After class is over, Thomas goes home.
8. Hyo visits the teacher's office if he has questions.
9. Oksana always hands in her homework on time.
10. I often see Tran studying in the library.

2. Present Progressive Tense

1 1. Nadia <u>is preparing</u> for her final examinations this week.
   She <u>has</u> a laptop computer to help her study.
2. Sentisouk <u>helps</u> his mother with housework every day.
   Right now he <u>is washing</u> the clothes.
3. Kerlen usually <u>comes</u> to every class.
   However, this week she <u>is staying</u> with her sick mother in Haiti.

4. Mike rarely <u>keeps</u> his room neat.
   His mother got angry, so he <u>is cleaning</u> his room at the moment.
5. Celia and Jenny often <u>play</u> ping pong after class.
   Today, however, they <u>are not playing</u> because the gymnasium is closed.

2 Possible answers
1. At the present time, the price of gasoline is rising.
2. Unemployment is not declining right now.
3. The war in the Middle East is continuing now.
4. The Earth is orbiting the sun at the moment.
5. Satellites are circling the Earth right now.
6. The cost of living is rising in Canada.
7. Fortunately, crime is not rising in New York City.
8. The population is growing around the world.
9. Our natural resources are dwindling.
10. Technology is changing at the present time.

3. Non- Progressive Verbs

1 Possible answers

   People <u>have</u> different types of worries about material goods, depending on their economic level. For example, most Americans <u>desire</u> a great number of material things: houses, furniture, computers, televisions, etc. They constantly <u>want</u> to acquire *more* things. The phrase "keeping up with the Joneses" <u>means</u> that Americans <u>seek</u> to have as many material goods as their neighbors. Often, they <u>feel</u> dissatisfied if they <u>don't have</u> the latest models of products. On the other hand, people with less money to spare may never <u>think</u> about buying the latest model of a car. They <u>worry</u> about how they can fulfill their basic needs. Acquiring food, water, and other basics <u>are</u> what they worry about the most. After they satisfy their basic needs, they may <u>desire</u> other material goods. Therefore, people of different economic levels <u>have</u> their own types of worries.

4. Subject-Verb Agreement

1 1. Some of my friends **have** bachelor's degrees from universities.
2. Taking notes in class **helps** me to succeed academically.
3. My classmate Javier always **sits** in the front row in class. He **wants** to hear what the teacher is saying.
4. It **feels** very comfortable when you study in your room.

5. This semester our class **is** reading the book *Dracula.*

6. If a student **doesn't** listen in class, he **doesn't** get good grades.

7. Computer skills **are** very important for us.

8. Now I **go** to school and work. That is very good for me because I **get** new opportunities.

9. Right now my brother and I **are** living in an apartment.

10. When students **are** listening in class, they should take notes.

2 A.   **A Great Tourist Destination**

One of the best cities to visit on the east coast of the United States **is** Washington. It **has** some of the most interesting landmarks and tourist spots in the country. There **are** many monuments to visit, such as the Lincoln Memorial, the Jefferson Memorial, and the Washington Monument (the tallest building in Washington). Washington also **has** interesting museums like the Smithsonian Institute. For more excitement, the area called Georgetown in northwest Washington **is** famous for its shopping, restaurants, and nightclubs. Nearby, there is Virginia Beach. It **has** nice beaches with features like horseback riding, sailboat rentals, and seafood restaurants. People **go** there in great numbers in the summer. Washington, D.C., is not as large or as famous as New York City, but it **has** an appeal all its own.

B.   **A Strange Dream**

Sometimes my friend Maria has strange dreams, and she **tells** me about them. She wants to know the meaning of her dreams. In one dream, Maria and a friend **are** walking through a city at night. In the next scene, they are sitting in a club. A band is playing jazz music, and all the people **are** smoking. A strange man **comes** up to her table and asks her to dance. Maria **feels** excited, so she accepts his offer. Then, while they are dancing, the man **changes** into a lion. Suddenly, the lion is opening his mouth, and Maria is running away. She **keeps** turning her head, and the lion follows her. Then, just at the moment when the lion is about to catch up to her, she **wakes** up. What do you think the dream means?

3 Possible answers

1. I always eat breakfast every morning.
   My classmate <u>Hana never eats breakfast</u>.

2. Many students at my college smoke cigarettes.
   Smoking cigarettes <u>is bad for you</u>.

3. Computers get less expensive every year.
   A hand-held computer <u>costs less than a laptop computer</u>.

4. At my university, international students pay three times the tuition that residents pay.
   My tuition <u>is not high because I am a resident</u>.

5. Oksana and Sergey are buying a new house.
   An apartment <u>is cheaper than a house, but a house is better</u>.

6. The students in Chinese 101 are learning to write Chinese characters.
   The Chinese language <u>sounds very different from my language</u>.

7. Flat-screen televisions with 24-inch screens cost about $7,500.
   A flat-screen TV <u>takes up less space than the TV that I have</u>.

8. People from all over the world celebrate the Carnival in Brazil.
   The Mardi Gras festival <u>seems very interesting to me</u>.

9. Children play in the parks and in the streets in my neighborhood.
   Playing in the street <u>is fun, but it can be dangerous</u>.

10. Some fast-food restaurants serve their customers in less than one minute.
    My favorite restaurant <u>takes longer than one minute to serve food</u>.

B. Past Tense Verbs

1 In **Group A**, the verb forms do not change from the present to the past tense. In **Group B**, all of the past forms sound alike and are spelled with *-ought.* In **Group C**, all the verbs have the "ee" sound in the present and change to the "e" sound in the past. In **Group D**, all the verbs change from the "i" sound in the present to the "a" sound in the past.

2   **Getting Lost**

Last week, I **went** to Summit Grove Camp in York, Pennsylvania. The camping trip for my church **began** on Friday night. All my friends went to the camp on Friday, but I had to work on Friday night, so I went to the camp by myself on Saturday morning. I **drove** alone about an hour on Interstate 95. In the early morning, there weren't many cars on the highway. I **felt** sleepy, so I thought I would get some coffee so I might feel better. I turned at the exit that said "service area." I **followed** the signs, but I **got** lost. I went on a road that **took** me into a forest. There **were** a lot of trees. I didn't see anybody there. I was very frightened. I turned back, but I got lost again. Luckily, I saw one car coming towards me from the opposite direction. It was a small road, so I **waved** him down and **asked** directions to get back to I-95. Once I got back on the highway, I drove straight to the camp. I **didn't** feel sleepy anymore because I was frightened. Finally, I got to the camp. I met my friends, and I had a good time.

C. Using Present and Past Tense Verbs Together

1   **Lee, the Computer Genius**

My friend Lee <u>did not touch</u> a computer before he <u>came</u> to America. He <u>bought</u> his first computer in 1998. In a five-year period, he <u>broke/has broken</u> two hard drives, two CD-Rom drives, and one modem, but he <u>gained/has gained</u> a lot of experience about caring for a computer. Now, he <u>knows</u> so much about computers that he <u>teaches</u> his friends how to maintain and repair them.

Lee often <u>gives</u> me advice about how to take care of my computer. He always <u>reminds</u> me that a computer is a machine. It <u>needs</u> good ventilation. As the computer <u>works/is working</u> it <u>produces/is producing</u> more heat. Lee <u>says</u> that when my computer <u>runs</u> slowly, or <u>gives</u> me a "system error" message, it may be overheated.

Last night my computer <u>froze</u> up on me two times. I <u>got</u> very annoyed because I <u>kept</u> having to restart it. Then I <u>remembered</u> what Lee <u>had told/told</u> me. I <u>shut</u> down the computer and <u>gave</u> it a break. This morning my computer <u>is running/runs</u> fine.

Another tip that I <u>learned/have learned</u> from Lee about the overheating problem <u>is</u> to open up the cover of the central processing unit (CPU). Lee <u>says</u> that I can use a fan to cool off the CPU while its cover <u>is</u> off. I <u>tried</u> this one time, but I <u>thought</u> the computer <u>looked</u> very ugly this way. Also, I <u>was</u> afraid that a lot of dust would full into my computer from the fan.

Every time I <u>talk</u> to Lee about computers, I <u>discover</u> something new. Thanks to my friend, my computer <u>runs/is running</u> very well.

D. Present Perfect Tense

1 Possible answers

1. In 1995, Lara and her family <u>left</u> Russia and <u>moved</u> to the United States.
2. She <u>has had</u> many jobs since she <u>came</u> to the United States.
3. She <u>has worked</u> in a florist, a coffee shop, and a bakery. At present, she <u>works/is working</u> in a computer company. She <u>has worked</u> there since 2002.
4. Lara <u>has received</u> two diplomas in the United States. First, she <u>got</u> her high school diploma in 1997. Then, in 2003, she <u>graduated</u> from the university and <u>got</u> a bachelor's degree diploma.
5. Also, Lara <u>has been</u> very lucky in love. She <u>met</u> her future husband, Richard, in 2001. They <u>got married/were married/married</u> a year later.
6. Richard <u>started</u> to work as a pharmacist in 2001. He <u>has worked</u> in the same pharmacy since then. He <u>has known</u> Lara since 2001.
7. The only problem that Lara <u>has had</u> since she <u>moved</u> to the United States is her allergies. She <u>has had</u> allergy problems since 1997. Of course, she <u>met</u> her husband because of her allergies.
8. Now, Lara and Richard <u>own</u> their own home. They <u>have lived</u> there since 2003.

2 Possible answers

1. I have studied English for two years.
2. I have lived in my apartment for six months.
3. I have seen many movies in the past year.
4. I don't wear glasses.
5. I don't have any health problems.
6. I don't work in a restaurant.
7. I have never taken a computer science course.
8. I have traveled on a ship on the Black Sea.
9. I have visited Paris twice.
10. I have not chosen my major yet.

3 Answers will vary.

E. Passive Voice Sentences

1   Many new security measures <u>have been established</u> in the United States since the September 11, 2001, attacks. Police <u>have intensified</u> their searches of people and their belongings as they <u>enter</u> government buildings and other places. For example, security guards at popular monuments like the Statue of Liberty <u>are searching</u> visitors more carefully. Visitors' bags are scanned by electronic devices. Also, tours of the White House have been canceled as a result of security fears. Even the streets in front of government buildings like the Independence Hall National Park in Philadelphia have been closed to drivers. Across the country, police are setting up checkpoints outside of airports. For instance, police inspect vehicles at several key points on highways leading to Bush International Airport in Houston, Texas. The police stop drivers and ask them to open their car trunks. Even visitors to Disneyland and Disney World are stopped at the entrance gates. Police open their bags and look through them. All these security measures are being taken to prevent bombings and other acts of violence. However, they make life less convenient for many Americans.

2 Possible answers

1. **Active voice sentence** — We **showed** our tickets to the guard inside the airport.
   Passive voice sentence — Our baggage **was scanned** at the ticket counter.
2. **Active voice sentence** — Before I got on the flight, the guard **checked** my boarding pass.
   Passive voice sentence — I **was searched** by a guard before I got on a flight last year.
3. **Active voice sentence** — At the museum, the guard **looked** through our bags.
   Passive voice sentence — Our bags **were scanned** when we went to the museum.
4. **Active voice sentence** — At school, we **show** our ID cards to the security guard.
   Passive voice sentence — Our ID cards **are examined** by the guards.
5. **Active voice sentence** — Outside the high school, there **are** police cars.
   Passive voice sentence — Students **are questioned** by the policemen outside the school.
6. **Active voice sentence** — We **have to show** our library cards at the entrance of the library.
   Passive voice sentence — Our books **are scanned** by the clerk at the entrance of the library.
7. **Active voice sentence** — Students **have to show** their ID cards to use the computers.
   Passive voice sentence — Our ID cards **are scanned** by a computer at the door of the computer lab.
8. **Active voice sentence** — At the music concert, a guard **looked** in my backpack.
   Passive voice sentence — My backpack **was searched** at the concert.
9. **Active voice sentence** — The cashier **removes** the electronic device on clothing.
   Passive voice sentence — An electronic device **is attached** to expensive clothing in the store.

III. Other Verbs

B. Modal Auxillary Verbs

1 Possible answers

Your Nutritional Needs

1. Before you reach for a piece of pizza, you should think of more than the energy it will give you.
2. For good health, the number of calories in the food that you eat should match the caloric needs of your body.
3. Most nutrition experts believe that about 50 to 60 percent of a person's calories should come from carbohydrates.
4. At a meal, you usually eat more carbohydrates than your body can immediately use.
5. If you have a craving for sweets, eat naturally sweet foods, such as fruits and fruit juices.
6. Animal fats and the fats in dairy products can affect the cholesterol level in your blood.
7. When you are choosing the food you eat, always consider the amount and kind of fat that it contains.
8. You should choose three to five servings of vegetables and two to four servings of fruit every day.
9. Grain foods like bread, rice, and spaghetti are high in carbohydrates, so you need to eat six to eleven servings of grains per day.
10. When you want a nutritious snack, don't eat a doughnut. Instead, eat a piece of fruit.

2 Possible answers

1. If you are going on a vacation, go some place that will relax you.
2. When you walk in the city at night, look around you.

3. <u>Don't spend too much money</u> at the shopping mall.
4. <u>You must check for mistakes</u> before you hand in your paper.
5. <u>Let me know</u> if you don't want to go to a Chinese restaurant.
6. Before you leave for the airport, <u>make sure that you have your ticket</u>.
7. <u>Don't go swimming</u> if the water is very deep.
8. <u>You can call me later</u> if you want to go to the movies.
9. Whenever you have free time, <u>take a break</u>.
10. Before you lock the door, <u>check to see that you have your keys</u>.

3   **A.** Sample sentences for paragraphs:
Javier can continue his studies after he joins the Air Force.
He needs to have more confidence in himself.
He should not join the Air Force.
He will learn more English in the Air Force.
Studying at Berkeley might be better for his future.

B. Sample sentences for paragraphs:
Svetlana should try to speak more English.
She can talk to people in stores.
She should read books in English.
She can study to be a nurse.
She needs to get a better job.

IV. Gerunds and Infinitives

B. Infinitives

1   1. Taking five classes every semester is tough (for Sendji).
It is tough (for Sendji) to take five classes in a semester.
2. Learning to use Microsoft Excel is beneficial (for the students).
It is beneficial (for the students) to learn to use Microsoft Excel.
3. Studying Spanish in Costa Rica was amazing (for Lynne).
It was amazing (for Lynne) to study Spanish in Costa Rica.
4. Winning a scholarship was rewarding (for Gilberto).
It was rewarding (for Gilberto) to win a scholarship.

5. Performing in the International Festival talent show was enjoyable (for our English class).
It was enjoyable (for our English class) to perform in the International Festival talent show.

2   Answers will vary.

C. Gerunds, Infinitives, and Simple Verb Forms as Direct Objects

1   Possible answers
1. Our new neighbors appear <u>to be</u> pleasant people.
2. We all appreciate your <u>coming to</u> our party.
3. Can you be prepared <u>to leave</u> in half an hour?
4. More and more people stop <u>smoking</u> every year.
5. Michele stopped <u>to smoke</u> in the parking lot because she had not had a cigarette for several hours.
6. Have you begun <u>to plan/planning</u> your vacation?
7. Peter continued <u>to stay up</u> long after his friends had gone to bed.
8. What time do you prefer <u>to have</u> dinner?
9. Do you like <u>to write/writing</u> letters?
10. Do you want me <u>to go</u> to the movies with you?
11. Elizabeth asked us <u>to try</u> the cookies that she baked.
12. A friend let Walter <u>borrow</u> his car.
13. George helped his friend <u>start/to start</u> his car.
14. Mr. Kelly made his children <u>clean up</u> the garage.
15. We saw a dog <u>swimming/swim</u> in the river.
16. I noticed a dog <u>sitting</u> in your driveway.
17. Do you like <u>to swim/swimming</u>?
18. It is expected <u>to rain</u> tomorrow.
19. We are tired of <u>studying</u> English grammar.
20. Are you accustomed to <u>living</u> in your new apartment?

2   Alberto was studying English 091 (High-Beginning Writing). He was serious about his studies, but he had to work full-time. Sometimes Alberto didn't have enough time to do his homework. Once he tried a timesaving way <u>to do</u> his homework but learned a lesson instead.

In the third week of class, his teacher asked him <u>to write</u> a paragraph about his country and turn it in one week later. Unfortunately, Alberto postponed <u>doing</u> his work until the night before it was due. He tried <u>to think</u> of something to write, but he had no ideas. He considered <u>asking</u> his teacher if he could hand in the paper late, but he didn't do it because he wanted to make a good impression. He also wanted to get a good grade on the assignment, so he found a Web site with information about his country. He wrote one sentence of his own. Then, he began copying/to copy sentences from the Web site to add to his paper. The next day he turned it in with a smile. He expected to get a good grade.

Two days later, he was surprised when his teacher handed back the paragraph. It was unmarked except for a short message: "Come to my office after class." Later, his teacher asked: "Would you like to explain where this came from?" Alberto denied copying the paragraph. The teacher looked unhappy. "If you expect me to believe that, you must think that I'm stupid," she said. Then, Alberto's teacher asked him to open his folder. "*This* is your writing," she pointed. Alberto felt embarrassed and started to sweat/sweating.

In the end, the teacher made Alberto write the paragraph over, so he didn't save time after all. He didn't make this mistake again.

3 Answers will vary.

V. Nouns and Pronouns

B. Article Usage

Articles with Proper Nouns (specific names of places and people)

1   **The** *Amistad*

In 1997, a film was made about the true story of a group of—Africans who were kidnapped in Africa.

The Africans were captured and transported across the Atlantic Ocean to ø Cuba on a ship named the *Tecoro*. On the journey to ø Cuba, about one-third of the Africans died. They had shortages of ø food and ø water, so the sailors put about 50 Africans in a net weighted down with heavy balls and threw the Africans into the sea.

When the remaining Africans arrived in ø Havana, they were sold as ø slaves to two Spanish landowners. On the trip from ø Havana to the owners' sugar fields, the slaves got free and killed the sailors. They forced the two owners to sail the ship, called the *Amistad*, back to ø Africa. However the owners tricked the Africans. At night, they sailed back toward ø Cuba.

Eventually, the *Amistad* ran aground near New York. A U.S. ship captured the Africans and put them in a/Ø prison in Ø Connecticut. When the court case started, a few Americans who opposed slavery spoke in favor of the Africans. A lawyer defended the Africans. The Africans won their first court battle; however, the case was appealed to the U.S. Supreme Court.

In the end, the Africans won, and they were allowed to return home to ø Africa.

C. Pronouns: Subject, Object, and Possessive Pronouns

1 1. If you look up the term *adult* in the dictionary, you will find the definition "fully developed and mature."
2. Certainly, most people reach maturity, the state of being full grown, by their late teens or early twenties.
3. If a person has been healthy and has had adequate nutrition and exercise, he or she is likely to reach his or her physical peak during young adulthood.
4. One major concern of young adults is finding an occupation at which they are effective, productive, and satisfied.
5. Although work can be rewarding, it also can be a source of stress.
6. Young adults may live at home or away from their families. When young adults live away from home, they may experience a sense of loss. Getting together with their family members for special occasions can help them adjust to life away from home.
7. You are more likely to form lasting friendships during young adulthood because as a young adult you have a better sense of who you are.
8. In addition, most people marry during young adulthood. People usually select their marriage partners on the basis of shared age, education, and social background.

2 1. A young boy doesn't know how to behave. **His** parents have to teach him since he is young.
2. Some people copy songs from the radio onto a cassette tape, but **they** are not good quality.
3. Nowadays, everyone wishes **he or she** had more money to make **his or her** lifestyle better.
4. Some people are scared of robbers who will get into **their** house.

5. You have special qualities, so **you are/you're** different from everyone else.

6. When I meet children, I feel like their mother and their teacher. I like to play with **them** and make **their** lives more interesting and fun.

7. The key to happiness is to learn how to live with what **you** have.

8. My friends and **I** can travel around the world if I am rich.

9. Nowadays, if a person wants to buy something, he just turns on **his** computer. He just clicks or types some words and he can buy something quickly.

10. Technology changes so quickly that **it's/it is** like trying to jump into a fast-moving vehicle. Technology improves so much every day that it is difficult to keep up with **its** speed.

3 1. **People** may want to change **their** behavior, character, or physical appearance.

2. **Computers have programs** to protect **their** files from viruses.

3. The **children** played in front of **their** house. **Their** dogs were running with **them** and **their** father sat on the lawn and watched his **children** play.

4. My **friends** finally reached the highway. When **they** were sure that **they were** not lost, **their moods** became better.

5. The **noises** bothered me. **They were** shrill and loud. **Their** sound gave me a headache.

4 1. When I got angry, I yelled at my **brother.** I threw the television remote control at **him.** Then, **he** got hurt. After that, I apologized to **him.**

2. I love my new **car. It's a** beautiful red **Honda. It has** clean, soft seats, and I don't let my friends eat food inside of **it.**

3. **A pretzel is a salted piece** of bread. **It is** twisted like a **knot.** Most people don't know where **it** came from, but some say that monks first made **it** in Italy.

4. If **a person has** trouble going to sleep, **he or she** should imagine a beautiful, peaceful place. **He or she** can think about the place, and this will help **him or her** to fall asleep.

5. **A flight attendant gets** excellent benefits. Enjoying new scenery is part of **his or her** daily work routine. **He or she** also gets bargain prices on airline tickets when **he or she takes his or her** own vacations.

VI. Parts of Speech

A. Common Noun Endings

1 Possible answers

1. illustrator = a person who illustrates books, stories, etc.
2. overeater = a person who eats too much
3. strainer = a tool used to strain foods, etc.
4. novelist = a person who writes novels
5. pharmacist = a person who dispenses drugs
6. guardian = a person who guards (cares for) someone or something
7. vegetarian = a person who eats only vegetables, no meat
8. Cuban = a person from Cuba
9. armory = a place for storing arms
10. bakery = a place where baked goods are made and/or sold
11. circulation = the state of moving around, i.e., blood, money, newspapers
12. hesitance = the state of not being willing to do or say something
13. encouragement = an action that helps someone become confident
14. phonetics = the science of speech sounds
15. parenthood = the state of being a parent
16. terrorism = the use of violence to obtain political demands
17. seriousness = the state of being serious
18. hardship = something that makes your life difficult
19. simplicity = the quality of being easy to do or understand

2   History of Genetics

The hist<u>ory</u> of gene<u>tics</u> began with a monk named Gregor Mendel working in the garden of a small monas<u>tery</u> in Europe. He joined the priest<u>hood</u> at the age of 25. In 1851, Mendel was sent to the Univers<u>ity</u> of Vienna to study science and mathematics. After he graduated, he taught high school and took care of the monas<u>tery</u> garden. Here he conducted experim<u>ent</u>s on pea plants to see if he could find a pattern in the way certain characteristics were handed down from one generat<u>ion</u> of pea plants to the next.

Although Mendel did not realize it at the time, his experim<u>ent</u>s would come to be considered the beginning of the science of gene<u>tics</u>. For this reason, Mendel is called the Fath<u>er</u> of Genetics. Gene<u>tics</u> is the study of hered<u>ity</u>, or the passing on of traits from an organ<u>ism</u> to its offspring.

3 Answers will vary.

B. Common Adjective Endings

1 Possible answers
1. limitless = having no limits
2. senseless = without sense
3. restful = peaceful and quiet
4. youthful = young
5. breakable = able to be broken
6. taxable = able to be taxed
7. stormy = full of rain, strong winds, snow, etc.
8. needy = full of need
9. ambitious = full of ambition
10. victorious = successful
11. Vietnamese = relating to or originating in Vietnam
12. stellar = relating to stars
13. coastal = relating to the land next to the ocean
14. devilish = very bad, difficult, or unpleasant
15. angelic = very kind or helpful; like an angel
16. feminine = having qualities of a woman
17. obedient = obeying laws, rules, or people
18. imaginative = able to think of new and interesting ideas
19. secretive = behaving in a way that shows that you do not want to tell people your thoughts, plans, etc.

2   **Breeding the Perfect Cat**

Did you know that cats are more popul<u>ar</u> than dogs as pets in the Unit<u>ed</u> States? Many people adopt home<u>less</u> cats from anim<u>al</u> shelt<u>ers</u>, and oth<u>ers</u> prefer to buy purebred cats from cat breed<u>ers</u>. Two of the most popul<u>ar</u> kinds of purebred cats are Siam<u>ese</u> cats and Pers<u>ian</u> cats. Both of these breeds are very old. Siam<u>ese</u> cats have long, thin bodies. They are short-hair<u>ed</u>, with dark markings on the face, feet, and tail. Pers<u>ian</u> cats are long-hair<u>ed</u>, with short, stock<u>y</u> bodies.

In the 1930s, these two breeds were combined in a series of genet<u>ics</u> experi<u>ment</u>s conducted by scient<u>ists</u> at Harvard Medic<u>al</u> School. The scient<u>ists</u> were trying to find out how certain traits in cats are inherited. The result of their work was a new, artifici<u>al</u> breed of cat called the Himalay<u>an</u>. The first Himalay<u>an</u> cat was born in 1935. The kitten had long hair like a Pers<u>ian</u> and the markings of a Siamese.

After the birth of the first Himalay<u>an</u> kitten, profession<u>al</u> cat breed<u>ers</u> took over. In the 1960s, Himalay<u>ans</u> were recognized by groups such as the Cat Fanc<u>iers</u> Associat<u>ion</u>.

3 Answers will vary.

Adjectives with *-ed* and *-ing* Endings

1   Last summer my friends and I took a trip to the Grand Bahama Island. The night before we left, we were so excit<u>ed</u> that we couldn't sleep. I was a little frighten<u>ed</u> by the plane ride over the ocean, but by the time we arrived I was completely relax<u>ed</u>. The first surpris<u>ing</u> thing that we saw was that everything was green: the palm trees, the grass, and the plants. Our hotel was beautiful, and the view from our room was very invit<u>ing</u>. We couldn't wait to change into our swimsuits and take a refresh<u>ing</u> dip in the ocean. After we swam for an hour, we were tir<u>ed</u>, so we rested on the beach. It was interest<u>ing</u> just to watch all the people riding on "banana boats" and playing volleyball. We spent four excit<u>ing</u> days on the island, and next summer, we plan to go again.

2 Answers will vary.

VII. Comparative Forms

A. Adjectives and Adverbs

1 Possible answers
1. A village is smaller than a town.
2. A refrigerator is more expensive than a toaster.
3. Watching television is more restful than running.
4. Yogurt is healthier than ice cream.
5. Laptop computers are larger than hand-held computers.
6. Sending an e-mail is faster than sending a letter.
7. Married men are more responsible than single men.
8. College is more difficult than high school.

2 Possible answers
1. My best friend is older than I am.
2. She is more athletic than I am.
3. I am lazier than she is.
4. My best friend has a lot more friends than I do.
5. I have a better sense of humor than my best friend.
6. My best friend works harder than I do.
7. I eat faster than my best friend.
8. She sleeps better than I do.

B. Nouns

1 Possible answers
1. My old school has a smaller library than my present school.
2. The food at my present school is better than the food at my old school.
3. There are more students at my present school than there were at my old school.
4. My present school has more buildings than my old school did.
5. The classrooms were cleaner at my old school than they are at my present school.
6. My present school has higher tuition than my old school did.
7. My present school has a better reputation than my old school did.
8. There are more computers at my present school than there were at my old school.

2
My Two Boyfriends

I am very lucky to have two boyfriends. The first boy is named Leo. I have known him about seven years. The second boy is named Sammie. I met him about three years ago. Both boys are wonderful, but they are very different from each other, in particular, in their personalities, habits, and background.

First, the major difference between the two is personality. Sammie has a **milder** temper than Leo, but he is not **as** independent as Leo. Sammie always makes me happy when I feel sad. Also, he has a **better** sense of humor than Leo. Sammie likes to talk, and he makes people feel relaxed. Leo is **more** mature than Sammie. He is quiet and independent, but he never makes me **as** happy as Sammie does. When I am with Leo, the only thing I feel is bored!

Second, I have discovered many different habits between Leo and Sammie. Sammie plays pool better **than** Leo. When Sammie plays pool, I always stand by his side and watch. He always beats everybody very quickly. On the other hand, Leo is a **more** skilled tennis player than Sammie, but I don't like tennis. At least, in the same way, they both like sports.

Third, Leo and Sammie have extremely different backgrounds. Leo is **richer** than Sammie because Leo owns several restaurants. In contrast, Sammie only works in a restaurant. Also, Leo speaks perfect English and some Chinese, unlike Sammie, who only speaks a little English but is **better** than Leo in Chinese. The thing that is similar about them is that they both come from China.

Each of these two men has his individual character, and they are very different. I like both of them, but in my opinion, I feel Sammie is the one that suits me better.

3 Sample sentences for paragraphs:
The Bahamas vacation is shorter than the Mexico cruise.
The cost of the cruise is higher than the cost of the Bahamas vacation.
The Mexico cruise has more entertainment than the Bahamas vacation.
The food on the cruise ship is better than the food at the Bahamas resort.
The rooms are better in the Bahamas than they are on the cruise ship.
Taking a cruise will be more interesting than staying in a hotel in the Bahamas.

VIII. Reported Speech Sentences

Verbs to Introduce Reported Speech

1
1. A professor at Beijing Normal University said that Beijing had been considered the best city in China in which to study, but that was changing. He explained that students now wanted to stay in the south or be on the coast because they had more opportunities and could make more money.
2. Lester Pearson, a former prime minister of Canada, said that the best defense of peace was not power, but the removal of the causes of war.
3. A Japanese garden architect commented that when he was arranging one stone after another, he was always entangling the stone with his dream and pursuing an ideal world of beauty.
4. One [male] writer says that he still likes Bangkok because it is a city of secrets.
5. A journalist who visited Rio de Janeiro, writing about the city's slums, or *favelas,* reported that the houses, built illegally on hillsides or swampland, generally consisted of wood planks, mud, tin cans, corrugated iron, and anything that came to hand.
6. One journalist observed that throughout Siberia, boats plied rivers only in the summer, and winter turned artery into bone. He added that on the frozen surface, transportation was far easier.

7. An old proverb says that Moscow is the heart of Russia, and St. Petersburg is its head, but Kiev is its mother.

8. One Eritrean, speaking after Eritrea, won its independence from Ethiopia, declared that there was almost a demonic determination to get things done. He commented that it was one of those things that came out of suffering.

9. Jawaharial Nehru, first prime minister of India, speaking hours before India's independence, declared that at the stroke of the midnight hour, while the world slept, Indians would awake to life and freedom.

10. A United Nations special delegate to Sierra Leone claimed that Africa never ran out of surprises. The delegate said that the lesson there in Sierra Leone was that things could always change for the better, and it was never too late to save a situation.

IX. Punctuation

A. Sentence-End Punctuation

1   **How Can I Decide on a Major?**
Question

My older brothers and sisters and most of my friends seemed to know what they wanted to do right out of high school. That's not the case with me. When I first came to college, I wanted to go into physical therapy and be an athletic trainer, but I don't know if there's a future in that. I've also considered teaching, but many teachers I know work other jobs to make ends meet. I want to work only one job so that I have time to do other activities that I like.

It seems like every day one of my brothers has a new idea for a major for me. Sometimes I tell people I'm thinking about it just to get them off my back. Lately, I've been thinking that I'll just major in business or liberal arts because those can be applied to just about any field. Can you offer a few suggestions for how I can decide on a major that's right for me?

—Hector Perez, Student, University of Idaho

2 Answers will vary.

B. Commas

1 1. When you're doing something that you like, time seems to pass quickly.

2. Shenxin knew that he needed to write his essay, but he just could not think of a topic. Perhaps if he took a little rest, he could work on the paper later. On his way to his bedroom, he suddenly stopped. He told himself, "You can do it."

3. Chirag did well in high school, so he thought that college would be easy. He didn't realize that he would have to work, study, and maintain a social life at the same time.

4. You can learn a lot about your interests by taking college courses. For example, taking an anthropology class may teach you that you have a passion for learning about diverse cultures, or you may take a photography course and learn that you have a real artistic talent.

5. Doing research without having a clear purpose is like driving without knowing where you are going. Therefore, before you go to the library always decide what you want to accomplish before you begin.

6. If you receive a federal grant, you need to budget your grant money. For example, a $1,200 grant for one 14-week semester equals about $300 per month.

7. It's important for students to have positive self-images. Successful students tell themselves, "You are smart, strong, and hard-working, so you will succeed."

C. Comma Splices

1   **The Africans' Problems**

The Africans from the *Amistad* faced two difficult problems. First, they needed to escape from slavery, and second, they needed to communicate.

The Africans faced a problem when they were kidnapped and taken as slaves. They were held by chains in the ship. They couldn't move or eat. Cinque, the leader, helped them to be free from the chains. Then, they killed the sailors. After that, they left the ship to get water. They were in a small boat. When they came back, they heard some sounds. There were men who shot at them with guns. Some of the Africans jumped into the sea. Cinque jumped, too. He heard his wife's voice. She called him back to their home. After that he came up out of the water and found a gun pointed at his head. He was enslaved again.

Afterwards, the Africans faced a lot of difficulties because of language. In the court, their lawyer tried to prove that the Africans were not slaves. **T**hey were free men before. However, there wasn't any proof that showed that. The Africans needed to talk about how they were kidnapped and who brought them there, but they couldn't speak English. This was another problem for them. With English, they could answer the judge's questions. **T**hey could defend themselves. They needed to find someone to communicate with them. **T**hey could use sign language or draw pictures. If they could do that, they would solve the language problem.

In the end, the Africans solved their problem of slavery by solving their language problem. **A** former slave from Africa translated for them in the court, and they were finally set free.

2 1. In Morocco, we lived with my entire family. **O**ur house was very large with many bedrooms and two stories. In the United States my house is small because I live here by myself.

2. All people need to dream every night. **N**obody can remain sound if he or she is deprived of dreams for a long time.

3. Sometimes dreams lead to creative solutions or ideas about waking problems. For example, before I decided to immigrate to America, I saw a dream where the military was fighting a losing battle. I abandoned the battlefield. **M**y war was over. When I woke up, I was ready to leave Russia.

4. Vietnam is a poor country, and it is a very small country. Vietnam is only as big as the state of Texas. Vietnam has only one big city: Ho Chi Minh City. **I**t has many small districts with many poor inhabitants.

5. In New Orleans, the weather always changes. **T**he people must follow the weather and wear clothes accordingly.

6. I was very excited when I took a vacation to Puerto Rico last year. It had been two years since I last saw my parents. **T**hey were so happy to see me.

7. My wife wants to return to college, but she has to work full-time. We have to talk about how both of us can go to school and still pay for our expenses. **I**t's lucky that we own a house, so we don't have to pay rent.

8. In the supermarket where I work, I practice speaking English. **T**he customers ask for things in the store, and I show them where to find them. I'm learning a lot of English in my job.

X. Capitalization Rules

1   **The Importance of Education**

I know now that **e**ducation is very important, but I didn't always have this idea. I remember when I was younger, I didn't like **s**chool. I thought that I would never need **s**chool in my life because I thought that school would never get me anywhere. I remember every time my **m**other used to send me to school, I pretended I was sick. I told **h**er that I couldn't go to school. **A**fter I graduated from **h**igh school I realized that **e**ducation is one of the best things in my life. I realize that I won't be able to get a good job without **e**ducation. **i**t's easy for anybody to find a better job with school knowledge. In **s**ome places when you apply for a job, the first thing they ask you is if you graduated from **h**igh school. **W**hen you are educated, you get more respect than somebody who doesn't have school knowledge. **N**othing can make you succeed better than education.

XII. Common Editing Symbols

1   I live **in** Chicago.
I have **a** large family.
His **parents** own a dry cleaning business.
My sister **works** at a Chinese restaurant.
My **daughter's** name is Alina.
When I was a child, my family **visited** Agra.
I **am from** Vietnam. OR I **come from** Vietnam.
I am happy to live in a **free** country.
She **told** me to go home.
We took a train. **W**e got lost.
I bought **a** car last summer.
She **is** going for a walk.
My classes end on **May** 15.
I **am always** late for class.
My best **f**riend is named Joan.